Routledge Revivals

Public Expenditure in Practice

Education, Health, Social Security, Transport, Defence, Law and Order—these essential services are provided for the community by the community. But how are decisions about such expenditure made? Where does the funding come from? Why isn't there more money available? Who ultimately benefits?

First published in 1975, *Public Expenditure in Practice* investigates and answers these critical questions from the decision centre of the world's most advanced system of public expenditure control at the time. The book begins with an exploration of the nature and scope of public expenditure, followed by an examination of the political debates surrounding its expansion or limitation. It outlines the roles of central and local government, as well as public corporations, and explains how taxation and charges are used to finance these services, how the tax burden is distributed, and how this compares to the benefits received.

The core of the book focuses on decision-making within government, particularly the Cabinet, and the dynamics of governance through "creative tensions". It provides a detailed account of financial and efficiency controls, emphasising the need for modern cost-benefit systems alongside traditional Parliamentary scrutiny. The responsibilities of the Treasury and the Minister are thoroughly analysed, culminating in a discussion on broadening the democratic foundation of decision-making processes. This book remains a valuable resource for students and researchers of economic history, public administration, and political science, providing a deeper understanding of the evolution of public expenditure control and governance.

Public Expenditure in Practice

Lord Diamond

Routledge
Taylor & Francis Group

First published in 1975
by George Allen & Unwin Ltd

This edition first published in 2026 by Routledge
4 Park Square, Milton Park, Abingdon, Oxon, OX14 4RN

and by Routledge
605 Third Avenue, New York, NY 10158

Routledge is an imprint of the Taylor & Francis Group, an informa business

Publisher's Note
The publisher has gone to great lengths to ensure the quality of this reprint but points out that some imperfections in the original copies may be apparent.

Disclaimer
The publisher has made every effort to trace copyright holders and welcomes correspondence from those they have been unable to contact.

For Product Safety Concerns and Information please contact our EU representative GPSR@taylorandfrancis.com. Taylor & Francis Verlag GmbH, Kaufingerstraße 24, 80331 München, Germany

A Library of Congress record exists under LCCN: 76356976

ISBN: 978-1-041-22235-4 (hbk)
ISBN: 978-1-003-73143-6 (ebk)
ISBN: 978-1-041-22258-3 (pbk)

Book DOI 10.4324/9781003731436

Public Expenditure in Practice

LORD DIAMOND

Foreword by Professor Alan Thompson
A. J. Balfour Chair of Economics of Government,
Heriot-Watt University

London George Allen & Unwin Ltd
Ruskin House Museum Street

First published in 1975

ISBN 0 04 330258 0

Set in 10pt Times Roman type

Composition by Linocomp Ltd
Marcham, Oxon

Printed in Great Britain
by Biddles Ltd, Guildford, Surrey

Foreword

By Professor Alan Thompson

A. J. Balfour Chair of Economics of Government,
Heriot-Watt University

Lord Diamond has written a wise, practical and hopeful book. Of his wisdom, and the breadth of his practical experience, ample testimony exists in the variety of posts he has held (including Member of Parliament, Chief Secretary to the Treasury, and member of the Cabinet) and the regard in which he is held by financial and economic experts in many fields.

The striking note of his book, however, is the hope that it gives us, that in spite of the appalling complexities and pitfalls that bedevil public expenditure (both in theory and practice), as a nation we are developing new skills and techniques to improve the effectiveness of public spending, and to ensure that it serves the community needs which are its *raison d'être*. If more public money is sometimes spent than has actually been planned, the response of those who favour less public spending is, as Lord Diamond points out, to claim that 'public expenditure is out of control'. Those who favour more public spending counter-attack with the claim that 'public expenditure is being managed with wise flexibility'. In the book, Lord Diamond steers a neat course between the 'out of control' and the 'wise flexibility' schools.

Lord Diamond's appraisal is a useful complement to the more abstract and theoretical works on the subject. The theme of public expenditure, both in this country and abroad, has attracted some of the best minds in the field of economic theory, and there is an impressive output of literature from which the student can choose. Lord Diamond deals with the main issues in a simple and direct way, which, I believe, will be extremely helpful to students when they proceed to more advanced reading on the topic, and will provide them with fresh insights, particularly with regard to the practical application of some of the policies involved.

For these reasons I consider the book to be valuable not only to economics students, but to students of politics, government, social administration, accountancy, business organisation and environmental planning, as well as the general reader who takes an informed interest in national affairs.

Lord Diamond's impressive command of financial and economic techniques is combined with an awareness of some of the deeper philosophical issues. He does not shirk the central problem that efficiency of public provision has to be reconciled with the satisfaction of individual choice. Lord Diamond is a democrat, and he speaks and writes in the great British tradition of political economy which recognises that efficiency must take place within the context of parliamentary government. There are echoes of Bentham, John Stuart Mill, Walter Bagehot and other nineteenth-century thinkers in this book, and not the least of its value is that in dealing with a thoroughly contemporary subject in the most up-to-date manner, it alerts its readers to those issues of personal liberty and the quality of life, which from *The Wealth of Nations* onwards have been the distinguishing characteristic of British economic thought. No less important, this book effectively acquaints economic specialists with some of the realities of contemporary political and parliamentary decision-making. Equally, I would like to think that it can help Members of Parliament and practising politicians at all levels, to understand the economic significance of what they are doing. The extension of the select committee system (a subject in which I am specially interested) in recent years in the House of Commons, has opened up new avenues of communication between the executive and backbenchers, and exposed them both to new economic ideas from outside experts over a wide range of subjects.

There are a number of issues concerned with select committee developments which are still the subject of controversy. These include: the relative merits of 'departmental' select committees which are concerned with a single department and 'subject' select committees which investigate a number of departments; the extent to which these 'watchdog' committees should intrude upon the executive function; the different degree of enthusiasm which different Ministers show towards their select committees; and the range and quality of economic evidence to which the committees manage to gain access. There is the further question of what new forms of economic and financial scrutiny should be applied to units of local and regional government. These bodies will be spending large sums of public money, and it can be argued that new controls may be needed, perhaps partly modelled on some of the forms of parliamentary scrutiny which Lord Diamond has described.

It is true that there is still a tendency for academic experts to act as advisers to Ministries rather than to parliamentary select committees, and to show more interest in advising central rather than local government. I would like to see an increase in independent academic advice in all these spheres. (I also believe that academic thinking and teaching can be helped – in economics and finance at any rate – by exposure to the opinions and behaviour of politicians, and by a better understanding of the pressures – party, regional, industrial, constituency – under which they operate.)

These issues – and many other topics of current argument in the sphere of economic and financial control – can be all the more effectively debated in the light of the material and arguments which are here presented by Lord Diamond.

Lord Diamond has provided us, in his book, with a meeting-place for experts, politicians and the public, and he demonstrates a sense of purpose and constructive thinking which could hardly be more timely.

Contents

Chapter 1

The Nature of Public Expenditure

Public expenditure is about living standards – yours and mine. It is not a remote, technical topic, something which 'they' (the Government) do, and which, apart from the fact that we have to pay for it, does not concern us. On the contrary, it is of everyday concern to everyone; for it is nothing less than the devising of everything around us, with the sole exception of those things which we choose and provide individually.

Public expenditure is the reflection of man's desire for community living. One could, perhaps, just manage to dissociate oneself completely from public expenditure by living as a hermit in a wood; but in real life we live together as communities, sharing the use and sharing the cost of a whole host of goods and services which we have jointly provided. If there are added the goods and services which we choose and provide individually, then the total constitutes in effect our standard of living.

Public expenditure is defined as the expenditure of the public sector. 'Expenditure' includes capital as well as current expenditure; the cost of building a new hospital or school as well as the cost of maintaining the building and manning the service carried on in it. 'The public sector' is the area of economic activity for which the Government has some executive responsibility. It includes local authorities as well as the central Government; for not only is local government of the same nature as central Government and equally to be distinguished from the private sector, but in addition the central Government is closely concerned with, and takes responsibility for, many of the aspects of local government activity. There is continuous and close consultation between Whitehall and the town hall, with the result that in effect a partnership exists between them for the purpose of carrying out community decisions. To the individual citizen the impression is of a single authority, which looks after the services everybody uses and for which he pays, in a general way, rates and taxes; and he, by contrast, provides the personal and individual items. Personal items paid for individually, ordered to fit his personal circumstances and chosen according to his taste, constitute his private expenditure: the rest is public expenditure, whether it relates to central or local government activities.

The public sector also includes the public corporations – in the main the nationalised industries – in so far as their capital expenditure and any government subsidies are concerned. Here again there is a measure of government responsibility and the necessary finance is provided by the community as a whole.

The size and importance of public expenditure is well illustrated by some of the figures given in 1964 by Sir Richard Clarke, then of the Treasury. He pointed out that at that time the public sector employed directly nearly 25 per cent of the nation's manpower: but of those with full-time higher education, the public sector probably employed about 60 per cent – a startling revelation. The public sector owned some 40 per cent of the nation's capital assets and was responsible for nearly 45 per cent of the nation's annual fixed investments. The various government agencies financed about 60 per cent of the nation's scientific and technological research and development. So far as certain private industries were concerned, such as agriculture and aircraft production, their size and structure were in effect determined by the decisions of Government in the field of public expenditure; and for other private industries, such as construction, pharmaceuticals, electronics and telecommunication equipment, the purchases of the public sector provided a large or even the dominant part of the demand for their products.

Such was the important impact of public expenditure in 1964. It had grown markedly since the beginning of the century and it has continued its growth since. A simple comparison between the two figures of public expenditure and gross domestic product (GDP) reveals that in the early part of the century public expenditure was equivalent to about one-tenth of GDP. In 1964 the proportion had increased to 45 per cent; in 1973 to 50 per cent. Perhaps an even more significant comparison is that of the share of national resources absorbed directly by the public sector. In 1960 the share had reached 25 per cent: by 1970 it had grown to over 28 per cent. The broad figures are given below:

	£ million	
	1960	*1970*
Public authorities' current expenditure on goods and services	6,676	9,539
Public sector gross domestic fixed capital formation	2,523	4,188
Total public sector	9,199	13,727
Consumers' expenditure	23,595	28,865
Private sector GDFCF	4,722	5,583
Exports, less imports, of goods and services	–846	–161
Gross domestic product	36,670	48,014
Net property income from abroad	379	581
Gross national product (at 1971–72 factor cost)	37,049	48,595

Source: *Public Expenditure* by Goldman, HMSO, 1973

What emerges is that public expenditure is an extremely important element in the life of every individual within a community, important because of its size and its quality – and of growing importance. A community cannot exist without certain common services: to the extent that these are provided by the community the cost of provision features as public expenditure. These public services have not been thrust on an unwilling public: they have been increasingly demanded by an articulate one. One must not confuse the age-old unpopularity of the tax gatherer – a feeling which has not been diminished by the passing of some forty centuries and an even larger number of Finance Acts – with the popularity of the services which have been provided 'free' out of the taxes so gathered. The financing of public expenditure is an extremely important matter which will need to be separately examined. But it is a different – though obviously not wholly unrelated – issue. The organisation of the provision of the services is also something which needs separate examination but is again not at issue here. What is evidently the case is that increasingly informed individuals, able to make their voices increasingly heard in an increasingly democratic system of self-government, press for improvements in the public services and, as a result, for increases in public expenditure. Sometimes what is being pressed is the provision of an entirely new service: more often it is the extension of existing services and an improvement in the facilities available. But the upward pressure goes on incessantly and the action of a government in reducing certain services always meets with criticism. For what is being withdrawn is part of the pattern of living of some group of individuals. What is happening is the lowering of their living standards.

As an alternative to reducing services a government may make a charge to the recipient of the service. The service continues but part of the cost of providing it will be offset by the amount collected from individual recipients in the form of charges. The full subtleties of the financial impact of such a charge will be discussed in a later chapter. What needs to be made clear at this point, in the context of the very close relationship between public expenditure and living standards, is that for the average user of the service the imposition of such a charge will result in a fall in his living standards. For if he continues to obtain the benefit of the service by paying the charges he will no longer be able to afford some other element in his standard of living. The publicly provided part of his standard of living would be maintained: the privately provided reduced. Thus the result is the same so far as the user of the public service is concerned, whether the cost of providing it is reduced through the lowering of the service or through the imposition of a charge – he suffers a fall in his standard of living. Nor is this statement invalidated by the fact that the saving in public expenditure may be reflected in a reduction in taxation in a way which benefits the user of the service: for the tax benefit – other than in the exceptional case – will be smaller than the loss suffered.

The concept that has now emerged is that of a standard of living which is provided partly through public expenditure; and that indeed is the essential fact of the situation. That is why the topic is of such importance: for it affects everybody in the achievement of something to which they devote the greater part of their energies.

Nor is it an exaggeration to refer to 'everybody', especially when it is borne in mind that the various amenities which contribute so markedly to the quality of the standard of living are often just as important as the amount of an individual's consumption. For it is not sufficiently appreciated how much the well-to-do, as well as the poorer members of the community, are affected by the benefits of public expenditure. The well-to-do taxpayer might find himself in pocket upon the reduction in a public service. The tax saved might be greater in amount than the value to him of the discontinued service of which he never availed himself. But there are other aspects; and they are the more numerous. There are the many areas of public expenditure which he has not contracted out of and would not – or could not – do so, so long as he is a member of the community. They are too numerous to list but a few examples will suffice to make the point. In his privately provided home, comfortably furnished and pleasantly decorated by him at his own cost and to his own taste, surrounded by articles of his personal direct choice – even in such surroundings, insulated as far as possible from the bustling community outside, he finds himself heavily dependent upon publicly provided, or publicly controlled, services. For the fact is that public expenditure is about the way people – all people – live.

Assuming that the morning starts in the usual way, he will quickly make use of several publicly provided services. He will go downstairs and switch on the light, secure in the knowledge that the publicly devised and controlled regulations will prevent him from getting a shock through contact with the current supplied by a public authority. He will turn the gas on under the kettle which he has filled with water from the cold tap; water which he knows to be pure because of the steps taken to secure that desirable end by another public authority. He will make a pot of tea with labour-saving tea-bags which hide no impurities. He will then add the tuberculin-tested milk (produced from a controlled, foot and mouth disease-free, herd) and take the tray of tea back to his wife. By this time the light is sufficient to enable him to admire the view from the bedroom window and to thank heavens that those officious chaps in the County Planning Department have decided that in order to preserve the public amenity of the area no building should be permitted in the adjoining fields!

Now it may be thought that the simple decision to leave a field as a field cannot involve public expenditure. But it does, surprisingly enough: and quite substantially. For the decision to be a valid one all sorts of expensive things have to be done. An Act of Parliament must have been passed providing the necessary powers. The preparation of that Bill will have meant the expenditure all told of a great deal of time of Ministers, civil servants, draftsmen and other experts. The passage of the Bill through both Houses of Parliament will have involved the further expenditure of time by many of the same individuals and many new ones – MPs, advisers, consultants and the host of officials, police, doorkeepers, electricians, cleaners and postmen (to mention but a few) who are needed to keep Parliament going.

But that is by no means the end. The would-be developer, to whom the neighbouring fields belong, may appeal against any decision of the planning authority which would prevent him building an estate of much-needed houses and shops for the benefit of scores of would-be occupiers and his bank manager. This could be followed by months of inspection, public hearings, arguments and all the other processes of a healthy democracy – and all at some cost in terms of public expenditure. The fact is that, like the rest of the community, the well-to-do taxpayer is utterly dependent on public expenditure for part of his standard of living. He cannot contract out of this situation whilst remaining a member of the community: by himself he cannot, at no matter what personal expense, secure the international safety and the internal law and order which he needs and which he quietly enjoys but which pertain to the community and are provided by community expenditure. He can of course press for an improvement in this or that public service – and frequently does. But he cannot determine that element in his standard of living by himself unaided: he depends – as the rest of the community does – on the decisions made by the community's chosen representatives and all he can do is to seek to influence them. For not only does he depend upon public expenditure; he is unable to decide, on his own, what form and size it will take. That is another characteristic by which public expenditure is differentiated from private expenditure. In the latter case the individual decides himself and pays specifically for what he has decided upon; in the former he has extremely little – far too little – to do with the decision; and pays, not the sum which precisely represents the value of the benefit to him, but a share of the public cost calculated by reference partly to his capacity to pay, and partly to the amount of his total spending.

Having given some thought to the nature of public expenditure and how it differs from private expenditure, it is now necessary to get the measure of public expenditure – to see how much is spent, the purposes it is spent on and who does the spending. At this stage it will be wise to avoid detail, remembering the French proverb that the houses prevent us from seeing the town. Nevertheless the detailed figures are, for reference purposes, shown in the Appendix.

The figures are changing the whole time, but the year ended 31 March 1973 will serve as a typical example. Public expenditure totalled some £28,000 million for that year, using round figures. (By way of comparison, GDP amounted to about £56,000 million, that is to say roughly twice as much, as already indicated.)

The purposes on which the money was spent, again in round figures, were the following:

	£ thousand million
On the social services (including education, health, welfare and social security)	12½
On the environmental services (including housing, roads and law and order)	5
On defence and external relations	4
On assistance to both sides of industry (including private and nationalised)	4½
On debt interest	2
Total public expenditure for 1972–73	28

One has only to think of new schools, hospitals, houses and roads and of new plant and buildings for industry, to realise that a great deal of the £28,000 million must be capital expenditure, the benefit of which will last for many years although the expenditure has been incurred in one year. In fact £7,000 million all told was capital expenditure and the balance of £21,000 million current expenditure therefore. On the other hand, all the schools, hospitals, houses and roads previously provided out of public expenditure were running down and wearing out during the whole of the year, and in the interests of simplicity rather than precision it is as well to regard half of the capital expenditure of any one year as merely maintaining the stock of capital goods.

The actual spending of the money is in the hands of three types of spending authority: central Government, local authorities, and public corporations. There is a clear distinction between government expenditure and public expenditure, although it should not be thought that the Government has no powers in connection with the expenditure of local authorities or public corporations. The amounts of public expenditure for which each of the three categories of spending authority has the final responsibility were, for the same year 1972–73:

	£ thousand million
Central Government	18
Local authorities	8
Public corporations	2
Total public expenditure	28

At first sight the proportion authorised by local authorities seems surprisingly large. But they are very big spenders on the social and environmental services – over £5,000 million on the two. Hence the relationship of Whitehall to the town hall is of considerable importance, particularly in those two fields. Local authorities' capital expenditure is in fact subject to a measure of government control; but for their current expenditure, control by Whitehall is indicative rather than positive. It results from arrangements which must take account of the large number of operating units in local government; of the fact that the members of local authorities are elected representatives; and of the fact that at the end of the day local authority expenditure is financed to a considerable extent from local rates.

Every year discussions take place between the Government and the various local authorities for the purpose of agreeing the estimates of total local authority revenue expenditure for the following year: and it is those agreed figures which form the basis for determining the contribution from national taxation known as the rate support grant. But the actual amount of revenue expenditure incurred by each local authority on each of its services is the result of the decisions made by that authority, albeit in the knowledge that the total excess over the rate support grant must be met from the rates, and that the rate-payers are the voters at local authority elections.

The third category of spending authority comprises the nationalised industries and other public corporations such as the BBC, although it is the nationalised industries which account for nearly the whole of the expenditure. The development programmes proposed by the various nationalised industries are fully discussed and finally agreed with the government department concerned.

The pattern that emerges from this short examination of the relationship between the central Government and local authorities and between central Government and the nationalised industries, is of three categories of spending authority in the field of public expenditure. The Government has full responsibility for its own expenditure; it contributes to, and accepts some responsibility for, the public expenditure of local authorities and the capital expenditure of nationalised industries.

So far the figures have been analysed in three different ways: the first to show what the money is spent on, the second to show which part is of lasting value, and the third to show who does the spending. In each case the same money total has been broken down. The question accordingly arises: is the money cost the best way of measuring public expenditure? It is obviously a very convenient way: but it is not sufficient by itself.

The main reason for attempting to measure public expenditure is so that the necessary facts shall be available to assist in resolving the major issues that inevitably arise. Without considering them – or their resolution – just yet, it is obvious that one such issue will be whether the nation can afford the total sum of public expenditure; and another, whether the various categories are in reasonable relationship to one another.

In any period a nation has only got its current resources which it can allocate for one purpose or another – that is, unless it proposes to get into debt by taking the products of other nations without giving its own products of equal value in return. So the question as to what a nation can afford must be interpreted in relation to its current resources and the competing purposes to which they can be put. The most helpful measure of public expenditure in total will therefore be, for this purpose, one that can readily be compared with national resources in total. The measure generally used for the latter is in fact the current money cost: so the current money cost will serve for total public expenditure too.

But immediately one attempts to compare this total with the figures of previous years, one realises that a simple comparison will be misleading, for the measuring rod itself will have shortened in the meantime. The pound of one year commands less resources than the pound of five years previously. Hence the current money cost of public expenditure for each year will have to be adjusted to take account of the fall in the value of the pound.

This adjustment will need to include a particular refinement to take account of the somewhat different nature of public expenditure from that of the national product as a whole. For whereas the nation's resources as a whole are devoted to the production of goods and services, the resources involved in public expenditure are in the main devoted to the production of services. With the production of goods the increased money cost is to some extent offset by the saving arising from new and more economic methods of production. With the production of services there is not the same degree of saving. Accordingly the net effect is that the fall in the value of money is more marked where services are concerned than with goods, and this difference needs to be taken into account in adjusting the public expenditure figures for different years so as to make them truly comparable with one another. The resulting adjusted money cost is a useful but not an all-embracing measure of public expenditure: for it does not take account of the fact that a given sum of one kind of public expenditure will require more of the nation's resources than the same sum of another kind. It is easy to picture the activity resulting from a decision to build a new hospital wing at a cost of £1 million – to see the bricklayers climbing their ladders, the carpenters sawing their planks of wood, the electricians, plumbers and others carrying out their manifold tasks – a great bringing together of human and material resources. On the other hand a decision to buy for £1 million an existing privately owned building, in order to provide additional accommodation, will result only in some activity in a solicitor's office. It is, however, much easier to demonstrate that different kinds of public expenditure have different demand effects on resources than to measure the demand with reliable precision. Suffice it to say at this stage that there is a difference which will need to be borne in mind.

It is perhaps inevitable that with a subject such as public expenditure, quality and quantity should be incapable of being dealt with in separate compartments. Both are important and both enter into the standard of living. Where so many are affected – indeed everyone in some degree – it is not surprising that the subject is of keen political interest and some party controversy. The issue is shortly described as being between private decision and public provision. The reformer sees public expenditure as one of the main instruments of change: one of the least painful ways of securing, via the public purse, those services and that alleviation of hardship which could not otherwise be afforded by the individual – and without the taint of charity. Others argue that only by private provision and individual choice is it possible to secure the kind of living standards that each one desires for himself. These are large issues requiring careful consideration.

Chapter 2

How Much Public Expenditure?

Having considered what public expenditure is and what it in fact amounts to, it would be interesting to consider the intriguing but much more difficult question, what should it amount to? Is there a specific absolute sum or a specific proportion of the national product which it would be 'right' to spend on the public sector? Or even if it were not possible to be quite so specific, ought not the attempt to be made to arrive at the limits within which public expenditure should be accommodated? And should it be a fixed sum; or should it be increased or reduced over a period? Or should it be a fixed percentage of the GNP or not? When the figure was 10 per cent, was that wiser than when it was 50 per cent? Has the growth, in absolute and in percentage terms over the years, been too great or too small? Indeed, has sufficient consideration been given to these questions by those responsible?

Before attempting an answer – or a series of answers – a number of considerations need to be discussed. Nor can the discussion be avoided by the simple device of finding out what most people want and giving that as the answer: for there is not much doubt that a public opinion poll which asked the question 'Do you think that there are too many civil servants and that they spend too much of our hard-earned money on running the country?' would come out with a fairly unanimous 'Yes'. Of course the wording is deliberately slanted so as to exaggerate the point: but there is no doubt that a large majority of people would want to see the total of public expenditure reduced.

Similarly if the pollsters posed the question 'Do you think the Government is mean in the petty economies it adopts which prevent the health, education, police and other services from being properly run?' there is no doubt that again the overwhelming majority would answer 'Yes'. The answer would be the same if the question were worded with complete objectivity. The fact is that most people want to see most public services improved: at the same time most people want the total of public expenditure reduced. One is therefore compelled to seek an answer on theoretical grounds, taking as the starting point the present figure and the present percentage. For the question of the right size for public expenditure is an essentially political question and in politics one starts by taking careful note of the current situation. Moreover any change to a different situation must have regard to the time which is likely to elapse before a sufficiently large number of the public can be brought to share the view that the proposed change is desirable and its consequences acceptable. In a healthy democracy this point does not need to be argued – merely remembered.

So the question that is to be considered is in what direction and at what pace should public expenditure move, having regard to the fact that the public want more money spent on many public services and less spent in total. Having fixed the starting point on political considerations, it would be logical to continue to examine the political aspects before turning to the purely economic and financial ones; and for this purpose to assess the pressures in favour of more and those in favour of less, so as to find out if possible which are likely to come out on top.

Among so many uncertainties one thing is certain: the desire of people continuously to improve their living standards. The acceptable standards of a bygone generation are totally unacceptable today; progress means having more and better television, kitchen equipment, housing, cars, leisure activities, holidays, general amenities and the possession of works of art. The list is almost endless and the desire is strong irrespective of the particular level of income enjoyed. It is not reasonable to assume therefore that those elements of the general standard of living which are publicly provided will be allowed to fall markedly behind the ever-increasing levels of those elements which are privately provided. The better equipment and furnishing of the home to which the citizen has become accustomed will need to be reflected in the standard of accommodation provided when he moves from a civilian occupation to one in the armed forces, for example, or when he goes into hospital; or when he moves into an old people's home. We need not here be concerned to examine exactly how these political pressures are transmitted and transformed into action; or the extent to which those who receive the benefits of the services and those who manage them and those who provide for them contribute to the improvement. The net result is to be seen all round: the television in the home is followed by the TV set in the hospital ward and in the old people's home. The process has been going on in the public services, the reasons for it are clear, and there is near-certainty that it will continue.

So too do the increasing standards of living enjoyed while at work need to be reflected in increasing standards during retirement, or while out of work, or while unable to work. The poverty which any self-respecting society seeks to eliminate is not a condition of need to be measured in absolute terms. It is comparative poverty: the lack not only of basic food, shelter and clothing of minimum standards but also of those amenities which are increasingly thought to be the essential right of every citizen to enjoy. The saying 'the poor will always be with us' takes on a new and permanent significance when 'the poor' is interpreted as meaning 'the poorest section'. It is for this reason that the cost of providing a basic minimum for those in need has been rising over the years not merely in money terms but, to a limited extent, in real terms also; and there seems to be no reason why that process should not continue, even though the rate of increase might be a little uneven.

For all these reasons one can expect a continuation in the real, as well as the money, cost of providing the relevant public services. Nor is it reasonable to suppose that the salary and other costs of the officials involved will not continue to rise as levels of remuneration and conditions of employment in the Civil Service catch up with the levels secured in the private sector. It is therefore difficult to think of any public services where these influences will not have their effect, either in increasing the real cost of existing services, as in the instance described, or in necessitating the provision of new services. Two examples of the latter process will serve to illustrate this; both relate to the reduction of poverty.

The first is the decision to provide a new cash benefit for those families which are beset by poverty notwithstanding that their breadwinners are in full-time work. The attempt to eliminate poverty already referred to has for some time been confronted by the problems of family poverty. Where this exists in spite of the breadwinner being fully employed, the two solutions which have been canvassed are an increase of one kind or another in family allowances and a minimum wage. Both solutions suffer from the defect that any provision which it would be realistic to contemplate would be inadequate to eliminate family poverty in all cases while at the same time providing additional income in many families where, on the current criterion of poverty, it was not needed. The solution now adopted goes some way to meeting this criticism by being based on a test of need, even though the imposition of a limit on the amount of benefit will mean that the need as so ascertained will not in all cases be fully met. Now it would not be unreasonable to suppose that this service will follow the pattern of other new services in being provided on a minimum basis to begin with and later improved. But the value of this example of a new service is that it demonstrates how developing ideas on poverty result in new responsibilities being undertaken by the State. Whereas previously the community had in effect accepted the responsibility of finding employment and therefore of subsidising those without employment to the extent necessary to avoid poverty, it has now accepted the responsibility of preventing poverty whether the breadwinner is in work or not.

Closely related to this decision to reduce family poverty by supplementing family income in certain cases, are the decisions to reduce family expenditure on rent and rates. Through rent rebates given to needy council house tenants; through rent allowances for the needy tenants of private landlords; and through rates rebates (reductions in the tax raised by a local authority on most residents in its area), public funds have been used in order to alleviate family and individual poverty. As special circumstances arose which made it appropriate to reconsider the level of this assistance from public funds, so the levels were increased. The decisions to provide the new services and the subsequent decisions to increase them are rooted in the same concept, namely the increasing responsibility of the community to eliminate poverty of the individual, poverty being judged in relation to the increasing living standards of the community as a whole.

It is reasonable, therefore, to suppose that these influences which have been at work in the past and the present will continue into the future and will result in some increase in public expenditure. But it would be wrong to assume that pressures to increase public expenditure could only arise in this way: for already it is possible to foresee other developments pointing in the same direction. Apart from the many known public expenditure proposals which are awaiting implementation – and it is only reasonable to suppose that some of them will in due course find their way on to the statute book – there are changes occurring in the attitude of the public to certain problems, which changes are very likely to result, at the end of the day, in increased public expenditure. One of the most important relates to pollution.

Public interest has increasingly centred on this issue. As evidence of existing pollution has built up, so too has a desire to prevent its spread and to reduce its existing level. The evident pollution of rivers and coastal waters caused by inadequately treated sewage has given impetus to the provision of better treatment at increased public cost. The pollution resulting from certain manufacturing processes has been followed by measures taken of necessity by individual factories to prevent a recurrence. These measures have resulted in increased private cost. But many acts of pollution or of the destruction of amenity – no firm line can be drawn between the two – still continue; and as the resulting level of pollution rises while at the same time so does the public desire for increasing standards of amenity, two-fold pressures are set up which will result in additional expenditure to the extent necessary to eradicate the pollution. The objection to aircraft noise at London Airport has resulted in additional insulation for nearby houses being provided at public cost. The avoidance of noise-pollution at any new London airport which may be built may result in the cost of flying being made more expensive; as for example through building in an unpopulated area albeit at greater cost.

Then again, there is the problem of noise pollution and loss of amenities affecting those whose homes are close to a newly built major road. Public funds provide the compensation for those whose land or property has to be acquired in order to build the road. But those living close to the new road are subjected to the noise of traffic and the smell of motor car exhaust fumes. Clearly their overall standard of living has been reduced and public expenditure will sooner or later have to shoulder the burden of compensation, on the basis that the additional amenity (of quicker communication and cheaper transport) provided for the many should not be at the cost of less amenity for the few. The receipt of the compensation by the nearby resident will enable him to improve his privately provided standard of living in some way or other, thereby restoring the overall standard of living to the level obtaining before the new road was built.

The prevention of pollution of the river by a manufacturing process, or of the air by a passing motorist, will then result in additional expenditure. The fact is that one man's profit is often another man's pollution. People have been enjoying their physical standard of living at an actual or potential loss to their amenity standards. As that loss comes to be appreciated and reduced or eliminated, as is already happening, additional private and public expenditure will be incurred.

Another – and quite fascinating – issue to which this appreciation of the loss of amenity gives rise is whether the kind of growth we have been experiencing over the past century is to be regarded as desirable. Has it added to the sum of human happiness? Would it not have been wiser to avoid the pollution and the loss of amenity even at the risk of much slower economic growth? Whatever the answers to these and similar questions – and a separate and substantial book would be needed for anything like adequate treatment of such fundamental issues – the political fact remains that people desire to improve their living standards in the ways described and are likely to go on doing so in the measurable future. Nor is there any likelihood that a switch away from such pollution-causing activities as noisy aircraft and smelly motor cars to quiet and inoffensive methods of travel would lessen the public's desire to attend universities or the opera. Technical progress may well come to be viewed more critically: a reduction in the pressures for more public expenditure is not an inevitable nor even a likely consequence of such a review.

There are then sound political reasons for believing that many public expenditure programmes will increase. Before attempting to measure the likely increase, consideration must be given to those political pressures, if any, which should lead to a reduction in the size of certain programmes of public expenditure in general.

Of those programmes only two seem to be worth closer examination: defence and aid to industry. So far as the former is concerned, there have always been those in the United Kingdom who have pressed for a reduction in defence expenditure, either to make room for increases in other public expenditure programmes, or for pacifist reasons, or because of the apparently non-productive or even wasteful nature of much of the expenditure involved. There is moreover the fact that, in spite of the reduction of the area for which Great Britain has accepted the role of world policeman, the proportion of our national resources devoted to defence continues to be greater than that obtaining on average during the inter-war period. Finally there seems to be growing evidence that a greater measure of success is likely to attend the efforts continually being made to prevent the risk of war against which the insurance premium of defence expenditure is paid.

There are on the other hand those who argue that defence is a prime responsibility of any government; that it is in the commercial interest of the United Kingdom that the country should extend its power and its influence; that the cost of defence against increasingly complex methods of attack inevitably increases and that it is the very methods of defence which have been adopted that have led to a general easing of the international situation.

It would perhaps be reasonable to conclude that inasmuch as the defence programme shares with other public expenditure programmes the experience of pressures towards increases in expenditure, but is one of the very few to experience pressures the other way, it is unlikely to rise at the same rate as other programmes or possibly at all. It would however be unrealistic to expect such a fall in the cost of defence and external relations programme as would have a substantial impact on the total of public expenditure.

Nor should such a result be expected in relation to the aid to industry programme, in spite of the increase in its cost over recent years. Whilst there are those who believe that industry will be efficient only when the weaker elements are eliminated through competition, and that state aid which postpones such a result is therefore short-sighted, there are many in industry prepared to press for special treatment for one reason or another. In cases where the national interest appears to be involved, such special pleas are likely to succeed. Where they fail, the resulting increase in local unemployment could be costly in welfare and other forms of public expenditure. It is unlikely therefore that a substantial saving will in future be made in public expenditure as a result of a changing attitude to the private sector of industry.

Nor is this conclusion invalidated by the changes which take place from time to time in the treatment of investment for tax purposes. All governments encourage investment by industry in new means of production as being a most important element in determining the rate of increase in the national product. This encouragement may take the form of a cash grant to the industrial investor – in which case for accounting purposes the cost is shown as an addition to public expenditure – or it may take the form of providing a measure of relief from taxation instead. In that case the cost will figure as a reduction in the tax receipts which go to finance public expenditure. Clearly the cost to the country is not altered merely by changing the form of the incentive to investment, and comparisons between the size of public expenditure in different years wisely ignore any difference in form.

The mention of taxation is a reminder that the taxpayer's unwillingness to pay the increased taxes needed to finance increased public expenditure is in effect the greatest deterrent to increases in public expenditure. How then should one assess the likely outcome of this pressure?

It is undoubtedly strong: nobody likes paying taxes and everybody dislikes paying more taxes. Nor is it the case that small taxpayers accept their lot with more grace than large taxpayers. Indeed there is some evidence to the contrary. Finally, it is not the case that a man would have to be an opponent of some element in public expenditure in order to become an opponent of some tax proposal, for tax proposals are rarely considered in the context of their likely impact on public expenditure in general and practically never in the context of a single item of public expenditure.

What is being argued therefore is that people dislike paying taxes whether or not they have particular views about public expenditure. The dichotomy between taxes and public expenditure is a very important factor in judging the likely effect of the anti-tax pressure and deserves further consideration. First it should not be thought that the sole purpose of taxation is to raise revenue for public expenditure purposes, and that the connection between the two therefore is immediate. Another and at least equally important purpose is to secure a balance between the total demands on, and the availability of, economic resources. Increases in taxation may also be needed to restrain the growth of private consumption and private investment to the extent necessary to make room for the growth of exports.

Then again different time scales are involved. Taxes are often designed to have an early impact and increases in taxes an immediate impact. Decisions on public expenditure on the other hand – as will be explained more fully in a later chapter – can rarely have an early effect and nearly always have a much longer-term effect. A short-term imbalance in the economy may well require an early adjustment in taxation and no adjustment in public expenditure.

Finally, even if one ignores differences in purpose and timing, one is confronted by the fact that it is not possible to relate a particular tax increase to a particular public expenditure proposal. Taxes are numerous and varied: they may be classified as direct or indirect – or sometimes neither one nor the other. The revenue coming in from this great variety of sources combines to form a large pool out of which public expenditure is met.

Nor, on that same assumption, is it possible to say that, the amount of revenue having been fixed, the amount of public expenditure must of necessity be accommodated precisely within the amount thus shown to be available. For that conclusion assumes that the nation's accounts are precisely balanced, revenue exactly matching expenditure each year. This is not the case: a Chancellor of the Exchequer budgets for an excess of one over the other – a 'surplus' or a 'deficit' – of the size that he regards as appropriate in all the circumstances: and it could not be argued that a slightly different figure, such as might be occasioned by a small increase or decrease in total public expenditure, would materially affect the nation's prospects.

It is of course true that the bill for public expenditure has to be met sooner or later. The delayed effect of an increase in public expenditure may well need to be matched by an increase in taxation in two or three years' time. The tax-restraining pressure will therefore still be there. But even so, two additional factors need to be borne in mind. The first is that although everybody grumbles all the time about the burden of taxation – and a lively democracy requires a harmless safety valve like this for letting off steam – it is usually the case that bitter complaints about particular tax proposals are fairly short-lived. They represent the kind of pressure that governments have learned to face.

The second is that there is no precise level of taxation below which the taxpayer is content and above which he will revolt. If one thinks of the different kinds of taxes, of the relative ease with which indirect tax is paid as compared with direct, and of the detailed gradation in the effective rates of direct taxation, it would indeed be surprising if the opposite were the case: for no one can tell when he is reaching a particular level of overall taxation.

To sum up this part of the argument, the pressures against tax increases, though strong, are imprecise in their impact; and increases in tax are not directly related to increases in public expenditure. It would be reasonable therefore to expect that these pressures would have nothing more than a general restraining influence upon the growth of public expenditure.

What remains to be attempted is an assessment of the likely effect of all the political pressures that have been discussed on the size of public expenditure. Such an assessment cannot be precise: the pressures vary from time to time and no method of accurate measurement exists. Nevertheless it seems reasonable to conclude that public expenditure would be likely to continue to grow if there are no strong economic or financial arguments pointing to a different conclusion.

Reaching a decision on next year's total public expenditure is an important element in the Government's management of the economy. It is necessary both to achieve a reasonable balance between the availability of, and the demand for, goods and services and also to ensure that sufficient resources are devoted to exports and to investment. Whatever resources are not so used are available for consumption and here again a government must ensure that adequate resources are available for that purpose. Now as 'consumption' and 'investment' include both the public and the private sectors, it is clear that the decisions as to the amount of the gross domestic product (GDP) to be devoted to public investment and public consumption are very important ones in this context.

Public investment relates in the main to the assets of the various public corporations (mostly the nationalised industries) and to the building of hospitals, schools and the like. As to the latter category, the economic arguments of the value of good health and the need to have a well-educated worker force merely add to the existing political and social pressures for increasing this kind of public expenditure. As to the former category, the economic advantage to the nation of devoting resources to the creation of assets managed by the public rather than to those managed by the private sector is not clearly established. Serious claims are made in both directions. However, the question as to whether to add to the public sector of industry or not is not a purely economic one: it is a political and social one also. It is therefore interesting to observe that although in basic philosophy the Labour Party is strongly in favour of national ownership and the Conservative Party strongly against it, in practice the public sector of industry tends to grow under both governments, albeit faster under Labour. Moreover the existence of a large public sector provides a very convenient tool of economic management to every government. For although a government may greatly wish, for economic reasons, to see the overall level of investment rising, it can do little in the short and medium term to secure that result so far as the private sector is concerned. With the public sector the position is very different: the government can, in effect, share in the decision-making. All told therefore, the economic arguments lead to the conclusion that investment in the public sector is, if anything, likely to grow.

Public consumption, which broadly means all public expenditure other than public investment, will, for the reasons already given in relation to public expenditure as a whole, tend to rise; and as it is more efficient for many services (defence is an excellent and very ancient example) to be carried out by the community rather than by individuals, each providing himself with the services required at a totally uneconomic level, it is reasonable to conclude that public consumption will be pushed ever higher. But there are two allegedly powerful restraints on this growth. The first derives from the argument that public expenditure, which has to be financed out of taxation, has reached such proportions that the consequential impact of taxation may well act as a deterrent to individual effort. The second restraint is based on the fear that so much of what an individual needs may have been provided by the community that an insufficient area is left for him to exercise his own sense of priorities in spending his own money. The first restraint relates to the earning of money: the second to the spending of it, a closely related aspect of the first. If the allegations could be substantiated they would give rise to the question whether the economy as a whole could be made more productive and the freedom of the individual enhanced by devoting less resources to public consumption and more to private consumption.

The proposition that high rates of taxation act as a disincentive – making managers unwilling to move to jobs of greater responsibility and workers unwilling to work overtime – has been examined on many occasions. Teams of university research workers, royal commissions, the Trades Union Congress and others have all looked at various aspects of it. The general conclusion drawn is that there is no evidence to show that high rates of taxation act as a disincentive: indeed many would express the conclusion in the more positive terms that the evidence supports the view that high tax rates do not deter extra effort and in some cases encourage it. This is by no means surprising, for what matters most to the average worker is what is actually in his pay packet, and if it is insufficient to cover his commitments it matters not whether the cause is low wage rates or high tax rates: the conclusion he reaches is that he must earn more. In this connection it was interesting to note that the workers interviewed on the radio at the end of 1970, after the news that the British worker worked longer hours than in nearly every other comparable country, said that the reason they did so much overtime was simply because they needed the money to make ends meet.

It may well be the case, however, that greater satisfaction is obtained from the direct purchase of goods or services with one's own money than from the consumption of those same services where they are state provided out of taxation. And it is certainly the case that the consumer is left with a greater area of choice when fewer elements in his standard of living are provided by the State and he is given the opportunity to provide them out of the resulting additional money available to him: and for the purpose of this argument one can for the moment assume that the reduction in taxation stemming from the reduction in public expenditure is broadly equivalent to the loss of public goods and services which he suffers. The act of spending money, rather than suffering its extraction, may to some seem an important exercise of power: the 'command of resources' and the 'power of the purse' are telling phrases.

It would be well therefore not to underestimate the psychological importance of leaving room for the exercise of personal choice by restricting the area of public provision. But that of itself does not invalidate any of the conclusions reached so far. It is still possible to argue that the desire to have free spending money encourages one to work that much harder when an increase in taxation has reduced the amount so available. One is really back to the incentive argument: and the psychological aspect, to the extent that it has not been fully taken into account in that economic argument, has been subsumed in the discussion of political pressures, where the psychological factors would surely have found their outlet.

It is sometimes alleged that it is the Welfare State itself that has produced a certain flabbiness in the economy. Human beings, so it is asserted, need the threat of poverty, hardship and unemployment to encourage them to give of their best: so that the way to increase economic health is to reduce public expenditure on the various forms of welfare. But there is no evidence to support this assertion: it could be argued equally well that the greater sense of security so induced has enabled men to concentrate their energies on production: and what is very evident is that people place great store on these welfare provisions, towards the cost of which they make substantial payments themselves every week. People, and governments representing them, have social as well as economic objectives: and a sense of security is one of the most important of them.

It would not seem to be the case therefore that either the assertion that the Welfare State saps the people's energy or the arguments about greater freedom to spend one's own money and about the disincentive effects of high rates of taxation cast any substantial doubts on the conclusion already reached that public expenditure is likely to continue to grow, in absolute if not in proportional terms. The main political, economic and even psychological aspects have been looked at: what remains to be examined is the financial one.

Here the question that has to be answered is whether considerations of financial cost point to an ideal or even a 'right' size for the total of public expenditure. It will be necessary therefore to be clear about what is meant by the phrase 'the cost of public expenditure'. For there are two ways of looking at it. The first is simply to take the total cost of every item involved in providing the goods and services that go to make up public expenditure. The second is to have regard only to the cost falling on the taxpayer. For not all public expenditure is provided by the taxpayer; a small part falls on the consumer. For example, part of the cost of the National Health Service is covered by charges for medicines supplied and for dental care which the patient is required to meet. The cost falling on the taxpayer is perhaps best described as the net cost, the gross cost being the total amount involved before deducting the charges to be made.

This distinction is clearly an important one: for if only the net cost needs to be considered, then by the simple process of charging the consumer for certain of the services provided for the public, the burden falling on the taxpayer will be less than it would otherwise have been, while at the same time the provision of the service will continue or even expand. At first sight the two opposing pressures previously referred to will be reconciled. Those who wish, for example, to see the Health Service expanding and at the same time to see no additional burden falling on the taxpayer because of it, will be able to have their wish granted. Indeed if this process were capable of being greatly extended it might be necessary to review, if not the substance of the conclusion reached on the likely growth of public expenditure, then at least the formulation. It might, for example, be necessary to say that although the size of the public sector was likely to continue to grow, the net cost falling on the taxpayer was not.

But the process of making charges is not such a neat and indeed almost magical solution, apparently leaving everybody happy, as to be capable of very wide application. It is nevertheless an important process, possibly of growing importance, and one which merits careful consideration.

Two preliminary points need to be made. The first is the obvious one that far from everybody being happy, the consumer who is called upon to pay for what he previously received free is very unhappy. For, as already explained, he will one way or another suffer overall a fall in his standard of living. The second preliminary point is that what is under consideration is not a system of universal charges, but one which seeks to impose a charge in selected cases, i.e. where the consumer is thought to be able to 'afford' it. In theory there is nothing to prevent a service being organised publicly on the basis that a charge is made to every recipient sufficient to cover the cost of providing the service. But public services are normally provided because there is felt to be a universal need for them, for example the maintenance of law and order and education, and either there is no suitable basis for making a charge (such as for the police service) or, as in education, the service provided is related to the academic need of the individual, not to his or her (or their parents') financial position, and therefore it would be impossible on practical grounds to make a charge related to the value of the service. It is administratively much simpler, as everyone benefits from these services at one time or another, to make everyone pay through their taxes and rates; and inasmuch as these are, to a greater extent in the case of direct taxes and to a much lesser extent in the case of indirect taxes and rates, based on ability to pay, it is roughly correct to say that the citizen can 'afford' the contribution he makes to the various social services through rates and taxes, where he could not possibly, as a consumer, afford charges based on the amount consumed. The fact is that the more children a man has of school age, the greater is the cost to the State of providing free education and the less is his contribution to the State in direct taxes at that time.

It is clear then that in a public service such as state education, to change the system of financing the service from taxes to charges would be a quite fundamental change. It could only be contemplated by a government which no longer took the view that education was an essential service. There is an entirely separate issue, unconnected with the issue of whether or not a charge on some basis or other should be made to the consumer of a public service; namely, whether the citizen should be free to organise a separate system of education on a more or less self-supporting basis. In so far as that issue affects public expenditure it will be discussed later: all that needs to be said at this point is that in many public services, such as education and the hospital service, the State does not insist on a monopoly, but that as public services are available to everyone, everyone is required to pay for them, through their rates and taxes.

It would be right to conclude, therefore, that to make a charge for the use of a public service would be a somewhat irrational way of proceeding; irrational because the very *raison d'être* of the service may well be the accepted impossibility of providing the service on a pay-as-you-benefit basis; irrational because every citizen through his direct and indirect taxes and rates is already making his contribution to the financing of the service. What then is the justification for making limited charges in selected cases?

There are broadly two. The first is that the service in question, though appropriately provided by a public authority, is not needed by more than a small part of the population, and is not likely therefore to be used by most citizens at some time or other. A public swimming bath is a very good example. While the act of public provision may be justified, it is difficult to see why everyone should be required to pay for what is a community need for some but pure pleasure for others (in particular the often-associated Turkish bath or sauna) and not used by most. The sensible solution is obviously to charge the user – the full cost in some cases, a smaller charge or no charge at all in others, according to what is generally felt to be the degree of need of the various categories. The need for schoolchildren to be taught to swim so as to avoid drowning in a quite minor accident is one which would be generally recognised as a community need, to be satisfied by the public provision of swimming baths and teachers at public cost. The fact that Johnnie's family is extremely poor is not held to be a sufficient reason to justify the risk of his drowning in the neighbouring pond when the ability to swim five yards would have saved his life. The schoolboy is one category; the businessman whose problems and official luncheons have led to tensions of a psychological or physical character capable of being eased through taking a Turkish or sauna bath comes into quite a different category. There is no reason why he should not be charged the full cost. There are categories in between these two extremes, such as the swimming club, where social policy would suggest a larger or smaller element of public subsidy.

The financial result of this system of charging is that the net cost of providing this service will be comparatively small and will be borne by the community at large on the grounds that it is a sensible act of public policy to teach schoolchildren to swim at no direct cost to them and to subsidise swimming clubs. As a matter of pure administration it is difficult to see any better way of arriving at that result.

The second justification for making charges is to avoid increasing taxes. Where a service, such as the Health Service, is serving a great public need and one which is likely to be felt by every member of the community sooner or later, it is obviously sensible that it should be provided and financed on a community basis. Doctors, medicines and hospitals are all equally part of the process of getting well. Why then pick on medicines for making a charge to the consumer? It cannot be justified on health grounds. What can be argued, however, is that the economic health of the community requires a limit to the level of taxation; that once that limit has been reached, additional public expenditure can only be provided for a particular purpose if there is a corresponding reduction elsewhere; and that within the Health Service itself it is generally agreed that the planned development of the hospitals should not be prevented by the size of the increased cost of prescriptions; and that the best method of reducing that increase as necessary is to charge the consumer in appropriate cases. It can also be argued that if – but that 'if' is important – the only practical system of prescribing leads to some waste of resources, then the act of charging may curb excessive prescribing. However, what is relevant here is the one point that selective charges may be made in order simply to save money and not in pursuit of a general line of social policy – indeed, in complete opposition to it.

The principle of a 'free' (meaning tax-provided) Health Service having been accepted, further charges may seem to conflict with that principle. The only apparent justification for such charges is that *users* should contribute the extra money being arbitrarily demanded rather than non-users. But in fact there is no logical reason for picking on users of this part of the Health Service rather than of any other; or for picking on a particular standard sum rather than on any other standard sum; and the stark fact emerges that money is simply being sought from where it can be got. Accordingly, where the consumer can afford to pay, he will be charged: and a system will be devised to select those who cannot, who will then have their charges refunded or be freed in the first place from the obligation to pay them. The administration of the system of selection will of course involve some financial cost – it may even be quite substantial in relation to the saving; and it may involve some emotional cost – to line up publicly with the minority who have failed to achieve a financial minimum can be very painful. So whether the saving is really worth while will require careful thought and calculation.

Two conclusions may therefore be drawn from this consideration of the principle of making charges. First, that where a publicly provided service caters for a limited public, it is right to charge for non-essential use so as to limit the cost falling on the general taxpayer to that of providing for essential use. Secondly, that where charges are made to users of what is for them an essential service, it is right to exempt those who cannot afford this additional arbitrary impost. The result would then be very broadly the same as if the amount in question had been collected by way of additional taxation – except that the cost of collection by that method would almost certainly have been much less.

One more aspect of charging remains to be considered. It may well be asked why, if it is right to describe charges for an essential service as 'arbitrary', 'illogical' and 'opposed to principle', all governments make charges of this kind to some extent. The answer is that this is not merely a method of saving money – it may well be the only method of doing so in the relevant period. Most public expenditure commitments are such that either it is impossible, or at least extremely wasteful, to reduce them in the immediate or near future. The need to reduce public expenditure may be very pressing. It could arise for example if a major item of public expenditure was running at a level far higher than that originally budgeted for and, owing to its nature, was incapable of being brought back to the intended cost. Prescriptions under the Health Service are just such a case. If the incidence of illness rises markedly because of a particular epidemic which requires an expensive drug for its cure, then the number and individual cost of prescriptions will rise substantially. By its very nature the cost of prescriptions cannot be accurately forecast; it is a so-called 'open-ended' commitment, not subject to control by a government. The fact that it had risen and was still rising – making that assumption for the purpose of elucidation only – would result in the need for a corresponding saving in some area of public expenditure if the overall ceiling was to be maintained; and that saving would have to be made in the immediate future, so as to coincide with the period of the excess expenditure.

Charges could be brought about quite quickly. Where a charge was already being made, the government would probably be able to increase it overnight by simple administrative action. Where the charge would be a new one for which the government lacked the necessary powers, the appropriate legislation and subsequent organisation could perhaps be achieved within a couple of months. Savings, in short, could quickly be made; and any government under severe pressure to reduce public expenditure would have at least to examine the question of charges as a possible solution and could well be right if it chose this method as the right course in the particular circumstances.

Before drawing together all the threads arising out of this consideration of the issues involved in making charges, a brief word on subsidies must be added in view of the similarity in certain respects between making a charge to the consumer and reducing a subsidy. Where the recipients of the subsidy are widespread, as is the case with the food subsidies in particular and to a less degree in housing, the effect of reducing the subsidies is to transfer the burden from the taxpayer to the consumer. Taxes fall and the cost of food and rent rises. For those in the middle income groups there may be little difference at the end of the day; for those in the upper income groups the tax reductions will outweigh the price increases. For the great mass who pay little or no income tax – because, having regard to their incomes and their family responsibilities, they cannot afford to do so – there will be clearly little or no tax relief to set against the substantial increase in rent and food. Many will be unable to find the extra money and selective help will need to be given. But the attraction to a government will be the possibility of making the saving in the near future.

It is now possible to return to the main questions which this chapter set out to answer: what should public expenditure amount to, either as an absolute sum or as a proportion of GNP? And has sufficient thought been given hitherto by governments and others to the consideration of what that answer should be?

The answer to the second question must be that governments have given increasing thought to the growth in the size of public expenditure – both in absolute and proportionate terms – over the decades. That is evidenced by the increasing interest expressed by governments, especially in recent years: by the number of government publications, the most important being on a regular annual basis; by the time spent by Parliament in debating the details and also the principles of public expenditure; and by the setting up in 1971 of a Select Committee of the House of Commons to examine all public expenditure programmes. But there does not appear to have been any serious examination of what the desirable size was. Views have been expressed that it is too large, or that it – and especially individual programmes within it – are too small; criticism of the rate of its growth have been widespread; but no clear view has been argued by any government or by any large body of informed opinion as to what it should be ideally over a long period. Short-term views have been expressed, but not closely argued. They are nevertheless worth quoting for the light they shed on this problem.

In their White Paper published in December 1969 (Cmd 4234) the Labour Government, having first declared that 'any forward plans for public expenditure as a whole need to be flexible', set out firm proposals for spending sums increasing at an average rate of 3 per cent per annum for the three years ending April 1972. They also explained that in their view 'the rate of growth of the nation's resources will be at the lower end' of 'a range of just under 3 per cent to about 4 per cent a year'. In other words the Government was intending to relate the rate of growth of public expenditure broadly to the rate of growth of the gross domestic product. Indeed they underlined this implicit intention by adding, in the same paragraph, 'But if experience were to show that a higher rate of growth [i.e. of the nation's resources] could be achieved . . . then it would become a matter for decision how far this additional output should be used to expand public expenditure programmes.'

In the follow-up White Paper published in January 1971 by the succeeding Conservative Government, public expenditure was planned to grow 'at an average annual rate of 2·6 per cent over the period 1969–70 to 1974–75. This is rather less than the increase in productive potential which has been taking place in recent years.' In other words the government was giving its view not on what GDP would be, but on what it could be; and was suggesting in effect that if, as would normally be the case, it grew nearly as fast as the recent increase in productive potential, then the growth of public expenditure would be in line with the growth of GDP.

The same theme is implicit in each of the White Papers published in the following two years. The rate of growth tends to nudge forward; the calculation becomes more sophisticated and less precise; and as a distant year becomes a current year with the passage of time, the actual cost tends to rise above the originally estimated cost. The variation in the pattern of annual increases in expenditure becomes more marked as lower-than-average increases are planned for later years to compensate for higher-than-average increases incurred in earlier years. The intention remains to increase public expenditure in line with increases in GDP; the performance tends to rely on the hope that the growth in GDP will be of a size to catch up with the growth in public expenditure.

The conclusions to be drawn from all this are that public expenditure has a momentum of its own; that the task of controlling public expenditure is essentially one of limiting its growth; that there is nothing like a carefully argued view of what public expenditure should, in total, amount to as a proportion of the national product and still less as an absolute sum; but that the view of the government – be it a government committed to increasing the social services and hence public expenditure, or a government committed to reducing taxation and hence to restricting public expenditure – is that public expenditure should be planned to rise over a period in line with the growth of national resources even if it has to be allowed in practice slightly to exceed that increase from time to time.

In essence, the decision as to the overall size of public expenditure is a political decision. This is not surprising, for public expenditure provides part of the nation's standard of living, and the rate of increase in living standards among the various sections of the community is a question which goes to the very heart of party politics. So the political aspects must inevitably be of prime consideration. Moreover a consideration of the other important aspects, economic, financial and even psychological (to the extent that that is not already covered by the political answer) does not seem to lead to a different answer, if it can be held to lead to an answer at all. In the final analysis, political considerations must be regarded as being dominant.

Now political decisions are taken in a wide context. They need to have regard, ideally, to all other relevant considerations affecting the community and – what is even more difficult – likely to affect it during the period covered by the decision. They must contain within them, therefore, the maximum of flexibility (so as to allow as far as possible for unexpected future developments) consistent with the certainty that is needed for the correct action to be taken by all concerned – which may be a very large number. It follows, therefore, that decisions as to the size of public expenditure will tend to refer to direction and relativity rather than to an absolute sum; and indeed all experience in the United Kingdom so far has shown this to be the case. The broad decisions have been based – as will be argued in more detail in the relevant chapter – on a variety of considerations and in particular on a stated relationship to general economic growth. The fact that the expenditure planned for a particular year produces a rate of increase which is higher or lower than average is not of great importance, for most public expenditure decisions inevitably cover a period of more than one year. The relationship of public expenditure to GDP must be looked at over a period of years therefore, certainly not less than three and mostly five; and a comparison of that kind will not only be more significant but will confirm that the calculation of the planned expenditure follows – in both senses of that term – the decision based on relativity.

Nor should the difference between what is planned to be spent in a particular period and what is actually spent be allowed to cloud the issue. Such differences, which are in any event not great and can be in both directions, may well be matters for comment in considering the control of public expenditure, but not in considering its planning. The principle remains fairly clear and supported by experience: the decision as to the amount of public expenditure is a political one and accordingly has in the past been, and will in the future tend to be, taken on relative considerations, even though it may need to be expressed in both relative terms and consequential absolute sums. The total figure, in short, derives in the main from the general decision, not the other way round.

It follows that the answer to the question posed a little earlier, namely what should public expenditure amount to either as an absolute sum or as a proportion of GDP, is that the first part does not arise. Once it is seen that the absolute sum is merely a derivative from a decision based on a relationship to GDP, only the second part of the question has reality; and the answer there must be that, being a political question, one must start with the present situation, then look at recent trends, and then consider the forces tending to speed up or slow down those trends. That examination has been attempted and the conclusion remains that public expenditure is likely over the long term to continue to account for an increasing share of the nation's yearly production of goods and services; and that in the short term it will, as a result of at least maintaining its share of a growing annual product, certainly grow in absolute terms.

Chapter 3

Who Pays and Who Receives

There are three simple questions which are always in mind when discussing any transaction involving money. Who pays? Who receives? How much? The last chapter dealt with the question 'How much?' This chapter is mainly about who pays, a question which generally arouses considerable interest; and to a lesser extent, about who receives.

The short answer to the question 'Who pays?' is that everybody does. The money for public expenditure comes, in the main, from taxes, including rates, and from direct contributions, including charges. Direct taxes, like income tax, corporation tax and capital gains tax; indirect taxes, like value added tax, tobacco duty, petrol tax and the duty on spirits, beer and wine; rates raised by local authorities on houses and commercial properties; National Insurance contributions and the Health Service charges – these are all important examples of the way in which the money for public expenditure is collected from the public as a whole according to a great variety of criteria. At one extreme the criterion is simply the use of the service provided; at the other, the ability to pay. In between the two extremes, a mixture of these two main criteria is involved.

It is necessary first to examine the various pieces in the puzzle before attempting to describe the final picture, and such an examination falls conveniently under the familiar categories of public corporations, local authorities and central Government.

Public corporations consist in the main of the nationalised industries, the nature of whose activities poses a number of difficulties in the calculation of public expenditure. In the ordinary course of events these industries carry on large-scale trading activities charging the consumer, as they are required by Statute to do, a price that will be sufficient to cover their costs. There is therefore no need to take account of these costs (current expenditure) for public expenditure purposes. Special circumstances do, however, arise from time to time. Their costs may have to be increased in order to accommodate government policy, where, for example, their investment programmes are specially accelerated in order to provide work for some of the unemployed. That acceleration is undertaken to meet a national problem and its attendant cost is an item of public expenditure in the same way as would be the cost of providing public works for the same purpose. Where special circumstances of this and similar kinds arise, the consequential additional costs are separately recorded for public expenditure purposes and accordingly the basic convention that the current expenditure of nationalised industries does not form part of public expenditure remains valid. It is therefore the consumer who, indirectly, pays for the ordinary current expenditure of nationalised industries; it is the taxpayer who pays for the out-of-the-ordinary current expenditure incurred at the behest of the Government in carrying out national policy.

The capital expenditure of nationalised industries, on the other hand, does form part of public expenditure; but before concluding that the whole of it falls on the taxpayer it is necessary to examine how the amount is arrived at and whether any deductions should be made similar to those made from the nationalised industries' current expenditure in respect of charges to the consumer.

Public expenditure is defined as the expenditure of the public sector, which includes central Government, local authorities and public corporations and which is to be distinguished from the private sector. What counts as public expenditure is only the final expenditure of the public body concerned. Financial assistance, in one form or another, by the central Government to a public body – be it local authority or nationalised industry or other public corporation – must be excluded from public expenditure to avoid double counting. The amount of such assistance may well be relevant to a consideration of the financial relationship of one body to another within the public sector but it is not relevant to the calculation of the final expenditure of the sector as a whole. It follows that the figure to be counted as public expenditure in respect of the capital expenditure of the nationalised industries is simply the total incurred by them irrespective of the extent to which it is financed by the Government.

Returning now to the question as to who pays for the public expenditure element in the nationalised industries, it is necessary to take account of the fact that they normally make a substantial trading surplus which, after providing the loan interest payable, in the main, to the Government, is available for meeting a large part of their capital expenditure each year – nearly a half in fact over the period from 1960 to 1972. The remainder is paid for with money borrowed from the Government. Looked at in these terms, it would appear that the cost of the capital expenditure of public corporations is shared more or less equally by the consumer and the taxpayer. But it is necessary to go deeper than the mere provision of cash. As in the private sector, borrowed monies have to be serviced. So long as the interest is paid, the loan of the money cannot be characterised as expenditure; it is in fact an investment, the acquisition of a financial asset. That view has to be revised however if ever it becomes clear that the loan cannot be repaid and that the money must be regarded as irretrievably lost. In that event the loss will be recognised by writing off the loan, or such part of it as has been lost, and to that extent the classification as investment must be disregarded and the sum in question must be re-allocated as expendiure. Such re-allocations have in fact had to take place and over the same period of a little over a decade have amounted to some £2,500 million. That figure therefore is the measure of the extent to which the taxpayer has had, during the period under review, to pay for the capital expenditure of the nationalised industries and other public corporations. The balance of the capital expenditure must be regarded as having been secured by the corporations themselves through their ability to service the relevant loans out of the monies provided by the consumers. During that same period the consumers of the products of the various corporations paid a total of some £66,500 million. A further £2,500 million, or $3\frac{3}{4}$ per cent, would have provided the cash needed to redeem the loans in question instead of writing them off. All told, therefore, the conclusion must be that it is the consumer who has paid for all the ordinary current expenditure and nearly all the capital expenditure of the nationalised industries; only a small fraction has fallen on the taxpayer.

This conclusion does not emerge from a superficial examination of the public expenditure White Papers, where the trading surpluses are ignored, where interest received by the Government from the public corporations is not deducted from the total interest paid by the Government and where the whole of the capital expenditure is included as public expenditure. All this can be justified on a number of grounds; but that is in the context of measuring the total of public expenditure. What is under consideration here is the separate question, who pays? In that context the price charged to the public by the corporation is seen to be all important. If the price charged is not sufficient to cover all the costs incurred, including the cost of servicing loans, then the deficiency will have to be met, sooner or later, by the taxpayer. This consideration is particularly relevant in a period of government price control. If a Government decides that it is in the national interest that prices in the public sector shall, in order to reduce inflationary pressures, be prevented from rising to the figure necessary to cover all proper costs, then at some stage, if the trading activity is to be fully continued, at least a part of the price deficiency will have to be met by the taxpayer. This process might well take the form of a payment each relevant year by the Government in the form of assistance to the particular industry. That would be the measure of the additional amount falling on the taxpayer, as would be seen by its inclusion, under the appropriate heading, in the published figures of public expenditure.

The question 'Who pays for the nationalised industries?' may therefore be broadly answered 'the consumer'. Of course, nationalised industries are used exceptionally as instruments of national policy, so that the consequential cost also falls on the taxpayer.

The financing of local authority expenditure – the second of the three categories earlier referred to – is a topic of never-ending interest and also of never-ending reconsideration. Three significant changes were made in 1958, 1966 and again in 1974. Other changes will undoubtedly follow in due course. But the task of describing the financing of local authority expenditure is not thereby rendered impossible, for it is just possible to discern those elements which will remain constant over long periods of time and also, in a general way, the limits within which variation in the other elements is likely to take place.

The comment was made at the start of this book that public expenditure is the reflection of man's desire for community living. It is now appropriate to add the comment that the local authority element of public expenditure is the reflection of man's desire to live in recognisable communities, and the same democratic principle of acceptance of the decision of a Government because of participation in its creation is at work whether the Government concerned is the national or the local one. Indeed it is more obvious in the latter case where the local authority tends to be 'us' than in the former where the national authority tends to be 'them'. Certain tasks – defence and the management of the economy are obvious examples – can only be performed at national level; others can be performed at local level, possibly with some loss of overall efficiency but certainly with some gain in democratic participation. As one moves down the scale in size of population, the greater becomes the sense of participation, the less the likelihood of achieving maximum efficiency. It will not be easy to reconcile these two major principles; every local council will argue for a wider sphere of final authority, either on the grounds of efficiency – if it is large – or on the grounds of democratic participation, if it is small. The same kind of argument will take place between national Government and local authorities, with public opinion swinging, sometimes in favour of greater power for the one, sometimes for the other, in response to events. There is no completely 'right' answer; there will therefore be no completely final arrangement.

But whatever the set of arrangements in force for the time being, they will include the exercise by the local authority of the final say in some expenditure, for that is a measure of the exercise of power; and they will include the raising by the local authority of some of the money it spends, for it is that which makes the exercise of power responsible; and they will probably result in the local authority spending more money than it raises, for that is in the nature of the problem.

The justification for this last statement is two-fold. First, these services, which, in the pursuit of the principle of sharing power, are most appropriate for local management, are expensive. Education is an example which immediately comes to mind. Secondly, apart from rates, the taxes which produce large yields are not local in character and are virtually incapable of being transformed into local taxes. The only way, therefore, of making local authorities wholly reliant on their own resources would be so to reduce their powers as to deny almost completely the principle of democratic participation and at the same time to ensure that men and women of real ability would not be forthcoming as local councillors because the challenge and scope of their duties would be insignificant.

One therefore has to start the consideration of the provision of finance for local authority expenditure on the premise that only part can be provided locally. At present the figure is about 40 per cent and is falling slowly each year. This is of course an average figure: the percentage could be as high as 60 per cent or as low as 10 per cent in particular cases. Of that 40 per cent, about half, or a little less, comes from the householder in the form of rates. The greater part of the other half is charged on commercial and industrial buildings and forms part of the costs of production and distribution which are ultimately paid for by the consumer. The actual amount of local authority expenditure under consideration is the figure arrived at after deducting any charges made for goods and services supplied by the local authority where the level of charge to the consumer is related to the cost of provision as opposed to being made for the purpose of raising revenue. But the cost falling on the consumer in this way is comparatively tiny – only for education does it amount to as much as 5 per cent – and any other treatment of these charges would not invalidate the general conclusion.

Domestic rates, then, provide for barely 20 per cent of the public expenditure incurred by the average local authority for the benefit in the main of the people living in its area. But even that can prove to be too heavy a burden in the case of the poorer householder, for although the house he lives in is presumably of less than average value and the rates accordingly low, they nevertheless represent a much higher proportion of his income than do the rates of the well-to-do householder. An attempt to meet this situation – that is to say, the regressive effect of rates – was made in the form of rebates for householders with small incomes and large families. A further step towards amelioration would be a special levy on business premises, thereby reducing the load on domestic rate-payers.

Finding the correct balance between the various arguments pointing in different directions is by no means easy, but it is an attractive problem because of the very fact that so many important principles need to be considered. To summarise them, they are, first, the principle of democratic participation which – apart from the issues of size and efficiency – calls for locally elected authorities with some locally raised revenue – enough to register with both elector and elected. This points straight away to rates as that is the only tax which has the three qualifications of being substantial in yield, appropriate for local collection and additional as a source of revenue. Next there is the principle that taxes should be buoyant (so as automatically to meet the rising costs of providing the same or somewhat improved services) and progressive; but rates are insufficiently buoyant and somewhat regressive. Then there is the principle of parity of provision with other local authorities at an acceptable standard. For a variety of good reasons people need to move from one area of the country to another and do so in large numbers. They naturally expect to find certain services, such as education, provided at a standard closely corresponding to that which they previously enjoyed. This can most conveniently be achieved by having the central authority lay down the standards and see that they are maintained, a proceeding which to a certain extent restricts local autonomy and impinges on the principle of local democracy, in that the obvious method of securing the maintenance of a standard set by an outside body is for that body to appoint its representatives, not for the local citizens to elect theirs. Some ways of strengthening the authority of the outside body and at the same time easing its relationship with the local body is required, and a substantial grant of money by the former to the latter serves both purposes admirably.

Finally there is the principle that what is good for the whole is good for the constituent parts. No area, however well managed its local affairs, could flourish if the economy of the whole country were seriously depressed. It is for the central Government, therefore, to manage the national economy well so that all areas may benefit; and this in turn means foreknowledge of the likely spending – that is, demand on resources – of all the localities together, coupled with some means of preventing wide variations between the estimate and the actuality. In its own interests, then, a local authority must accept some restriction on its freedom of action.

These would seem to be the dominant principles, though no doubt there are many other considerations which may affect the outcome in a minor way, and it should be possible therefore to draw the appropriate conclusions as to the broad shape of future local authority financing arrangements. First, they will rely fairly heavily on rates, albeit adjusted to the needs of the most difficult cases. For here is a worthwhile source of revenue, comparatively cheap to collect and evidently local, thereby corresponding to the requirements of local democracy. Few new local taxes or sources of revenue will be added, for the task of finding suitable ones has often been attempted and always found extremely difficult. The alternative of apportioning to each area, on some formula or other, part of a national tax serves very little purpose financially, for the same result is achieved with less difficulty by the existing method of providing central government grants. Nor does such a system of apportionment serve any democratic purpose, for it fails to produce a recognition of the close connection between the tax-payer and the elected local representative. The necessary identification by each of the other is missing.

For the reasons already given, it will be necessary to give to local authorities the final say over services the cost of which far exceeds the local revenues; and the excess will have to be – as in some measure it is in any event right that it should be – met out of grants from central Government. There are many bases on which these grants could be calculated and distributed, and having regard to the likelihood that they will account for well over half the necessary finance it is right that they should be most carefully considered and inevitable that new events and new political pressures will result in reconsideration from time to time. But certain elements are bound to be present. Local authorities vary considerably in the average wealth of their inhabitants, reflected in the value of their properties. They vary too in the make-up of their populations, in the proportion still at school, or needing care of some kind; as a result the demands on a particular local authority may be quite different from those made on another one of similar size. Some formula then will have to be relied on which attempts to take account of these variations so as to provide at least rough justice. Then again the healthy discipline of the need to make ends meet will have to be introduced, at all events over a sufficient part of the field to make the necessary impact. The alternative of giving in the form of central government grant whatever the local authority has spent in excess of its own resources will never do: that would soon result in each local authority vying with its neighbour to give ever-increasing services at ever higher standards, secure in the knowledge that the extra cost would be refunded by Whitehall. It would accordingly be necessary for a sizeable part of these grants to take the form of fixed amounts – fixed according to some reasonable and acceptable formula – so that any additional amount spent by the local authority in pursuance of its own decision to improve or extend some services would have to be met out of its own resources. These additional amounts would be sufficient to involve the principles of responsible management and democratic participation.

This then being the likely constitution of the continuing arrangements for financing local authority expenditure, it is possible to indicate where the burden falls and where it is likely to continue to fall – that is, to answer the question 'Who pays for local authority services?' The answer is that a small part is borne by the local residents as such, a small part by the consumer (wherever he may be) of the locally produced goods and services, and a large part by the general body of taxpayers, including those resident in the locality and including in the taxes so paid, all direct and all indirect taxes, all taxes on income, all taxes on expenditure and all taxes on capital. Given in those fairly general terms, the answer is not likely to be upset by the future course of events.

Having examined the financing of public expenditure so far as two categories of spending authority are concerned – nationalised industries and local authorities – it is now the turn of central Government, by far the largest of the three. In very round figures the amounts spent by each in 1972–73 were (in billions, i.e. thousands of millions, of pounds):

Central Government	18
Local authorities	8
Public corporations	2
Total public expenditure	£28

The largest item every year is social security – in 1972–73 it accounted for some £5 billion out of the £18 billion spent by the central Government. But that is the gross expenditure: the net expenditure falling on the public purse is much less, between a quarter and a third. The rest is separately financed and as this item is so exceptional, both in size and character, it is sensible to examine the financing of social security separately from the financing of the rest of central government public expenditure.

The cash benefits provided under the social security schemes are paid to very large numbers of people. There were nearly 8 million retirement pensioners in 1973, and their number was growing. There were 7 million children qualifying for family allowances and their number was growing too. But there is a great difference in the method of financing these two schemes. The first is paid for mainly by contributions to the National Insurance fund; the second out of the fund of general taxation. The other principal contributory benefits forming part of social security are sickness, unemployment and industrial injuries. The main non-contributory schemes cover supplementary benefits and war pensions as well as family allowances. It is only the contributory schemes, amounting to some £3½ billion in 1972–73, which call for special examination, for the others are financed in the same way as the rest of central Government expenditure and can conveniently be considered together. As what in fact takes place is very different from what is thought to occur, the financing of the contributory schemes will need to be looked at under two heads, fact and fancy.

The fact is that, as already indicated, about five-sixths of the cost of the contributory schemes is met by contributions from employers and individuals, the Exchequer contributing the balance. The truth is that National Insurance benefits are mainly provided through the efforts of those at work for those not at work at that time.

The general belief is quite different. It is that there is a pensions fund carefully husbanded by the Government; and that this fund receives Tom Jones's weekly contributions throughout his working life and, when he retires, pays out the accumulated proceeds in weekly contributions until he dies. The myth of the insurance fund is a very convenient one, for it engenders a number of beliefs which greatly contribute to the comparative ease with which the finance is obtained.

There is the belief by each person, for example, that he is saving up each week for his own retirement – which he is mostly willing to do – as opposed to his being called on to pay more taxes, which he is always unwilling to do. Then there is the belief of the retired man, that he is merely drawing his own savings in the form of a pension: it is his 'as of right'. He can feel independent, totally unaware of the fact that he is, like so many others, being supported by those at work. These are profoundly important beliefs contributing much to human happiness and not to be ignored in the search for greater efficiency.

Having touched on the special considerations attaching to the social security programme, it is now possible to deal very quickly with the financing of the rest of the public expenditure of the central Government. There are some receipts which are not in the nature of charges but which serve to provide part of the necessary finance. The amounts are mostly comparatively small and are paid either by the contributor (as in the case of the contribution to the National Health Service) or by the consumer, using that term in its broadest sense to cover the occupation of houses and the borrowing of money. Apart from these receipts, the public expenditure in question is financed wholly out of general taxation.

The enquiry into the question 'Who pays for public expenditure?' has been conducted under the headings of the three spending authorities, the nationalised industries, the local authorities and the central Government. The conclusions reached are that in the first case, the consumer and the general taxpayer pay; in the second case, the consumer, the ratepayer and the general taxpayer; and in the third case, the consumer, the contributor and the general taxpayer. Putting the three together, and without attempting yet the difficult task of assessing an approximate order of magnitude for each, the conclusion is that public expenditure is paid for by the consumer, the contributor, the rate-payer and the general taxpayer.

Now it was important, for the reasons given, to consider the nature and amount of local rates when considering the local authority part of public expenditure. But when what is under consideration once more is the total of public expenditure, irrespective of the spending authority, the distinction between local rates and national taxes becomes much less marked. Indeed the description 'local' vanishes because rates apply in every locality and are, therefore, of national coverage. What, then, is the essential difference between rates covering the whole country and taxes doing the same? Or, to be more precise, between taxes and domestic rates, for non-domestic are borne by the consumer? The answer must be none. Domestic rates are in essence just another tax, and as they only amount to about one-fourteenth of the amount collected in general taxation, it is clear that there is no sufficient reason either of quality or quantity to justify their separation from taxes in this general consideration. The conclusion, reformulated, is that public expenditure is paid for by the consumer, the contributor and the taxpayer.

The taxpayer pays for about three-quarters of public expenditure; the contributor for about one-eighth; and the remaining eighth, either directly or indirectly, comes from the consumer of nationalised industries' products, the borrower of money, the occupier of premises and the user of services. Those are the broad orders of magnitude and they are sufficiently precise for present purposes. They are conveniently set out in the first of the new annual series of public expenditure publications issued by the Government of the day in 1969 (Cmd 4234), and although the four subsequent ones have unfortunately – and unwisely – omitted this information, they contain some evidence to support, and none to confute, this broad conclusion.

One moves into a very different world when one attempts to proceed from the question 'Who does pay for public expenditure?' to the question 'Who should pay?' Nevertheless the answer must be attempted, and a considerable advance along this road will have been made if at all events it can be shown how the burden of providing for the public falls on the public. There will be differing views as to whether that is a 'fair' way of sharing the burden: the moral conclusion – whatever it is – can be based on the facts.

The third category – the consumer-borrower-occupier-user – is perhaps the most appropriate to consider first. The proportion is small, only one-eighth all-told. There is one criterion applicable throughout – the criterion of paying according to how much you get, whether as consumer of gas or electricity, or as occupier of premises or as borrower of a sum of money at a given rate of interest. Of course a case could be made out for gas and electricity being consumed as needed and paid for according to one's ability to pay. But that is not the present situation – nor the likely one in the foreseeable future – and in the meantime it is sufficient to say that that particular portion of one-eighth of public expenditure is paid for according to the amount used and that most people would regard that as a fair measure. Moreover as the essential characteristic of public expenditure is community provision rather than individual choice, it must be added that the whole of this category is somewhat peripheral.

The second category – contributions – has something in common with the category just discussed. It is very similar in size – again, one-eighth. It consists predominantly of National Insurance contributions from the employer and the employee (or self-employed). The employer's contribution must be regarded as an addition to the cost of his product which is ultimately borne by the consumer, again on the same criterion of payment for use. The employee's contribution is in the main a fixed sum unrelated to the size of his pay-packet, and to that extent is a simple poll tax bearing heavily on the lower wage-earner. The same remarks apply to that part of the contribution which is labelled the health stamp. It is a fixed sum and accordingly falls disproportionately heavily on the smaller wage earner. Although changes in the rates and variety in the insurance schemes themselves make it impossible to define with precision and permanence the proportion of the total contributions to the National Insurance fund which is paid for by the employer, it would be reasonable, and sufficient for present purposes, to put it at two-thirds. This means that the element borne by individual contributors is not very great when considered in relation to the total size of public expenditure finances. A third of an eighth, even allowing for a bigger-than-usual margin of error, is not a large proportion. In these terms, therefore, the overall size of the injustice stemming from the poll-tax type of treatment is not great, and the effect of the weighting in favour of the smallest contributor to the Graduated Pension, and of the special treatment of certain low-paid categories of flat-rate contributors, is to reduce the inequity. But the impact on a particular wage-earner can be substantial, as has already been indicated. The married man working to support his wife and children on a less than average wage will find himself with little or no income tax to pay. But the deduction from his wage packet for his flat-rate contribution will be perhaps 5 per cent of his wages, whereas the man earning twice as much, and paying the same amount, has only 2½ per cent deducted for the same purpose, and so on up the scale: the higher the earnings, the smaller the proportionate impact of the constant contribution.

The answer to the question as to who in fact provides that part – roughly an eighth – of the finances of public expenditure described as 'contributions' is, then, that the greater part comes ultimately from the consumer and the smaller – roughly 4 per cent of the total of public expenditure – from the employee, including the self-employed person. The question as to who should pay has largely been answered already. The criterion of the amount used or consumed is generally accepted as a just one, and the injustice of the poll-tax element in the employee's contribution to the National Insurance fund is made tolerable by being proportionately very small. Certainly the replacement of both employers' and, in particular, employees' contributions by progressive taxation would be more just, those with the broader shoulders being called on to carry the heavier burdens. Nor would such a change be more than an extension of existing practice. The Government would be meeting the whole cost of pensions and the Health Service instead of part only, as at present. But increases in taxation are unpopular and the idea of saving for one's old age is both popular and wholesome. The National Insurance fund may be an economic fiction but it is a political fact, and the conclusion would seem to be that it is unlikely that in the near future any Government would attempt to disturb the comparative contentment surrounding the present arrangement. Certainly all Governments have hitherto taken the view that while most people are, if not blissful, at least content to continue in ignorance of the absence of any funds in the National Insurance fund, it would be political folly to add to their wisdom.

Working back, one is left with the first category, taxation – by far the largest provider of finance for public expenditure. How does this burden fall upon the taxpayer and is it just and equitable? Obviously that is a complex question, and equally obviously a full study would be out of place in a book dealing essentially with public expenditure. But the provision of the finance for the expenditure is important enough to merit a short discussion of the impact of taxation.

Direct taxation – taxation on incomes – is progressive: that is to say, the rich man pays a disproportionately high share. This accords with the generally accepted sense of what is just, namely that a person's liability to tax should be fixed in relation to his capacity to pay – the bachelor more than the family man, the rich man more than the less well-to-do. Indirect taxation, on the contrary, is regressive: that is to say, the poor man, when he spends his money on things that are taxed, pays indirectly in tax a sum which is disproportionately heavy in relation to his means. One has only to think of the effective rate of duty on a packet of cigarettes, a pint of beer or a glass of whisky to realise the truth of that statement. Of course, there is a great difference between taxes on income and taxes on expenditure. The first are compulsory: the PAYE deduction is the practical reminder of that for the majority of people at work. The second are not: you can live without beer or whisky; you will probably live longer without cigarettes; and most food is not taxed. So one cannot simply marry the two types of tax in order to arrive at an overall rate. What, however, can be done is to ascertain the actual pattern of spending of different types of household with different levels of income and thereby to estimate what each pays in indirect tax. By adding the burden of direct taxation it is possible to arrive at the total tax borne by single and married people in all typical variations both of size of family and size of income. The broad answer that emerges is that taxes overall bear proportionately on the taxpayer. (*Economic Trends*, Nov. 1973, HMSO.)

The sense of fairness that the use of the word 'proportionate' creates is however only superficial, for what meets the general sense of justice is that taxes should bear on different individuals according to their capacity to pay. This means that the rich man pays above the average proportion on his income and the poor man less. Now the finances for public expenditure, to the extent that they are not simply provided by the consumer, fall to be provided, to a very large extent, by the individual citizen as taxpayer and, to a very small extent, by the employee. In the former case, each contributes the same proportion of his income; in the second, a fixed sum irrespective of his income. So in neither case does the equitable concept of progression apply.

But that is not the whole story. It is necessary to ascertain who pays for public expenditure so as to discuss whether that accords with generally accepted views of fairness. It was in particular essential to demonstrate that certain widely-held beliefs about the impact of total taxation in the UK were erroneous. But no general conclusion can be drawn about the fairness of the whole system of public expenditure without looking at what the various taxpayers get in return for what they pay. The judgement that would be reached if it were demonstrated that although the payment was proportionate, the receipt of benefit was disproportionately great in favour of the poorer section of the community, would be quite different from a judgement based on a spread of benefits which turned out to be broadly in line with the amounts contributed. The next task therefore is to examine the spread of the benefits of public expenditure among the various sections of the population.

The answer – again derived from the same exercise and from the same source – is that benefits are progressive; that is to say, they constitute a bigger proportion of low incomes than of high incomes. Benefits as a whole favour low-income households more than high-income households; they also favour larger households more than smaller households.

The next step is clearly to examine, for the same year, both taxes and benefits for the same typical households at various levels of income so as to find out their combined effect. The figures, both in absolute and in percentage terms, are given in the Appendix. They show, as was to be expected from combining progressive benefits with neutral taxes, that as in each of the three previous years, households with low incomes gain more on average from benefits than they pay in taxes and conversely that high-income households pay more in taxes than they receive in benefits. The figures similarly show that within a given income range the largest households, in general, gain most and the smallest gain least, from all taxes and benefits combined.

It hardly needs to be said that the figures given are subject to the normal reservations relating to definition, to margins of error, and to problems of allocation: or that averages as usual hide variations within them. Nevertheless the broad conclusions as stated are clear and unlikely to be disproved. They are drawn from statistics which are reasonably consistent over the years and are confirmed by external experience. A comparison has been made between the USA and the UK of the average taxes and benefits per household for 1968. The figures, which are again given in the Appendix, show that for the UK the combined effect of taxes and benefits was to produce on average a final income which was 84 per cent (not very different, incidentally, from the 1972 figure) of original income. For the USA the comparable figure for the same year was again 84 per cent. There is clearly nothing in those figures to throw doubt on the general conclusion that the combined effect of taxes and benefits is progressive.

Chapter 4

Making the Decision

Whatever the issue to be decided, the process of arriving at a decision is always of great interest and importance, for not only will the process be likely to affect the correctness of the decision but all those affected by it will accept the decision the more readily the more satisfied they are with the method by which it has been reached. The importance of the decisions reached in the field of public expenditure can hardly be exaggerated, so substantial are they and so great is their impact on the lives of all of us. As in other fields, however, a large part of arriving at the right answer is asking the right question, and it is that aspect therefore which first demands consideration.

Before 1961 the question that was asked was: is this individual proposal for expenditure within the public sector justifiable on its own merits? That is to say, is it necessary and desirable and is the method proposed of achieving a certain purpose better than alternative methods which have also been carefully examined? They were good questions, clearly; but they were not all-embracing – indeed, they omitted what is probably the most important element. Since 1961 – it is not really possible to draw such a marked dividing line but the Plowden Report of that year (Cmd 1432) is one of the most important of the signposts to the new, current approach – that element has been given its proper importance. The question now asked is the right one, namely: how does this proposal, which is shown to be justifiable on its own merits, compare in terms of social, political and economic priorities with other proposals in the field of public expenditure and can it be fitted in to the general scheme? In short, the question was: is it a good proposal? The question now is: is it a better proposal?

The explanation for this new approach – which had been developing over the years, so that its elevation by the Plowden Committee into recommended practice from its previous status of an idea worth discussing, was immediately accepted – has several strands. The first is that all British Governments had come to accept full employment as a dominant objective. This in turn meant that human and other current resources – for material resources are made available for use by human activity – became for all practical purposes fully used. The second is that British

Governments had also come to accept that the role of the public sector was substantial and increasing – and indeed it was already something like a hundred times as big as at the beginning of the century. The combination of these two meant that the public sector was an enormous user of resources in competition with the private sector and that a proposal for additional expenditure – involving, inevitably, additional resources – could only be met either out of a growth in resources or by diverting resources hitherto devoted to some other purpose. As to the first alternative, it was of course to be expected that resources would grow every year. As new machines replace older ones, the resulting saving in manpower means that human resources are set free for additional purposes. But the development of existing programmes of public expenditure will be likely to absorb them; so that no escape from the need to make a choice is likely to be found here. Nor is it to be found, other than exceptionally, in putting to use idle resources. For although there may be bouts of high unemployment resulting from some unexpected difficulty in the management of the economy, they will normally be eliminated in a comparatively short time and in any event cannot be counted on for programmes of public expenditure that will, once started, absorb resources for many years ahead – probably even in increasing measure. There may be the odd occasion when it is necessary to attempt to increase the use of human resources for a short period only, by a short-lived emergency programme of increased public expenditure. But that is the exception; the normal situation will be that a choice will have to be made between the particular public expenditure proposal under consideration and the use of the resources which it would entail for the alternative purposes of the public or private sectors or for the balance of payments. It is in that context that the question 'Is this a better proposal?' takes on its full significance.

Two further words of explanation are perhaps needed before that set of alternatives can be fully accepted, both centring around the balance of payments. When a country imports goods or services it is making available to its own inhabitants the products of resources used abroad. These must be matched by the export of goods and services arising from the use of domestic resources. In effect therefore the enjoyment of the goods and services produced abroad is only made possible through the use of domestic resources. This is the long-term picture: in the short term the matching may not have taken place fully, resulting in an imbalance – either a deficit or a surplus – which must be made good later on. Accordingly a country which has accumulated a balance of payments deficit over a period of years will probably need to earmark part of its resources over the next few years to making good that deficit; and to the extent that it is essential, during periods of imbalance, to limit the rate at which the deficit accumulates, a measure of unavoidable unemployment may arise during the period of switching resources from domestic purposes to exports. These are the circumstances in which the use of more resources for the balance of payments becomes essential and in which idle resources cannot be used for public expenditure purposes other than at the cost of exacerbating balance of payments difficulties.

In short, therefore, resources are used for the private sector or for the public sector or for the balance of payments; and given the full use of resources any new expenditure – which means the use of resources for that new purpose – can only be met out of a growth in resources or the diversion of existing resources. The questions for decision on public expenditure must therefore be framed in that context; hence the main Plowden Committee recommendation that public expenditure decisions 'should never be taken without consideration of (*a*) what the country can afford over a period of years having regard to prospective resources and (*b*) the relative importance of one kind of expenditure against another'.

The key words are 'relative importance': they repeat the essence of the famous dictum 'Gouverner, c'est choisir'. Indeed, a Government must make its choices, especially in the field of public expenditure. It must establish its own set of priorities, and Governments of differing philosophies may well have different views about the overall size of the public sector (i.e. the choice between resources being used for the public or for the private sector) and about the claims of competing programmes within the public sector.

Having got the right question one must set about getting the right answer. For this purpose the starting point is the realisation that there is no starting point – not, at all events, in the sense that one can start with a clean sheet and then list all the desirable public expenditure proposals. Rather is one confronted, at any point of time, with a moving, closely packed panorama. It will result from decisions taken at different times, some stretching several years back. The implementation of certain programmes may be in their early stages before they have built up to their full annual cost. Others may be increasing through government decisions to expand a particular service. Most will contain commitments for the future built into them. Few if any will be decreasing in size. Some will be largely uncontrollable – such as sickness benefit which depends on the fortuitous incidence of sickness and not on a governmental decision to spend a given sum. Others will be largely but not completely under the control of the Government – such as the vast amounts of local authority expenditure, where the final decision as to the amount spent is in local hands although in practice forecasts of expenditure agreed with Whitehall are generally not exceeded.

The first task in enabling the right new decisions to be taken must therefore be to get a clear picture of the existing situation; that is to say, what would happen if no new decisions were taken. The period covered by this survey would have to stretch sufficiently far into the future to enable new decisions to be taken in the knowledge of what flexibility exists in the periods ahead where present commitments will result in future expenditure, sometimes at an increased rate. It would also have to stretch sufficiently far into the past to enable one to see how the current pattern has been reached and the extent to which the circumstances on the basis of which past decisions were taken have changed. Such a survey would have to take place every time a group of new decisions had to be taken, which in practice means at least once a year. Equally important, the survey would have to include an estimate of the resources likely to be available on the basis of existing policies and past decisions.

Such a survey of public expenditure does in fact take place each year. The figures are analysed by reference to the purpose of the expenditure; and as Government as a whole is based broadly on departments serving different purposes, it happens that the analysis conveniently corresponds in the main to departments of Government. The period covered is five years and the recent past – although the record of the more distant past is always available if reference to it needs to be made. Five years is by no means the maximum period in the future over which current public expenditure commitments extend. Major capital projects frequently extend over a longer period than that, and major policy changes – such as increasing the number of doctors or of teachers – often take more than five years to show their full effect. On the other hand much can – and does – happen in a period of five years to invalidate current assumptions about both future expenditure and future resources. Which period contains most of the longer-term commitments and least of the figures which are unreliable is a matter of judgement. But all seem to be agreed that the five-year period is about right.

The effect of a decision to spend is to create a demand on current resources. The size of that demand can be conveniently, but not completely, described in normal money terms; for that is only one measure – and not the most relevant for public expenditure. Decisions of the same monetary amount may have different demand effects. The survey therefore includes the calculation of the demand effect of broad groups of expenditure, making it clear that owing to the difficulties inherent in such a calculation, the figures must be read with some reservations. At the same time information is obtained about manpower implications of the expenditure forecast so as to give supporting and very significant detail to the demand calculations.

Reference has already been made to the differing degrees of control over public expenditure exercised by the central Government. Accordingly the survey also incorporates an analysis of public expenditure by spending authority, such as local authorities and nationalised industries.

The picture thus given of the demands of the public sector at the time of the survey is now a fairly complete one, with all the more relevant and significant implications capable of being grasped and digested before new decisions are made – with one major exception. Nothing so far has been said about the resources available to meet the demands. Accordingly forecasts of the movement of the economy over the same period of five years are also prepared so as to enable the total of all demands to be related to the resources likely to be available. Although these figures, especially in the later years, will inevitably be subject to wide margins of error, without them it would be impossible to estimate what resources are likely to be available in total for the public and private sectors and for the balance of payments, nor, in particular, what resources are likely to be available to meet the combined demands of the various public expenditure programmes. It is that forecast which makes possible the 'consideration of what the country can afford over a period of years, having regard to prospective resources'.

This, then, is the starting point in the process of reaching decisions about future public expenditure. It can be seen that the annual survey is an extremely important document and it is appropriate therefore to consider its time-table and some of the difficulties encountered in preparing it. The initiating body is the department of Government which spends the money. Each such department prepares its own figures in the spring of each year and enters into discussions with the Treasury at official level in order to reach agreement on them, in particular about the precise effect of existing policy decisions over the ensuing years. By about May the figures agreed with each department can be assembled and are then submitted to a thoroughly representative and very high level committee of officials, known as PESC (Public Expenditure Survey Committee). They in turn present a report to Ministers showing where present policies will lead in terms of public expenditure at constant prices over a period of five years. This is produced about June and from then until October or November the report is considered by Ministers and decisions are taken on all the issues which arise affecting the amounts to be spent by each department on each public expenditure programme and the total figure. The period appears longer than it is; and it would be misleading to think that some four months are spent every year in close ministerial discussion. In fact this includes the holiday period when for some two months it is difficult to get a meeting of all senior Ministers of a kind that would be necessary in order to reach decisions on public expenditure. But of course many metings do take place at various levels and many difficult decisions have to be reached – in both senses of that term. The issues are frequently complex, and often the decision – almost invariably a majority, as opposed to a unanimous, decision – will be difficult for one or more Ministers to accept. Indeed it is not surprising that on occasion a Minister may feel that an unfavourable decision of great importance to his department, added to all the other pressures and inevitable frustrations and coming at a time when twelve months' work (often of an intensity far greater than is generally experienced in professional or commercial life) must have produced something close to complete exhaustion, has finally made ministerial life so intolerable that he must perforce consider – or even threaten – resignation.

But that is rather jumping ahead. The first difficulty is that of agreeing the figures for the cost, over five years, of existing policy decisions. These figures, when agreed, will form the starting point in the consideration of what further amounts should be spent, so they are of considerable importance. It is not difficult to imagine the kind of arguments that might arise. What part of the increased cost of a particular service represents the maintenance of the service in the altering circumstances of the future and what part a proposal, in effect, for improvement? How does one deal with the additional future cost arising out of a possibly fortuitous reduction in the past? Where a decision has been made to spend a given sum on an open-ended commitment, is the increase which is now seen to be very likely, a new decision or the maintenance of an existing policy decision? There are many examples which could be given of the difficulties which are inevitable when one is attempting to make estimates for the changing world of three, four or five years ahead. Moreover it will always be in the interest of the department concerned to argue for the higher figure. For the assumption is that every department – save possibly defence – will be entitled to an increase, and an increase can only be defined by reference to a starting point. The higher the starting point, the more will the department have to spend.

In these circumstances what is surprising is not that the difficulties inherent in the PESC approach lead to arguments, but that these arguments are almost always settled at official level – mainly between the Treasury and the department concerned – and that Ministers are therefore presented with a document setting out the agreed figures of existing public expenditure decisions. It is perhaps appropriate at this stage, therefore, to offer a comment on official, as opposed to ministerial, relationships, and in particular on relationships with the Treasury, for an understanding of the background atmosphere will undoubtedly help in appreciating the decision-making processes described below.

By the time an MP becomes a senior Minister he has developed the arts and attitudes of a skilled advocate. His function as a politician is not to display the strengths and weaknesses of his party's line on a particular issue and having compared them with the strengths and weaknesses of his opponent's policy, to attempt an objective summing up and a conclusion based solely on the merits (as he sees them, of course). Rather, having related that particular line to his general political philosophy, he will justitfy the conclusion, which by now he has absorbed, by every substantial argument in its favour which he can think of, only adding a passing reference to one, or at the most two, unimportant weaknesses in his argument to show what an obviously fair and broad-minded fellow he is. Similarly, as a Minister his task in Parliament will be to justify the policy conclusion reached by the Government and not to set out a series of arguments for and against, leaving it to the House to decide.

Not so the senior civil servant – at least, not to the same extent. He is not a partisan, his emotions are not involved, being permanent his perspective is different; and though the spokesman for and fully loyal to his department, his understanding of the other department's point of view may well have been strengthened by having worked in it, and as a loyal member of it, for a number of years.[1] He is therefore rather better situated than is his Minister to resolve differences of the kind which arise in the early stages of the PESC process. Nor is his attitude towards the Treasury quite the same as is, in general, that of his Minister; there are fewer causes for tension and minor resentment – but more of that anon. Sufficient has been said to indicate some of the circumstances surrounding the immensely difficult process of moving from the starting point to the finishing point – from the survey of existing policies and their public expenditure cost to the final document setting out the Government's proposals for public expenditure for the ensuing period.

It is also necessary, for a full understanding of the decision-making processes, to bear in mind that although the annual PESC exercise is likely to be the most important and far reaching of the occasions when public expenditure is under consideration by a Government, it is almost certainly not the only occasion during the year. There will be many occasions when individual proposals, or perhaps a small group of proposals, are considered and decided upon; there may be occasions during the year when the public expenditure programmes of many departments are reviewed and revised – upwards or downwards. For the background situation is continually changing. The world does not stand still and unexpected world events may call for an unexpected response in terms of public expenditure. The domestic economic climate alters and may call for the slowing down or the acceleration of certain programmes. None of this means that the annual exercise need not be carried out, or that the difficulties surrounding it are too great for any result to be meaningful or sufficiently permanent. But what it does mean is that the whole approach to public expenditure planning must be flexible.

The first big decision is obviously that as to the total size of the public expenditure bill for the year in question; and the preliminary questions which arise, although they relate to the substantial sum of £30,000 million and more, are not fundamentally different from the questions Mr Everyman asks himself when considering his own very much more modest budget: how much would he like – or does he need – to spend on the individual items; how much can he afford to spend in total?

[1] There is the amusing case of Miss Jones of Dept A who wrote a rather fierce and critical letter to Dept B before taking some leave and getting married. Returning as Mrs Smith she found she had been transferred to Dept B. Undeterred she wrote, as Mrs Smith, to Dept A, answering their criticisms and drawing attention to the faulty logic of Miss Jones's letter.

Ideally, he hopes, the two answers will coincide, when a decision will be extremely easy. In fact, he knows they never do: the desirable always exceeds the affordable (not least because by the time the affordable has grown to the size of what was earlier the desirable, what has been afforded has in the meantime given rise to new desires and so the desirable has forged ahead once more). Accordingly some kind of compromise must be reached in which the desirable is scaled down – more or less – to the affordable total, which in turn is stretched a little to accommodate some more of the desirable. For after all, as Mr Everyman's family will point out to him, just a little more on items D and F would make such a difference, while in relation to the total size of the budget the extra amounts would be hardly noticeable. And might not Mr Everyman get a rise next year or earn more in overtime pay? And who is to say that the amount set aside in the budget for a rainy day is either the minimum amount or essential this year? So the argument will run; and at the end of the day there will be a broad agreement – which is another way of saying a tolerable measure of disagreement – on the amounts to be spent on the individual items (even though somewhat less than desired) and on the overall total (even though somewhat more than could safely be afforded, unless an optimistic view were taken both of future earnings and the likely rainfall).

There is a considerable similarity between Mr Everyman endeavouring to make ends meet on his private budget and a Government doing the same for public expenditure. The first antecedent question in each case is 'How much can be afforded in total?' For a nation that is not an easy question to answer – indeed it is an impossible question to answer with the degree of accuracy that would import finality into the determination of the public expenditure total. For the answer turns on a number of complex questions of fact and complex issues of policy. What, to begin with, is the likely figure of GDP for the relevant period: that is to say, how much is likely to be available for all purposes, including public expenditure? How much of this total should be devoted to the other claimants, leaving what balance available for public expenditure? What would the effect be of such a conclusion on taxation policy? Alternatively, having regard to the difficulties of such an approach, would it be better to fix future public expenditure totals by reference to past public expenditure, by deciding simply on the rate of increase – or decrease? If the period chosen for the exercise is far ahead, may it not make the task of economic forecasting impossibly difficult? And if it is immediately in the future, may it not make the task of adjusting public expenditure programmes as required in the time available impossible of achievement? In any event is there any close connection in time between economic growth and the growth of public expenditure programmes; or should one adopt different time scales for these two? Each of the questions needs to be fully examined against a continually changing background and a full realisation of the fact that public expenditure programmes are dynamic affairs with their own built-in driving power: if nothing is done to the contrary they will have consumed nearly all, or all, or more than all the resources that will, on a final decision, be regarded as appropriate. It is not unlike considering the right route whilst riding a horse: the animal is pressing forward the whole time along the general line and at the pace already set, and being a strong animal with a will of its own, moving at a fair pace, it is going to require time and energy to do more than deflect it slightly.

The right period for the PESC exercise and the relative time scales of economic growth and public expenditure growth are probably the first questions to be examined. Here it is necessary to recall the timetable and to remember that the decisions reached by the Government in October or November are often merely proposals which must be approved by Parliament before they can become effective. These proposals are based on figures gathered together in the spring, so that something like nine months must elapse before the figures can be publicly discussed, and even longer before overall finality can be reached. Given that a year is the normal period for the consideration of budgets of this kind, which year – and a year in this context must mean the Government's financial year – is the right one? Clearly it is not the year covering the period of discussion, for by the time the figures are published the year is three-quarters spent. The following year – which for the sake of clarity had better be called Year 2 – is to a substantial degree ruled out owing to the very nature of most public expenditure programmes. Some of them have a time scale of seven years or more: that is to say, a decision having at some time been taken in principle, a commitment extending over several years exists. In other cases the commitment extends over a shorter period, but still a period of years. Of course the commitments are not completely inescapable: they can, in exceptional circumstances, be varied or extinguished – at some cost. But in normal circumstances the degree of commitment is such that only a comparatively small sum in Year 2 would be left completely free for decision, and the question under consideration is which is the right year to choose for the exercise of a Government's decision. Years 1 and 2 having been ruled out in this way, the choice falls naturally on Year 3; not because that year is likely to be entirely free of commitments – that is far from the case. But it is likely to afford a substantial area for decision-making; and, equally important, an even later year would create too many difficulties in forecasting so far ahead. For to choose Year 4 would mean forecasting something like forty-two months ahead on average. So Year 3 – the one starting some fifteen months after the date of publication of the figures – becomes the focal year, although neither Year 2 nor Year 4 are ignored in the process.

Closely related to this issue of the correct focal year is the question whether there is a necessary connection between the time scale chosen for public expenditure and the same time scale for the economy as a whole. In other words, accepting that public expenditure decisions should be taken in the context of 'what the country can afford over a period of years having regard to prospective resources', does the public expenditure decision for Year 3 have to be related to the likely total resources of that particular year, and similarly year by year? The answer must be that although such a comparison would be informative, it should certainly not be regarded as definitive. In the first place, there is no reason why twelve months should be taken as the right period over which to measure the growth of the economy. Powerful as may be the effect of the moon on the oceans, no one has ever suggested that the rate of growth in the economy is related to the passage of the earth around the sun. Various cyclical periods have been suggested in relation to the economy, but none as short as a year. If therefore the growth of the economy over a period of, say, four or five years is estimated to be such as to accommodate satisfactorily the total public expenditure planned for the same period, it does not in ordinary circumstances matter very much whether the path along which public expenditure climbs is identical with the path taken by the economy. It may, for example, be shallower to begin with and steeper at the end without affecting the outcome or the planned relationship. In extraordinary circumstances such as a severe balance of payments crisis, such flexibility might not be possible, but in those circumstances the appropriate special steps would be taken and the conclusion based on normal circumstances would be unaffected.

What emerges from the consideration up to this point is that the year starting some fifteen months ahead is the right focal year for deciding the level of public expenditure and that there is nothing in the relationship between the growth of public expenditure and the growth of the economy to tie the one to the other for precisely the same twelve months alone. There is therefore in normal circumstances no overwhelming argument arising out of the pattern of growth of the economy against that year being chosen as the focal year.

The next question that arises is whether the amount available can be assessed with such precision as to import finality into the determination of the total of public expenditure to be planned for the relevant year. Clearly it cannot, for it is impossible to be sufficiently precise in all the estimates involved. It is not merely that one is peering into the future without the possibility of controlling future events. For the same argument would apply, although with less force, if one were dealing with a period immediately ahead. As is later explained in more detail, the argument that arises in practice in relation to the overall size of public expenditure is not whether a proposed total should be increased by 10 per cent or by 5 per cent, but rather as to a variation of $\frac{1}{4}$ per cent or $\frac{1}{2}$ per cent or, at the very most, 1 per cent. That is to say, there is likely to be agreement that the appropriate measure of increase for the particular focal year is between 3 per cent and $3\frac{1}{2}$ per cent, for example, with some arguments pointing to 3 per cent and others to 3½ per cent. Now that difference may well represent a substantial sum: if the total were £30,000 million then it would represent £150 million. Such a sum could be of vast importance to a great number of programmes where an extra few million pounds might be held to make all the difference. But what is under consideration is not the needs of individual programmes but the order of magnitude of the total sum involved in relation to the accuracy with which growth in the economy two years ahead may be forecast. That sum, varying between ¼ per cent and 1 per cent of the total of public expenditure, is equivalent to between ⅛ per cent and ½ per cent of the GDP. But the growth of the economy cannot be determined with such accuracy, as oft-repeated experience has shown. The margin of error must be regarded as being of the order of 1 per cent – double the maximum and eight times the minimum. Nor, as stated above, would the difficulty be resolved by shortening the months ahead before the start of the focal period. For it is virtually impossible to affect the course of public expenditure in the immediate future, and it is only when the year has ended that GDP can be calculated within the required margin of error.

To sum up, then, the likely future growth of the economy is something which must be taken into account in determining the size of future public expenditure; but the amount of that growth cannot be determined with sufficient precision to dispose of the kind of arguments that are likely to arise in deciding the size of the total increase in public expenditure programmes in the focal year. In these circumstances it is only necessary to deal quite shortly with the other difficulties which arise in endeavouring to deduce from the total of GDP the amount available for public expenditure. From that total – itself a somewhat imprecise estimate – must be deducted the amount, if any, to be set aside for balance of payments purposes and the sum of the amounts to be allocated to the private sector for current consumption and for capital expenditure. Each one of these is clearly an enormously important issue, but it is only necessary in the present context to refer to the fact that the obvious complexity of the issues must inevitably involve the possibility of different conclusions being reached as to the precise amounts to be set aside. Thus a further uncertainty is added to the margin of error inherent in the original economic forecast. Indeed the possibility of error could by now be so great as to make it clear that little assistance, if any, can be gained from an attempt to arrive at the total of public expenditure by treating it as a residual item in a calculation of prior economic needs. But there are still more question-marks in this approach. The first relates to the amount to be set aside out of public expenditure for capital expenditure. This is a very important tool in economic management, for it is the method by which a Government can exert early influence on the level of the nation's spending on investment. All Governments attach great importance to investment as being a major contributor to future economic growth, and it is the case that whereas in the private sector investment decisions rest with private individuals who may or may not respond to government exhortations and fiscal encouragement – except perhaps embarrassingly late – in the public sector some investment decisions can be directly influenced. Now the slower the private sector responds, the greater is the pressure put upon the public sector to advance its investment plans. Inevitably, therefore, estimates on public sector investment expenditure must allow a measure of flexibility, and that can only add to the difficulties of calculating precisely the residual figure of public current expenditure.

There are still further substantial difficulties of assessment. What has so far been considered is the effect of private sector decisions on the residual size of the public sector. But the reverse must also be considered – the effect on the private sector of public expenditure decisions. Public expenditure involves expenditure on goods and services. The goods are largely supplied by the private sector – indeed the Government is the private sector's largest customer. The services include the salaries of thousands of individuals who habitually spend their money in both the private and public sectors. The calculation of the effect of these decisions must clearly allow for a further margin of error.

Finally there is the question of taxation – large, complex and sensitive. Fortunately, only one aspect need be touched on at this point. A decision to increase the total of public expenditure requires for its implementation a decision to increase the level of taxation correspondingly, assuming other things to be equal. Of course they never are: but making that assumption for the moment, one is even so faced with the fact that the relationship between variation in taxation and variation in demand on resources is complex and imprecise. As a result, an additional margin of error must be provided.

It is clear therefore that a Government cannot arrive at the precise figure for public expenditure for the focal year merely by the method of calculating what the available resources are. This is very far from concluding that the allocation of resources to the public sector should be decided without regard to the total resources available, but it does mean that the comparison must be more general and over a longer period of time than would be compatible with attempting to define public expenditure totals by reference to GNP estimates year by year. If a sufficiently precise answer cannot be found by examining what can be afforded, is the alternative approach of calculating what is desirable the right one? It has to be recognised that in relation to any single programme, provided it is a modest one, no argument based on what can be afforded in total can serve to demonstrate conclusively that the increase in a particular year should be 3½ per cent rather than the figure resulting from the new proposal of 3¾ per cent. That difference will not be sufficient to upset the general economic strategy decided upon, nor could it be maintained that such a proposal could not be financed out of increased taxation for there is no obvious finality to what can at a particular time be regarded as the nation's maximum taxable capacity. But it is never the case that only one proposal for increased public expenditure is put forward, and that a modest one. At any one time there are numerous proposals being pressed by the public, by interested parties, by Parliament and by departmental Ministers, all involving increased expenditure. It would be quite impossible to cater for all these demands. It hardly needs to be argued that the way to arrive at a sensible total is not simply to list all the proposals that are held to be beneficial and which would be put forward if there were no limits to the financial or physical resources that could be made available for the purpose; and having listed them to add up the cost and fix that as the figure of public expenditure for the year. That would be to fly against common sense and also against the recommendation of the Plowden Committee about considering 'what the country can afford'.

On the other hand proposals for increased expenditure cannot be ignored. Indeed, some proposals may by general consent be more beneficial and yet no more costly than existing programmes. The new proposals must clearly take the place of the old ones – phasing in the former and phasing out the latter are matters of consequential administrative detail. There may in any event be room for some new proposals: one department, such as defence, may be reducing its level of expenditure and the mere maintenance of the same overall level of real expenditure would mean that other departments could seek to fill the gap with their own proposals; or one particular programme may be coming to its natural end during the course of the year, and the responsible department may feel it has, as a result, a claim on those unused resources for one of its own new proposals. But more generally it may well be the case that a Government is going to decide that having regard to the growth pattern of the economy and the particular economic needs at the time, there is room for a small overall increase in public expenditure generally, in which case each department will naturally put in candidates for consideration. Nor will they be deterred from submitting a number of proposals, for at this stage no decision will have been reached as to the size of the overall increase, and each department will naturally feel entitled to the lion's share of any such ultimate increase having regard to the superior merits of its own proposals.

At this point a Government will have three very useful sets of figures relating to the expenditure of the focal year. First there is the full picture – in detail and in total – of the cost that will arise if no new decisions are taken; then there are the figures of what, in the view of the various departments and their Ministers, are the desirable additions to the bill; finally there are the economic forecasts and figures indicating, subject to decisions on taxation, what could reasonably be afforded for public expenditure, in round terms and subject to wide margins of error, if the various parts of the economic puzzle are to fit together so as to produce the desired picture. With all this information it will begin to be possible to form a tentative judgement – for that is all it can be at this stage – of the direction in which total public expenditure should move – that is to say, upwards or downwards – and, perhaps, as to whether the movement should be considerable or slight. At this point there will be nothing approaching precision, but if one were to describe on paper, in some suitable diagrammatic form, the size of public expenditure as presently planned for Years 1, 2 and 3, and if one were to add a shaded area around Year 3 (Year 1 being virtually over and Year 2 being firmly committed) indicating the proposed additions, and if one were to draw on a separate sheet of transparent paper, but to the same scale, a diagram which would necessarily be very shadowy round the edges, of what could be reasonably afforded on various assumptions, and if one were then to superimpose the second on the first, one would not be likely to find anything approaching coincidence, but what was common to both diagrams could be seen and an indication of the way ahead would be given.

In all this one has spoken of the total figure as if that were the first figure to be very tentatively arrived at. That is indeed so, for no Government can escape reaching a conclusion on this total, however it is arrived at, and the importance of that decision makes it natural, if not inevitable, that a tentative starting point should be here. But first a further test must be carried out, namely, to discover what kind of percentage variation on the previous year's figure would be represented by the tentative total. For if the variation does not come within the range of what is politically acceptable it cannot even be considered as a tentative figure. Public expenditure is a highly political issue and the pressures for increases of nearly every kind are such that, given the continuation of the growth of the economy, a planned decrease in expenditure would not be politically possible. A Government would have to plan for an increase, however small. It could be as little as 1 per cent provided the economic circumstances of the time can be shown to require it. But political necessity demands some planned increase, and the mere fact that, as in 1969–70, certain estimates proved excessive with the result that the actual total expenditure incurred was fractionally less than in the previous year, does not invalidate that statement. By the time the figures of the amounts actually spent in a particular year – the 'out-turn' – are available and published, general interest will be centring on the planned increase in public expenditure of several years ahead of that. Few will be interested in the out-turn and even they will regard it as past history. So the central political fact remains that the minimum plan for public expenditure for the focal year must be a measurable increase on the preceding year and for all practical purposes a reasonable interpretation of that minimum would be 1 per cent.

Now it is just possible to envisage circumstances in which at this stage of the decision-making process a minimum figure for the proposed increase would be a relevant consideration. But it is highly improbable; in fact it will almost certainly be the case that the problem will resolve itself into defining the ceiling rather than the floor. The point is not, however, purely academic, for it illustrates the importance attached to the growth of public expenditure expressed in percentage terms. Indeed so important is this, that irrespective of the route followed or the method pursued in arriving at the tentative figure of total public expenditure, it will need to be expressed in terms of a percentage increase on the previous year. That is the information which Parliament and the public seeks; that is the figure against which each department will ultimately set its own percentage increase. One has only to look at the annual reports presented by the Government to Parliament for ample confirmation of the practice of expressing public expenditure figures in terms of percentage variations from year to year.

At this stage one can define the issue a little more closely. What is being sought is a total figure for public expenditure in the focal year which will represent an increase, in money terms at constant prices, of not less than 1 per cent above the previous year; which will accommodate some of the pressing proposals for increased expenditure; and which will not be inconsistent with the country's economic needs, having regard both to likely resources and to the value of the public sector to the private sector. To these qualifications a further one can now be added, namely, that the implementation of the total programme will not necessitate unacceptable increases in taxation. 'Unacceptable' in this context means politically unacceptable. Public expenditure, as has already been argued, is a highly political issue; but equally – if not more so – is taxation, and the two pressures work in opposite directions.

The subject of taxation was earlier touched on to show that it did not provide the kind of inflexible barrier which would prevent a single modest proposal being added to a tentatively fixed overall figure for public expenditure. Indeed in Chapter 2 it was additionally argued that in the long run taxation would be found to accommodate itself to moderate annual increases in public expenditure. What we are now concerned with is whether, in the short term, the kind of increase that might best fit in with the various factors already listed will be such as to require early legislative proposals for increases in taxation which, in the opinion of the Government, would not be generally acceptable. All tax increases are of course unpopular, but the question is not as simple as that. A large number of political and economic considerations will have to be taken into account, including general expectations, and the Government will in the end exercise its own judgement: it will conclude that public expenditure proposals become increasingly difficult to finance out of taxation the more they add up to new tax legislation and that there is a figure beyond which the consequential additional tax proposals are politically unacceptable.

Three related comments need to be added at this point. First, the assistance given by an examination of the tax aspects is valuable but, again, indicative rather than definitive. It will indicate the kind of increase that could possibly be accommodated and the kind that could not. Second, even such a tentative statement overstates the position, for it is not the case that every increase in public expenditure would require to be financed out of a corresponding increase in taxes. Chancellors of the Exchequer do not seek a precise mathematical balancing of their budgets: they budget for a surplus or a deficit according to the needs of the occasion. Additional public expenditure might well, it could be argued, be financed out of such a surplus – or by increasing such a deficit – without affecting the general strategy of a budget. That would be a matter for argument and would clearly depend largely on the amount of the proposed expenditure and the size of the surplus (or deficit). But all this serves to underline the point already made that the level of public expenditure cannot be determined with complete precision by reference to tax considerations.

It is the third comment, however, that is the most important one. It would be quite wrong to conclude that the amount of taxation to be raised in a particular year is decided upon with the figure of public expenditure in mind – or even mainly so. It is necessary to understand that although public expenditure is of great social, economic and political importance, and although it is mainly financed out of taxation, the decisions about taxation are taken in a different context, the economic one. The level of taxation is a most important consideration in the management of the economy and it is getting the right economic climate that matters most. It is necessary to point out this simple truth in view of a tendency to confuse the relative functions of the Budget and Public Expenditure Survey Committee (PESC) exercises. It is the Budget which, through its effect on the whole of the economy, can help greatly in the creation of more resources for the nation. It is the PESC exercise which will determine whether a large part of those resources are wisely spent. Certainly full account will have to be taken of public expenditure in arriving at the Budget judgement which in turn will lead to decisions about the level of taxation; and equally, as has been explained, taxation levels will have to be borne very carefully in mind in deciding the total of public expenditure. But it is economic considerations which are – and must be – dominant.

An additional difficulty arises out of the particular years being considered. The focal year for public expenditure comes up for consideration twelve months before it becomes the focal year for Budget purposes. In both cases consideration is not limited to one year, for the decisions taken will affect years further ahead. Indeed it is mostly the case that Budget decisions will not have anything like their full impact until the year starting some twelve months after Budget day, and in this sense it is the same focal year as for public expenditure. But the fact remains that the amount of public expenditure for the year of the

Budget will have been decided some fifteen months before Budget day – which may prove to be an added complication for the Chancellor of the day. Similarly an added complication arises in the consideration of the focal year for public expenditure in that any weight which needs to be given to tax considerations will be the more difficult to assess.

The conclusion that emerges from all that has so far been said on this topic is that the task of deciding even tentatively on the overall figure for public expenditure must be a very complicated one; and that is certainly the case. The indications are imprecise; there is much room for argument. Clearly no figure can be demonstrated to be the 'right' one to the exclusion of all others. But a great deal of information will have by now been put together, and a judgement will be starting to form in the minds of Treasury Ministers as to the kind of percentage increase which should satisfy the economic and taxation requirements and might also satisfy social needs and political aspirations. The 'kind of percentage increase' will be a band rather than a single figure – stretching, for example, between 3 per cent and 3½ per cent on the basis that anything well above 3½ per cent would result in unacceptable tax problems and create undesirable economic pressures; while anything substantially below 3 per cent could not hope to satisfy reasonable political expectations or to accommodate the essential improvements in, or additions to, public expenditure programmes. The band would at this stage be a tentative one: in the example chosen of 3–3½ per cent the final increase might conceivably be 2¾ per cent or 3¾ per cent – both could be shown to be justified. That would still allow a very substantial increase in expenditure, sufficient to accommodate any number of disputes about possible candidates for additional expenditure. By the mid-seventies, for example, a difference of 1 per cent would represent £350 million or so at current prices – a very substantial sum in terms of additional expenditure.

It will, then, be for the Treasury – in effect the Chancellor of the Exchequer in consultation with his Treasury colleagues and taking into account the advice of his officials – to form a tentative view of an appropriate percentage increase. The responsibility cannot fall on any other department of Government: it is the Treasury which will have amassed all the relevant information; it is Treasury Ministers and their senior advisers who familiarise themselves throughout the year with the background to problems of this kind and who will have absorbed the relevant facts and figures; it is the function of the Treasury to form a view in all these financial, fiscal and economic matters; and it is the Treasury which can take an impartial and informed view of the competing claims of the various spending departments. That it can take an impartial view stems simply from the fact that it is not itself a spending department; that it is in a position to take an informed view results from the fact that there is within the Treasury – at all the appropriate levels – sections dealing with each of the departments and familiarising themselves with their problems. It is only in this way that the Treasury is able to carry out its normal function of examining departmental estimates and proposals. Accordingly, in the process of forming a tentative view on a possible public expenditure figure, Treasury Ministers will have informed themselves not only of the views taken by their officials on the merits of the various departments' proposals for additional expenditure but also of their officials' estimates of the weight attached by each department itself to each of its own proposals. Treasury Ministers will thus be able to form a view as to what kind of increase might ultimately be acceptable to their ministerial colleagues, and to judge the likely response to any figure which might be in other respects satisfactory. As has been made very clear, all this is very tentative at this stage, and estimates of other people's reactions could be wrong in either direction. Nevertheless what has also become clear is that the Treasury will by now have collected sufficient factual material on the basis of which they will have been able to form a number of conclusions which, when put together, and viewed in the light of the various indications also available to them, will enable them to form a judgement as to the band of percentage increases within which final agreement inside the Government might be reached.

It is that agreement which is going to determine the issues as to individual programmes, departmental allocations and the grand total of public expenditure, and it is necessary at this point, therefore, before describing the steps taken to reach that goal, to explain what that goal is. Underlying the whole of the discussion in this chapter is the assumption that there is, for each year, having regard to all the relevant circumstances of that year, a figure for public expenditure which is broadly the right figure. What that is can only be arrived at by a process of listing all the relevant circumstances, ascertaining as far as possible (and within the time available) all the facts and likely developments with regard to those circumstances, weighing all the arguments with great care and patience, and reaching a judgement as to where the balance of argument lies. The right figure will not select itself – it has to be sought. Nor will it define itself. The only definition can be the joint view of all those who have accepted the responsibility of reaching an agreed conclusion and, in carrying out that responsibility, have equipped themselves in every possible way to reach a wise conclusion. In other words there must at the end of the day be a joint government view; and that is indeed the case, for a decision must be reached. Without a decision, the process of governing stops. The total amount must be decided so that the money may be provided so that each programme can be carried out in the way proposed. Theoretical views are not enough; a band of figures is not enough; there must be a precise figure and a precise instruction for all concerned. That is the goal – an agreed precise decision.

That it is going to be difficult to secure agreement is obvious. Weighing arguments is an individual process; we all tend to carry our own special pair of scales. We attach different weights to the same argument. That difficulty is somewhat lessened by the process of party government: that is to say, those who at any one time have accepted the responsibility of making the decision will all share broadly – but very broadly – the same political philosophy and are therefore likely to attach, within broad limits, the same kind of weight to a particular argument. But the difficulty, though reduced, is not thereby disposed of. A well-chosen Government will include members holding views representing a cross-section of all those electors who voted for them – something like half the population of the country. That kind of broad agreement will be of little help in determining some of the issues involved, and more than political philosophy will enter into some of the discussions affecting the favourite proposals of individual Ministers. In short, there will be disagreements; yet an agreed decision is required.

No department of Government will be unaffected by the public expenditure decision and all Ministers will therefore be concerned; but departments can in practice have only one departmental view and it is among the Ministers who are heads of departments that agreement must be sought. It is well known that where disagreement exists the Cabinet will have to resolve it, and in any event a public expenditure decision of this kind is of such importance as inevitably to be brought before the Cabinet. But it would be unwise in the extreme to regard a reference to Cabinet as an alternative to the process of endeavouring with understanding and patience to reach agreement. The minor reasons are that Cabinet is not a suitable forum for settling individual disagreements and would soon become bogged down if all such disagreements were referred to it. The major reasons are that until that kind of open-minded exchange takes place, no one can be certain where the truth lies. Moreover one is not in Cabinet engaged in the judicial process of assessing how much should be paid by A to B or B to A, they being two litigants who are involved in a commercial dispute and who are unlikely to see each other again. Here one is concerned to reach an understanding between colleagues who are jointly engaged in the extremely difficult task of governing and who must continue working together, helping one another and wishing to help one another. As far as possible, therefore, differences of view need to be resolved in such a way that both sides feel that each has contributed to a meeting of minds rather than that one should feel that he has been compelled to accept a decision based on numbers against what he still believes to be the right view.

The task that is now seen to emerge, therefore, is that of winning agreement on a precise figure within – or at least very close to – a band of figures, from colleagues who – or some of whom – are going to find it very difficult to come to an agreement; and to win it in such a way that there will remain a sufficient fund of mutual goodwill to enable the same colleagues to resolve similar difficulties in other areas of government which are bound to arise in the very near future. It is not only the goal but the method of reaching it which will need to be borne in mind in every action that is taken from this point onwards.

There is more than one way of proceeding at this stage: which one is adopted will depend on the circumstances – including the atmosphere – existing at the time and the degree of success which was experienced on the last occasion the same approach was tried. It is a reasonable assumption that men and women of goodwill and good minds, broadly sharing the same philosophy, will, when confronted with the same issues, be likely to go through the same processes of thought and to reach the same – or similar – conclusions. But they will not necessarily jump to those conclusions; they must be given not only the opportunity to traverse the same mental journey, but adequate time to move by logical steps from place to place. So there is obvious merit in the argument that a Chancellor should at this point give his colleagues the opportunity of examining the facts and the arguments and reaching the same conclusion – in much shorter time than he himself took because the route will by now be suitably signposted; but they must be given adequate opportunity none the less. What they will be invited to agree is that all the facts, indications, trends and arguments relating to economic, social and political needs – in short all the relevant factors – lead to the same broad, tentative conclusion as he himself has reached. He will probably not wish to be more precise at this stage; but to secure broad agreement on that general proposition will mean a great deal. It will, for example, mean that if the details can be fitted into that total, the tentative conclusion referred to will have become a final conclusion. Moreover, the matters which will have to be raised in the discussion will be some of the most important in terms of good government. Discussions and conclusions of that importance will almost certainly be regarded as appropriate for the Cabinet – the supreme committee of Ministers, chaired by the Prime Minister himself – even if, as sometimes happens, there also exists a special committee of Ministers charged with the duty of advising the Cabinet on major public expenditure issues. If such a committee were in operation, no doubt it would be asked to consider any proposals of this kind first. But for present purposes it should be assumed – for reasons which will be discussed later on – that no such committee exists and that the matter goes straight to Cabinet.

The Prime Minister works at No. 10 Downing Street, the Chancellor at No. 11, next door. It is very easy for him to walk along the corridor connecting the two houses without even having to go outside his own front door. A few paces will enable him to discuss personally with the Prime Minister any matter of importance on which he would find the latter's preliminary views very helpful before displaying the issues before his colleagues generally. A proposal of the kind under discussion would be very appropriate for such a consultation, and presumably that is what the Chancellor would next do. Assuming that the Prime Minister reacted favourably, he would then arrange for a paper setting out all the considerations and drawing the desired conclusion to be circulated to his colleagues for consideration at a fairly early Cabinet meeting. He might also take the opportunity of describing to one or two of his colleagues, in a quite informal manner, the way his mind was working on this issue and mentioning that a paper would be put before Cabinet shortly. He might – but this would depend entirely on the circumstances – be in a position to estimate, in answer to the enquiries of those particular colleagues, which of the programmes to which they attached great importance were likely to be accommodated within the broad band he had it in mind to recommend.

The stage would thus be set for a useful discussion of the Chancellor's still tentative proposals. In the meantime all the members of the Cabinet would have the paper before them, together with the comments and advice of their senior officials. They would presumably form preliminary – but no more than preliminary – conclusions, in advance of the Cabinet discussions. But the important consideration would be that given at the meeting itself, for no discussion on paper can move minds to the same degree as the spoken word – and it is the moving of minds in the desired direction that is the task confronting every Minister who puts a paper to Cabinet.

So far this description of the process of reaching a decision on public expenditure has centred on the vast amount of information which has had to be gathered and digested and the trends and attitudes which have had to be assessed – all told a highly logical process. But it would be wrong to assume that the final decision owes everything to logic and nothing to emotion. The part that emotion can play will vary with the circumstances and especially with the topic; but it would be difficult to think of a single political issue where it does not play some part. Public expenditure decisions in particular range over a host of extremely human issues – schoolchildren without milk; old-age pensioners without coal; the survival of a firm employing many thousands in an area of high unemployment; withdrawing from the Far East and so saying goodbye to old glories. So many of the problems must be approached with a warm heart as well as a cool head. But the printed – or the typewritten – word contains little warmth as compared with the spoken word and will accordingly carry less persuasion. Then again, quite apart from the human content of the issue, only the spoken word with its inflections and accompanying facial expressions can bring an argument alive. Finally, only the two-way process of question and answer, of argument and counter-argument, and of implicit assumption and explicit testing of assumption, can evoke a meeting of minds. So it is necessary for a Minister carrying the heavy responsibilities of a Chancellor to be skilled – more skilled than most of his Cabinet colleagues – in the art of presenting a case and of replying to counter-arguments. It is a very great art requiring great clarity of mind, great depth of understanding, enormous self-discipline, endless patience and great sensitivity – to mention but some of the qualities needed. Making a case in Cabinet is quite different from making a case in Parliament and very different indeed from making a case on a public platform.

It may be asked why such importance is attached to the art of persuasion if it be true – as was earlier claimed – that people of ability in these circumstances are likely, when confronted with the same problem, to go through the same thought processes and reach the same or similar conclusions. The answer lies in the willingness or otherwise of the individual Minister to accept arguments which would lead to an unwelcome conclusion. A lot will, of course, depend on the circumstances and the atmosphere at the time; but a reasonable assumption would be that there are some members favourably disposed, some unfavourably, and some neither one nor the other. On this issue the second category will comprise those who feel sure that to agree to the Chancellor's proposals would be likely to exclude the possibility of their getting such an increase in their departmental allocations as would permit of much-desired programmes being accommodated. Now two things are required of such a Minister. The first is that he should join with his colleagues in an objective search for the wisest policy decision in the interests of good government; the second is that he should advocate his departmental causes. There is no doubt that they will merit his advocacy – they would not have got thus far, receiving the blessing of the Minister and his senior advisers, if they had not been worthwhile. As in so many matters coming before Cabinet, the issues at the end of the day will not be between good and bad proposals, but between good and good, or perhaps between now and a little later on. So a Minister will have no difficulties of conscience in promoting his departmental point of view. Moreover he knows that if he does not do so, it is most unlikely that anyone else will and the issue will go by default. In these circumstances he will naturally be less willing to accept certain arguments than he would were he a non-departmental member of the Cabinet.

This does not mean that the decision of the Chancellor in the first place to put a paper to Cabinet was unwise. For if the discussion has gone reasonably well he will have satisfied or persuaded a substantial number, perhaps the majority, of his colleagues that his proposals should be adopted. He will in any event have pleased all his colleagues, including those he has failed to persuade, by giving them the opportunity to express their dissenting views at this early stage before his proposals have taken on a more precise form; the alternative course of not sharing his thinking with them might have produced or permitted a marked hardening in their attitudes. Equally he may have been influenced by some of their arguments and felt justified in indicating that he would reconsider certain aspects in the light of what his colleagues had said. Finally, he will have been able to form, as a result of the discussion, a closer estimate of the size of the difficulties he would have to overcome in obtaining a decision at the final stage. For all these reasons he will have been helped forward by the Cabinet discussion.

There might well be one or other outcome to a Cabinet discussion of that kind. The first – and the more likely – would be a summing up by the Prime Minister to the effect that there was broad agreement in Cabinet that the Chancellor should proceed to the more detailed consideration of the year's public expenditure programmes on the basis of his general proposals. The Prime Minister might perhaps add, having regard to what had been said on all sides, that Cabinet had noted that the Chancellor would, during the course of that consideration, give special weight to the need to do so and so. The second possibility is that the discussion had persuaded either the Chancellor or the Prime Minister – who, not being involved so directly, would have been able to assess accurately the way the discussion was developing – that there was too much involved in the proposals for them to be digested satisfactorily at one meeting, whether or not an adjustment of one kind or another would be likely to help them forward. At that point a short whispered conversation between the two – in most Cabinets the Chancellor sits immediately on the Prime Minister's left, the Cabinet Secretary immediately on his right, and the Foreign Secretary immediately opposite – could well have taken place so as to establish an identity of view on this particular aspect, with the result that the Prime Minister would choose a suitably early opportunity of suggesting that perhaps Cabinet had progressed as far as it reasonably could at that first discussion of the Chancellor's paper and that it would be returning to it again when everybody had had an opportunity of considering carefully everything that had been said (and perhaps, if this had arisen in the discussion, in the light of the further information which the Chancellor had undertaken to circulate in regard to a particular aspect).

The outcome which can be dismissed as being wholly improbable is that of Cabinet rejecting the Chancellor's proposals completely. The proposals would not have been framed or worded in such a way as to attract a conclusion of that kind; they would not, however framed, have been put forward if the weight of argument had been so heavily against them – and that is the only circumstance in which Ministers would reach such a conclusion; and if, in spite of the care that had been taken reasonably to prepare the ground, the discussion had, as a result of some entirely unexpected turn of events, developed very unhelpfully from the point of view of the Chancellor, he would, through the Prime Minister, have secured the second outcome just described – and at a suitably early stage.

In that event discussions would follow between the Chancellor and the two or three colleagues mainly concerned in voicing doubts and difficulties during the Cabinet discussion. Both sides would be aware of the views of the majority of their Cabinet colleagues; both would be anxious to find at least a partial accommodation with one another.

Moreover the further passage of time and the further consideration given will have familiarised the Ministers with the problems involved. If a counter-proposal suggested by one of the Ministers in question were critical from the Treasury point of view, the Chancellor would have to be quite firm in explaining that that was the case and the Minister would almost certainly accept the position. If the counter-proposal were not critical, the Chancellor would endeavour to meet the Minister to some extent, taking great care not to go so far as to give any justification to a possible complaint from other Ministers that this Minister was being singled out for favourable treatment because he had made a fuss. The matter would then come back to Cabinet, possibly in a somewhat informal way, when approval on the original or slightly amended lines would probably be secured after quite a short discussion. Once Cabinet has had a deep discussion on a particular issue it tends to show a marked disinclination to spend long on the second encounter. Ministers' minds will in the meantime have become more familiar with the problems and more aware of the trend of the argument: they will be very conscious of the likely outcome as indicated by the first discussion; those who were opposed will have had the satisfaction of a further discussion and possibly also of a small concession; and by this time many new issues will be pressing. For all these reasons there arises a general desire to dispose of the matter quickly, and one can assume that the Chancellor is now in a position to move forward to the next – probably the final – stage in reaching his goal. But before leaving No. 10 for the various Ministries in which negotiations are now going to take place, it would be appropriate to add a few further comments about Cabinet and its committees, even though this is a topic to which further reference will need to be made in later chapters.

Reference has already been made to the importance of the spoken word, to the part played by emotion, to the great skill required of a Minister who needs to excel in the art of persuasion among a body of expert practitioners in that art and to the need to press a departmental point of view. None of this detracts from the supreme part played by logical argument: the spoken word will have no more effect than the written one if it is part of an illogical case; the skill of the habitual persuader will achieve nought if the case put forward lacks logic; and the wells of emotion soon dry up if logical argument makes plain that what was being called forth was in reality sentiment in favour of the superficial. Logical argument does indeed play an important and pervasive part; but it does not suffice. Where important decisions of the kind under discussion come to be made, they are made by men and women meeting jointly to exercise their judgement, and at their meeting personality, emotion, persuasiveness and the feeling of one human being for another all play their additional part.

Partly for these reasons, Cabinet tends to be very unpredictable. One simply cannot foretell how a particular discussion will go – assuming, that is, that large-scale canvassing of views has not taken place beforehand. Not only may the mood of Cabinet have been affected by some very recent event; even a change in the order of the agenda may affect the outcome on a particular issue to a certain extent. The pressures and strains surrounding the resolution of a complex of issues taken early on the agenda may so affect Ministers temporarily as to require an almost light-hearted treatment of the following item. A slip in the presentation of a case or an impatient comment may get a discussion going in a very different direction from that intended; and one cannot recall the spoken word. The order of speaking may affect the issue: at a critical stage in the argument when the issue is in the balance, a strong and authoritative intervention by *A* might succeed in pushing the argument in the desired direction. But if at that point *B* is called to speak and makes an equally strong and authoritative speech in the other direction, by the time *A* finally puts his view forward opinions may have hardened sufficiently to be unaffected by *A*'s arguments. It is simply too exhausting to hold an open mind about issue after issue; at a certain stage the mind seeks relief by coming to a conclusion – not jumping to a conclusion, but deciding that enough weighty material has been put forward to justify forming a particular view and to justify paying scant attention to any new arguments in the opposite direction.

No Minister is likely to bring a matter before his Cabinet colleagues for resolution if he feels sure he is going to be overwhelmingly defeated. There is simply no point in his doing so. There may be the odd occasion when a Minister is desirous of obtaining his colleagues' support for a proposal which is not pressing and which he feels may, because of its novelty, need more than one discussion to accustom them to the idea. In that event he may well put a paper to Cabinet so as to secure a discussion – giving his idea a preliminary airing so that it will not seem strange on its second introduction at some later stage. But he will not seek a decision at this early stage – to do so would be to court disaster.

In the ordinary course, then, a Minister will try to avoid bringing before Cabinet an issue on which he is going to suffer a major defeat. For by doing so he will not have advanced his case at all; on the contrary, he will most likely have denied himself the possibility of bringing the issue forward at a later date, which he otherwise might have desired to do. On the other hand he will have damaged his own standing a little by demonstrating that his judgement was wrong; and he will have suffered a most unpleasant and, though not humiliating, a demoralising experience – and he needs all the resources of morale he can muster to cope with the burdensome difficulties of his job. Yet every Minister will have experienced unexpected defeat at Cabinet and many an unexpected victory.

It is necessary to be aware of this characteristic of unpredictability as well as of the part played by human relations and by emotion in order to understand the perils with which the journey to the desired goal is fraught. All this is the habitual concomitant – certainly of healthy democratic government, where public views and pressures have to be assessed and taken into account. Unfortunately the assessment tends to vary from one Minister to the next.

The job of government would, of course, be a lot easier if differing views did not have to be reconciled; if arguments only had to be counted, not weighed; if emotion and human attitudes never entered into it. But government would in consequence be a lot worse. For all its defects the committee system does work: it produces decisions. At its worst it produces decisions which are so vague and ambivalent that one has to wait to read the minutes before one can be sure what the decision was. And yet even then the fudging may have been deliberately chosen as the only way of avoiding worse disasters. At its best, Cabinet can be extremely impressive. It is not merely that it presents the opportunity for a number of really big men and women to grapple with really big issues, aided by their own high intelligence – at one stage nearly half the members had obtained 'firsts' at their universities and in addition there were those who had left school at fourteen or fifteen and whose understanding was at least as profound – and by that of some of the best brains in the Civil Service. That is, of course, impressive; but what is even more impressive, and much more difficult to describe, is the occasion – after a series of excellent contributions in which Ministers have not merely dealt with the issues as originally presented, but, as discussion has gone on, have responded fully to the new points made and have dealt with the issues in their newly-emerging shape – when there begins to emerge a consensus of opinion which is greater and more profound than any single one of the views put forward. It is as if the arguments, instead of opposing each other at the same level, were adding one to the other and taking the discussion to an ever higher level until the true solution is clearly revealed. No single member of the Cabinet may have put forward a view which commanded general support, yet each has made a contribution towards reaching the essential truth. Cabinet as a whole has once more been able to achieve more than any individual member could have done.

Time spent on describing the working of Cabinet – a separate book would be needed to do so at all adequately – is by no means time wasted. For it is in Cabinet that the important decisions are made, and no matter how carefully the ground may have been prepared, Cabinet has a life of its own and reaches its own decisions. But it would be right now to take up the thread once more at the point reached; namely of Cabinet having decided, whether in one bite or two, to confirm the tentative approach proposed by the Chancellor. What remains to be done is to hammer out agreement – as far as possible – with individual Ministers on individual programmes in a way that will be approved by other Ministers and, where agreement cannot be reached, to refer the issue to

Cabinet for decision. The methods by which agreement will be sought are many; the difficulties which will be encountered are great; the total picture will become very blurred before it finally emerges in the form of a series of departmental allocations adding up to an acceptable total. The process is going to be extremely painful to all concerned; but everyone knows that agreement simply must be reached and that there is a not-too-elastic time limit. Added to those two helpful factors is the knowledge that a framework exists in the decision of Cabinet – not a rigid one, but one that indicates, if not the exact size of public expenditure, then the order of magnitude of the percentage increase.

On the other hand, there is no established machinery which might provide precedents and guide-lines for resolving difficulties so as to ease the journey somewhat. Different Governments have considered different methods. The suggestion which immediately occurs to one is to appoint a committee of senior Ministers charged with the responsibility of examining departmental proposals, weighing one against the other, and making recommendations to Cabinet. The committee would as far as possible consist of Ministers without departmental responsibilities and would naturally be chaired by the Chancellor of the Exchequer. Such a system has a lot to recommend it: it is thoroughgoing and it gives every departmental Minister the opportunity of appearing before his colleagues and explaining the merits of his departmental proposals. But it is not, in fact, a very successful method. First, there are manning problems. There are very few Ministers in a Cabinet of normal size who are free of departmental responsibilities, and it does not necessarily follow that they are the best equipped to carry out the rather specialised task involved. Then there is the fact that a committee is not the appropriate forum for arguing detailed points. These have to be discussed between a Treasury Minister and the Minister of the spending department just the same – there is no saving of time there. But the main weakness of this arrangement is that the time necessarily spent by all concerned is wholly disproportionate to the results achieved. It does not get down to grips with the situation, and the issues involved are such that little progress can be made unless one gets down to very close grips. Differences of view are not resolved in the course of the bipartite discussions between Treasury and departmental Ministers because both sides to know that the arguments will have to be repeated before the committee and neither will agree to anything less than is hoped for when the committee stage takes place. In the same way, at that committee stage no departmental Minister is going to agree to anything less than he hopes to be able to persuade Cabinet to grant. In fact, far from resolving differences the advisory committee process encourages the adoption of negotiating positions and the hardening of attitudes accordingly. Its main advantage is that those members of the committee who are members of Cabinet are better informed when

Cabinet comes to consider the matter than they would otherwise be. So although that system may conceivably be a suitable one in the circumstances of a particular year, it is not sufficiently useful in practice to become an established method of resolving public expenditure issues of a major kind.

In the absence of special machinery, resort must be had to the normal machinery and to bipartite discussions between Treasury and departmental Ministers. The normal machinery comprises the various committees of senior and junior Ministers by means of which proposals of individual Ministries are processed before being adopted by the Government as a whole. The broad purpose of the committees is to ensure that these proposals, which will have been processed inside the department and will have secured the approval of the relevant departmental Minister, are examined and justified before a group of colleagues so constituted as to include every Minister who is likely to have a departmental interest in them. If it is a proposal which will result in additional public expenditure – as is very often the case – then the Treasury will be represented on the committee. Proposals of this kind arise throughout the course of the year; the aspect of public expenditure is very important and will require separate discussions. What is under consideration at the moment is any method by which agreement may be reached between the Treasury and the department, after Cabinet has indicated the broad framework and before the final figure has been decided upon, in respect of public expenditure proposals for the focal year. The normal committee machinery provides one such method in that if the relevant committee – or Cabinet itself if for some reason the matter requires to be considered by Cabinet – decides on merits that the proposal should be put into effect and the Treasury representative concurs, then it follows that the necessary finance must be made available.

Similarly where departments have proposals of a kind which do not need to be processed by any committee of Ministers, then agreement by the Treasury of the consequential addition to public expenditure will again result in that proposal being included in the public expenditure figure for the focal year. But the number of proposals likely to be cleared in these two ways is very small, and Treasury Ministers will need to be absolutely sure that in agreeing to the proposals of one department they are not going to run into difficulties with other departments. For no matter what the circumstances, some proposals will have to be omitted, and it will be open to the departmental Minister sponsoring such a proposal to maintain that it would have been included had the finance been available and that the finance would have been available had it not been earmarked for one of the proposals agreed under either of the methods described, and that no opportunity was given to him to register his objection at the time. It is for these reasons that Treasury Ministers will need to be very circumspect in everything they do in this connection.

The greater part of public expenditure relates to large programmes of a continuing nature, such as education and the Health Service. Various aspects of the policy underlying these programmes are discussed in Government and debated in Parliament from time to time in the ordinary course of events. All basic programmes are subject to review from time to time, when decisions are taken affecting their cost over the ensuing years. But the best time to undertake such reviews, essential as they are, is not at this period when decisions must be reached on the total of public expenditure for the focal year. Indeed the Government machine would be completely overloaded if that were attempted; the essential task of deciding public expenditure budgets would never be completed.

At this stage, then, in the process of reaching a decision the assumption must be that all existing programmes are included in the tally at the agreed PESC figures. These will automatically include any variation, upwards or downwards, resulting from the latest review, whenever that took place. It is on new programmes and the development of existing programmes that discussion will centre. There will also be the need to agree a figure to meet any unexpected turn of events. A rough calculation will show the extent to which public expenditure, if provision were made to meet all demands, would exceed the tentatively agreed rate of increase. (There is no need to consider the opposite alternative, for it never arises in practice; and even if it did, there would be nothing to prevent immediate agreement.) It is the total excess which presents the problem, and its size will indicate the severity of the attitude with which the problem of reconciliation will need to be approached.

It will not normally be the case that equal severity will have to be applied to the examination of the claims of each department, and a breakdown of the total increase between departments will be of some assistance. Again the resulting figures will be indicative rather than definitive. It will be a simple matter to see to what extent each department's total claims represent an increase on the figures of the previous year and also of those for several years back. The departmental trend can easily be plotted and extrapolated into the future; comparison can be made with total trends, with the required figures, and so on. All this may yield some generally acceptable conclusions; on the other hand it may simply provide statistical ammunition for sustaining the dispute. An increase of 2 per cent per annum in each of the past three years' expenditure of a particular department indicates, so the Treasury will argue, that next year's proposal of 4 per cent is too high. The department, on the contrary, will insist that as expenditure has been kept down to such a low figure in the past, a substantial increase in the future is inevitable. It is not difficult to imagine the kind of arguments that will be used to justify any trend or comparison shown by the figures or alternatively to condemn it. So although a detailed examination of the figures may enable the abnormal to be segregated and some conclusion drawn as to the normal, not a great deal of assistance can be expected from this kind of analysis.

All that is left now, therefore, is to face up to the onerous and painful task of bipartite argument on each new proposal ('agreed' proposals having already been eliminated from the dispute) with a view to reaching agreement – as far as possible – on which should and which should not be included. This process may be assisted by a device which is fraught with difficulties but which has something to recommend it. It is to invite each department to express its own sense of priorities with regard to its marginal proposals. The initiative is in a sense transferred from the Treasury to the department – that is to say the initiative with regard to taking action aimed at reaching agreement, and initiative of this kind amounts to more than simple consultation. If, for example, the total tally at this stage looked like being x per cent in excess of any figure that the Treasury could contemplate, each department could be asked to submit, without prejudice, a list of those proposals, totalling about $(x+1)$ per cent which it regards as the least essential judged by the criteria of the department. The proposals would be set out in order of priority, thereby indicating the expenditure the denial of which would cause the least damage, and so on.

The proposals thus listed would probably be those upon which the Treasury themselves had reached the same or similar conclusions; on the other hand they might include surprises. But they could only be obtained on the basis that they were given without prejudice, and to discuss only those listed would have disastrous results. The department would feel that it had been improperly induced to disclose weaknesses in its own case. Indeed this feeling would arise if even a year or two later one such proposal was sought to be excluded at that time on the grounds that it had earlier been so listed. One or more departments might refuse to produce such a list, claiming that to do so would be tantamount to yielding the case without even discussing it. It might in those circumstances be necessary to go back to Cabinet to obtain the necessary approval on the basis that this was a better way of proceeding than not ascertaining departmental views of possible exclusions and that if some departments had to comply, all should do so. But any such decision against the strongly held views of a particular departmental Minister would not be likely to improve relations between him and his Treasury colleagues, and reliance on the big stick of Cabinet would be avoided as far as possible. It might conceivably happen that a departmental Minister, faced with the necessity of complying with a procedure which he regarded – not completely without justification – as being ill-conceived, would react by deliberately including in his list proposals the retention of which he knew his colleagues would regard as absolutely essential. Unless the inclusion in the list was obviously a ruse – and no department would be likely to be so inept – the proposals would not be challenged with a view to exclusion and the supplying of the list would not have advanced the argument at all. The whole question of whether or not to use the device of seeking lists of this kind must clearly be considered with great care; the special circumstances of a particular time might necessitate its use, but to attempt its use every year might well be self-defeating.

In the bipartite discussions which now fall for consideration, the Ministers concerned – that is to say of the Treasury and of the relevant department – might concentrate on detailed proposals or might prefer to attempt to reach tentative agreement on an overall departmental total. Although such an agreement would have to be regarded as tentative until it had been approved by Cabinet at the same time as all other proposals, this kind of approach has much in its favour. The Treasury would know that any departmental figure which it was able to recommend would fit in with the overall scheme and would be likely to be acceptable to colleagues whether judged by the absolute size or by the percentage increase. The departmental Minister would know that any figure he was able to accept would at a pinch accommodate those programmes he regarded as absolutely essential and that any total figure he suggested to Cabinet with the Chancellor's support would be likely – but not without some discussion and explanation – to be approved. The question of merit – as opposed to comparative merit – of the individual proposals would not be in question at this stage, as previously explained. The departmental Minister would feel some satisfaction in being left with the decision as to which of his own proposals to include and which to exclude, and the Treasury Minister would reckon that the desire of the departmental Minister to accommodate as much as possible of his total programme within the agreed figure would encourage him to seek all possible economies.

There remain the bipartite discussions on individual proposals. One year there may be many; another year – where economic circumstances are perhaps less restrictive – only a few. The discussions are unlikely to follow a regular pattern; each will develop differently according to the circumstances of the case and the characteristics of the Ministers involved. All Ministers tend to be strong of mind and purpose: but most are co-operative and all realise that agreement must be reached within a fairly short time. Occasionally a Minister is found who regards it as his responsibility, as the spokesman of his department, to yield no ground under any circumstances. Inevitably issues will have to be referred to Cabinet in his case, and it is unlikely that the other members of Cabinet, most of whom will have had to make compromises for the sake of reaching agreement with regard to their own departmental programmes, will be very sympathetic towards such a display of inflexibility. On the other hand there will be issues where the Treasury may regard the economic arguments as the more weighty but the Cabinet – or a majority of the Cabinet – may well regard the political issues as dominant. Where this is clearly going to be the case, the

Treasury will be compelled to seek agreement at a higher level of expenditure than would otherwise be the case – though hopefully still below the level originally put forward by the department. For there is a limit to the extent to which the Treasury can afford to see its authority being chipped away by losing cases taken to Cabinet, especially at this time. For it will need its full strength and authority to fight the major issues which will finally have to be settled at Cabinet level. These will consist of items of expenditure, not necessarily the largest in amount, which depend on policy issues of such a nature as to require the approval of Cabinet; of others of less political or social importance where for one reason or another – including the personalities involved – it has not been found possible to reach agreement; and of the overall figure of public expenditure for the focal year.

It can be assumed that the process of bipartite discussion has been fully used and that nothing further can be achieved by continuing in that way. The stage is therefore now set for the all-important Cabinet meeting – or, more likely, meetings – at which these questions will be finally settled. The Chancellor will have in mind the total figure for public expenditure which he would regard as satisfactory for the year in question, and also the maximum figure which he would regard as tolerable in the existing and expected economic circumstances. He will accordingly know what margin, if any, exists for the disputed increases in expenditure arising out of the issues still open. He may still be able to afford concessions here and there, especially where the resource content is small and the political or social content large. Not all items have an equal demand effect for each £1 million of financial expenditure, and he may therefore be able still to accommodate a comparatively substantial financial increase where the increased demand on resources is relatively small. Accordingly much may depend on which items are approved. On the other hand he may have very little room for manoeuvre left and his tactics at the meeting will have to be quite different. In all this there is one item which will play a useful part and which has not so far been touched on – the contingency allowance.

The essential reason for a contingency allowance in a public expenditure budget is the same as in any other budget – it is not given to any man to know the future. A Government has in the exercise of its functions to take account of, and perhaps respond to, a number of unexpected events outside its control. There will be the actions of other Governments; natural catastrophes abroad and at home; developments in world trade and world currency practices; and the unexpected increases in expenditure of those items of public expenditure which are beyond, or to some extent beyond, the control of the central Government. It will not be possible to forecast the consequential increase in public expenditure; but that there will be some increased expenditure is beyond doubt and unless the planned expenditure of approved programmes is to be reduced – more or less without notice – in order to make way for it, then separate provision is necessary. The normal method of calculating the amount to be provided in most budgets is a percentage of the total, and experience over the years will show whether the percentage chosen is reasonably appropriate. But the percentage will need to be increased as one peers further into the future: it is a matter of experience that the further ahead the period to which an estimate refers, the greater is the likelihood of it being exceeded (at constant prices).

In the same category, but working in the opposite direction, are two provisions to cover possible underspending. The first relates to the capital expenditure of the nationalised industries, the second to expenditure overall. Both will require examination at a later stage: all that needs to be noted at this point is that complete accuracy in estimating future expenditure is incapable of achievement. Although a Chancellor would be unwise to approve more public expenditure than he thinks manageable in the hope – or even expectation – that it would not in fact be spent, nevertheless a Chancellor would be unwise to be completely inflexible in considering a precise limit for public expenditure some two years ahead; there are too many unknowns.

A second purpose served by the contingency allowance is to provide for possible increases in public expenditure arising from the development of programmes or changes in policy. That element of flexibility is essential for wise administration – it would be ridiculous for a Government to regard itself as bound to a particular course because of a decision about the consequential public expenditure taken two or three years back. The contingency allowance does therefore provide a little more room for manoeuvre and it enables a disappointed departmental Minister to console himself with the hope that circumstances may permit of some increase beyond planned expenditure; in which case his temporarily rejected proposals may be accepted and financed out of the contingency reserve. Indeed he may have withdrawn his proposals on that very condition.

Before the final Cabinet meeting the Chancellor will circulate a paper setting out all the public expenditure issues. He will remind his colleagues of the earlier decision regarding the total increase in public expenditure and perhaps set out what has been agreed and accordingly within what figure the remaining proposals have to be accommodated. The paper will then set out the opposing views on each outstanding issue – there will be no need for the dissenting departmental Ministers to put in separate papers explaining their respective points of view if their representations have been described in their own words in the Chancellor's paper. The Chancellor will present the paper to his colleagues at the meeting and will indicate the kind of conclusion he hopes will be reached, and there will follow a detailed discussion on each of the disagreed items in turn, with the relevant departmental Minister justifying his viewpoint as far as he can. At a fairly early stage there will be likely to develop a general consensus of opinion as to whether the overall figure suggested by the Chancellor and falling within the band previously agreed by Cabinet is about right. If so, then the individual items will be discussed not only on their comparative merits but also on the basis that they will all-told need to be of a size capable – more or less – of being accommodated within that total. In this way the discussion will be driving to a common goal and only the really sensitive political issues will cause great difficulty. But in every year there are likely to be two or three such, and mutual understanding of a very high order will be needed to enable agreement – or, failing that, an acceptable conclusion – to be reached. It is true that all that is immediately under consideration is the effect on public expenditure of a policy decision, not the policy itself. But clearly it would be illogical to include a provision for the cost of a particular policy unless it was agreed that that very policy was going to be implemented in that period. If there was some doubt as to whether events would move in such a way as to necessitate the expenditure at that time; or as to whether, if they did, the Government would wish to carry out the particular proposal, then the appropriate conclusion would be not to make any specific provision in the public expenditure budget but to accept that this might constitute a claim on the contingency reserve at that time. A decision to make such a specific provision must therefore follow on a decision approving the policy in principle and suggesting a scale of implementation.

The policy underlying any new proposal must therefore be decided either at this time or earlier; and clearly this is the best time, not of course the only time, for such a discussion because several proposals – some large, some small, but all politically difficult and therefore important – will have to be considered at the same time and will, as a result, be compared with one another and, if a given total is the agreed goal, be in competition with one another to a certain extent. This is the realisation of the Plowden recommendation that public expenditure decisions 'should never be taken without consideration of . . . the relative importance of one kind of expenditure against another'. In making this recommendation the Plowden Committee was not pronouncing upon a difficult issue: it was merely stating the obvious, the inescapable truth. Decision about the use of a country's resources are decisions about alternative uses: if the resources are applied for a certain purpose they simply cannot be used for a different purpose. The decision to use them for the first purpose was in fact a decision, whether implicitly or explicitly stated, not to use them for the second purpose. Clearly the process of consideration is likely to be more rational and better informed if both possible uses are taken together.

It is therefore in the interests of good government that the various outstanding public expenditure issues should be discussed at the one meeting, even though tempers may as a result get a little frayed and the physical and mental resources of Ministers be taxed to the utmost – as they will most probably be. For these will not be impersonal discussions as to whether instructions should be given to somebody else to continue doing the same thing or to start doing something different. They are discussions as to whether a particular Minister sitting at the Cabinet table, who has devoted very many years of gruelling service and suffered many painful experiences in order to qualify for that seat, shall be allowed to carry out a proposal which his department considers essential, which he himself very much wants to see implemented and which probably represents a point of view he has held for years and in the promotion of which he has devoted a great deal of his time and invested a great deal of himself. It is not a question of whether the proposal is of great merit: all his colleagues are satisfied that it is in the best interests of the community. It is a question as to whether priority ought to be given to his proposal or to that of a colleague – for at some stage all have to accept that resources cannot be stretched any further. He must not only justify his own sense of priority: he must question that of his colleague. And all are conscious of the fact that a decision now is probably a decision for all time; for who knows what the situation will be when a further opportunity for discussing the proposal presents itself, if indeed it ever does? Nobody can be certain that he will retain the same responsibilities, or still be a Cabinet Minister, or that the same Government will be in office; and in any case much water will have flowed under many bridges.

Painful as some of these discussions will inevitably be for certain Ministers, they are perhaps not the most painful. For what has been envisaged so far has been the type of issue that centres around a new proposal. Where the issue is whether an existing programme should be run down, even greater difficulty will be experienced. These questions may sometimes cause such difficulty that they would probably not be tackled were it not for the pressure of scarcity of resources; and accordingly the PESC review becomes the only occasion where this can happen. By the time this final Cabinet meeting takes place the particular issue will have become clear to Ministers as a result of papers circulated by the Chancellor and by the relevant departmental Minister – for a really large issue of this kind will need to be separately and fully set out – and perhaps by an earlier discussion among those most closely involved at the relevant ministerial committee. The discussion that is now beginning will therefore quickly centre on the heart of the problem with the main contendents explaining why their judgements differ. The basic facts should not be in dispute, although some estimates may well be matters of opinion.

There are several reasons why this kind of issue is likely to present many difficulties. First it will be realised that the decision to cut expenditure in this area will have to be justified publicly, for it is not a decision to omit a proposal which no one outside Government has been aware of: it is a decision to vary an existing policy which has been brought to public notice in some form or other in the past. It might even have been justified – on its own individual merits – in a recent debate in Parliament. But it is in any event implicit in the fact that it is an existing programme that it had been approved by the Government – probably by Cabinet – at an earlier stage. Some Minister then will have to stand up at the despatch box and explain to the House of Commons that whereas in the circumstances existing previously it was right for the Government to incur this expenditure, in the changed circumstances now prevailing – and likely to prevail in the future – it is right for the Government to curtail the expenditure or to cancel the project. Where there has been a change of Government this difficulty will be much reduced. All the new spokesman will have to say is that his Government had always made it clear when they were the Opposition that they were unhappy about this particular item of expenditure; or, alternatively, that although they had supported (or never dissented from) the proposal previously, now that they were in Government they had had the opportunity to consider all the factors at first hand and so had concluded that a change was needed. But in the normal circumstances of a continuing Government it may not be easy to satisfy the House that a change in circumstances took place at that particular time sufficient to justify the new decision. Those who have long been opposed to the particular item will argue that the change in government policy should have been made long ago; those who support continuing the expenditure, that the new circumstances are not sufficient to justify the departure from previously approved policy. What adds to the difficulty is the fact that the Minister whose duty it will almost certainly be to justify the new decision is the very Minister who is engaged in opposing it tooth and nail at Cabinet. He cannot very well escape that task. All British Governments proceed on the basis of joint Cabinet responsibility – indeed nothing else would work under our system. The Minister in charge of the department is the Government's spokesman in matters affecting his department and the appearance of any other Minister at the despatch box will signify that the responsible Minister is not prepared to support the new policy. The effect of that will merely be to bring the dispute out in the open, and the now obvious division in the government ranks will be widened by hints being dropped as to who was on which side of the argument. The alternative of the Prime Minister making the announcement is available when the matter is of sufficient importance, but that is not always the case and in any event this alternative merely serves to postpone this particular difficulty because in practice it will be found that sooner or later the departmental Minister has to speak and act on the new decision.

Then there is the responsibility of that Minister to his own department, of which he will be fully conscious, and especially so in regard to his senior advisers. They will have shown him great loyalty and he will wish to demonstrate his loyalty to them and to the department in return. For the decision may mean more than a temporary loss of prestige: it may mean that a particular activity will cease and that the services of those connected with it will no longer be required.

All these problems, together with his own conviction that his point of view is the right one, add up to a very considerable difficulty for the Minister – as all his colleagues recognise. But they devoutly trust that he will not feel so strongly as to consider resignation from office as the proper course. That would be embarrassing and probably damaging to the Government, at all events for a time; and it is likely to be damaging to the Minister. There are the few glorious exceptions, but generally resignation has meant the end of a ministerial career. From the national point of view this could be a great loss: really big men are very few on the ground. Nevertheless, he may feel so strongly as to warn his colleagues that if they reach a certain conclusion he will have to 'consider his position'. In that event, as he knows, Cabinet will have to give even closer consideration to the issues involved in search of some compromise that will retain his services without flouting the previous Cabinet decision as to the overall figure. This may mean a measure of sacrifice for other Ministers who will see expenditure on some of their programmes being cut down to make room for the compromise. In reaching their decision they will have to assess the position very carefully. They will have to decide whether the threat of resignation, though understandable in the light of the Minister's difficulties, was only made in a moment of despair; or whether the Minister had, for other political, personal, physical, or financial reasons, already got near to the point of resignation, so that if the present issue did not provide the actual occasion for it, the next issue would; or whether the issues involved made it impossible for the Minister not to resign, in which case all should make some contribution – including the Chancellor – to prevent that happening. The outcome might well rest on a knife edge for some time; but gradually on this, as on nearly all big issues, a consensus would emerge and the matter be resolved one way or the other.

Probably relieved, but certainly somewhat exhausted, Cabinet would then turn to the next difficult issue, and at this point in the narrative it would perhaps be right, if only by way of providing some light relief, to describe the conditions under which Cabinet works – at all events, as seen by one member.

The Cabinet table is coffin-shaped. No moral is intended; the shape is allegedly designed to enable those sitting at it to see one another with the minimum of gymnastics, notwithstanding that the room is ill suited for the purpose because of its narrow, rectangular shape and inadequate size. Cabinet members sit at the table in strict pecking order, the most senior at the waist, the most junior at the head and feet. With a Cabinet of normal size the table is just big enough to accommodate those attending – Ministers and officials – provided they do not have too many papers. As a good deal of paper is required for most Cabinet meetings, a certain amount of confusion between one's own papers and those of one's neighbours is perhaps inevitable. On the other hand this promotes a healthy exchange of information between colleagues who have been briefed by their respective departments to oppose one another. Hearing what is said is somewhat difficult, partly because of background noises – the knocking out of pipes into ash-trays, the endless rustling of paper as one Minister after another searches for some important piece of information temporarily mislaid, the frequent whispers between Ministers commenting in a good-humoured if not highly complimentary way on what another Minister has just been saying – and partly because of the disposition of Ministers around the table. Natural courtesy requires them to address their remarks to the Chairman, the Prime Minister, who sits half way down the table, facing the windows. Accordingly any Minister addressing him from the same side of the table turns away from those colleagues who sit on that side even further from the centre, and who must bear this loss of yet a further pearl of wisdom as best they can.

Smoking is not allowed in the Chamber of the House of Commons, with its extremely high ceiling and efficient air-conditioning. Cabinet used to obey the same rule. Then, around the early thirties, so it is said, a change of Government produced a situation in which only one Cabinet Minister had previously served as such. He knew that smoking was never permitted; on the other hand, he enjoyed a smoke. So at the first meeting of the new Cabinet he lit up, just to see what would happen. What happened was that most of his colleagues proceeded to light up also and thus a new tradition was born. This tradition is well sustained; indeed to a non-smoker it would seem that a haze develops within fifteen minutes of the start of any two-and-a-half-hour meeting. The Cabinet room is a pleasant one, its windows overlooking the garden at the back of No. 10. The windows are, however, mostly kept shut, presumably to avoid the smoke escaping and polluting the air around the michaelmas daisies. There were occasions when a silent gesture to a sympathetic official resulted in a window being opened slightly; but this was always followed very shortly by the very reasonable complaint by a lady member – puff – that there was a hell of a draught down the back of her neck.

Beyond the garden wall one can see the Guards' parade ground. It is of course reassuring to be made aware of their frequent presence by the sounds of martial music produced by powerful men on powerful instruments of brass. It is only fair to add that on the other side of the room the double doors and the green baize effectively prevent the entry of the slightest sound or the smallest current of smokeless air.

It has been said that the job of a Cabinet Minister is a gruelling one, and attending a long Cabinet meeting tends to support that view. For anyone who feels faint, a glass of water is provided. But a cup of coffee, which might at a certain stage restore the inner man, relax the atmosphere, and enable the business of Cabinet to proceed more briskly, is strictly taboo. But enough of this squeamishness: back to the serious business of the Cabinet meeting grappling with the problems of public expenditure.

In fact little more remains to be said in describing the process of making all the decisions for the focal year. Similar difficulties to those already described may be encountered, but the whole Cabinet realises that these must all be overcome and a general will exists to drive forward to the final conclusion. As more of the individual issues are resolved it will become clearer what percentage increase on the previous year the final grand total is likely to show. It has been assumed that at an early stage in the meeting Cabinet agreed on the kind of increase to be sought. That was a reasonable assumption, for there would be no point – as all would recognise – in proceeding with the detailed examination if there was a major difference of view between the Chancellor and the majority of the Cabinet as to the final total. It is in fact inconceivable that a Chancellor would have circulated a paper for Cabinet decision against that background; the final stage would have had to be postponed until further discussions – assisted perhaps by the Prime Minister himself – had established a closer correspondence of viewpoints. At the very least, and assuming the discussion to have developed unexpectedly badly from the Chancellor's point of view, it would have been possible to proceed on the formula of 'let's carry on and see where we get to', the implication being that both sides would somehow or other reconcile their different views at the end of the day, and it is this process of reconciliation which now has to be undertaken. It may present little difficulty; the total provisionally arrived at may be within, or within acceptable distance from, the band originally contemplated. It may on the other hand be a sufficient distance away to require further examination of all the relevant elements. Perhaps some Ministers could be prevailed on to seek greater economy in implementing their programmes without cancelling any of them; perhaps others would agree to postpone the start of some new proposals, thus saving expenditure in the focal year; perhaps the Chancellor would review the demand content of the revised proposals to see if after all there had been a smaller increase in demand terms than the many figures would indicate. So the search will go on, the total figure dominating the detailed proposals but the detail having some impact on the total figure, until the difference is resolved.

The difference may even be resolved only conditionally; that is to say, some proposals may have to be left over for reconsideration in six or twelve months' time on the clear understanding that if the economic situation – or some other factor – improves sufficiently, the Chancellor will then agree to the inclusion of the proposals – or a proportion of them – in the focal year (which will still not have started). In one or other or a mixture of these ways Cabinet's determination to reach a conclusion will finally be fulfilled. The publication of the annual report to Parliament containing all the more important statistics on public expenditure can then go ahead, though a reference to 'the need for flexibility in the light of economic developments' may be required to cover the one or even two cases of conditional approval. Ministers can now breathe a sigh of relief, for one of the most painful meetings of the year will be over and thoughts can now be turned very constructively to the tasks of preparing for the implementation of some new proposals and the expansion of some old ones, all within the terms of the Cabinet decision. Interestingly enough, some Ministers may be thinking that the Plowden Committee has been proved right, for not merely was its main recommendation that public expenditure decisions should be taken in the light of their relative importance and of what the country could afford (as will have just been done), but the report went on to say that in administrative and political terms it would not be easy to carry that out.

The occasion of the PESC review is however not the only occasion when public expenditure proposals or programmes fall for consideration, either singly or in groups. As already indicated there are perhaps three main causes for this: first, that some existing programmes may call for review; secondly, the unexpected development of the economy; and thirdly, the need to respond to external events. The necessary decisions will probably be reached more easily than at the annual survey and everybody will be greatly assisted by the existence of an established framework, but it will be much more difficult to ensure that decisions are taken in the light of 'the relative importance of one kind of expenditure against another'. It is quite impossible to postpone consideration of all new public expenditure issues to the next annual review. That would certainly ensure their relative importance being considered; it would equally certainly ensure that some old and unnecessary expenditure was incurred and that some new and essential expenditure was not. The simple fact is that there are some proposals which, by their nature, do not require immediate decision and can be accumulated for a reasonable period and then considered together. Equally there are others which require immediate decision, if necessary singly. The comparison with other kinds of expenditure can be made; but the absence of competing claims will make the exercise a theoretical one only.

Normally the initiative in reviewing existing programmes is taken by the department concerned. A frequent cause will be a development necessitated by new circumstances not envisaged when the programme was first decided on – which may well be several years back. The methods and scope of the existing public service may have gradually become inadequate or unsuitable. The department may even have proposed the development during the course of an annual review and found that it could not then be accommodated. Whatever the history, it will be suggested that the time has now clearly come when the development should take place. On merits there may be no dispute. On comparative merits there probably will be; for there may be other departments with precisely similar claims, arising out of similar circumstances, in relation to public services which they administer. Again there may be new proposals about to be made by other departments which, though quite new and not developments of the old, may nevertheless be thought to be of higher priority. How then can the stage be set so that the actual comparison takes place, and how can the amount available be determined in such a way that competition for the scarce resources ensures the determination of priorities? The short answer is that neither can be fully achieved. In a perfect world the Treasury might circulate all departments saying that Department A had put forward the proposals described in the paper and would any department which thought it had proposals of similar importance please put them forward within the next two months, at the end of which period the decision would be made – in the appropriate way – as to which proposals should be approved having regard to existing and prospective resources. At best that would merely result in six 'annual' surveys each year; at worst it would provoke an uncontrollable scramble. It would probably be reasonable to postpone consideration for a few weeks and then to consider together in the appropriate committee – not necessarily Cabinet – all the other public expenditure issues which had arisen in the meantime. But it would be difficult for practical reasons to go much further than that along the road of securing effective comparison.

Nor would it be possible, except at a comparatively late stage, to be precise about the resources available. Assuming no evident change in economic circumstances as compared with those contemplated at the time of the annual review, then the only resources available will be whatever amount remains unallocated in the contingency reserve. But in the early stages, before the claims likely to be made on the reserve during the rest of the year can be assessed with any degree of accuracy, great caution will need to be exercised in allocating sums in this way. It will be a matter of judgement, not of precise calculation.

Another possible approach would be to make the Treasury an arbitrator on interim public expenditure claims so as to secure consistency of judgement and decision; but such an approach would be likely to appeal more to Treasury Ministers than to their colleagues, who would feel that they must retain the right of appeal to Cabinet where the issue was of sufficient importance.

It is possible for the development proposed by a department to be of such high merit and of such modest financial and resource requirement that the Treasury would be able to agree without further reference to colleagues and to allocate the necessary funds out of the contingency reserve. There will in practice be several such cases during the course of an average year, and of course with experience accumulating over the years it should be possible to forecast and provide a contingency reserve which will accommodate the really pressing claims likely to be made on it during the succeeding twelve months. So the problem of the provision of funds need not be such a difficult one other than for the quite exceptional case; that is to say a case which raises issues of such an order as to need the full treatment of the annual review although being of an urgency which prohibits that.

In the event of the proposal not being agreed by the Treasury there are several ways in which the issue can be resolved. The normal practice of taking the matter to the appropriate ministerial committee and finally, if necessary, to Cabinet must be considered by both sides with care. That the proposal will have considerable merit is not really in doubt: it would not have got this far otherwise. The only question in public expenditure matters is whether a particular proposal has, not great merit, but greater merit than other proposals. So Treasury Ministers will hesitate to take the proposal to the judgement of colleagues in circumstances where the departmental Minister will be able to demonstrate its great merit and where the real question of its greater merit is not likely to arise in concrete form. On the other hand the departmental Minister will hesitate to take to colleagues a proposal to extract from the contingency reserve substantial sums which those very colleagues might prefer to be devoted to proposals of their own and which Treasury Ministers will make painfully clear can only be used once.

Suitably restrained by these calculations the two Ministers are likely to discuss possible compromises. The proposal could, for example, be scaled down. Alternatively it could be postponed till the next annual review on the Treasury's promise to treat it sympathetically at that time. Alternatively, without scaling it down, the department could meet part of the additional cost by economising further on one or other of its own existing programmes. Alternatively, the Treasury might feel that here at last was an opportunity to get rid of an old programme which in its view had outlived its purpose but which the department still wished to continue for the time being. Now it is very difficult indeed to halt an old-established programme; the forces making for its continuation seem to grow stronger with every year that passes. Programmes which, if they did not exist, would not secure ministerial approval will nevertheless be able to secure ministerial approval to their continuation, and departments tend to fight hard to maintain that continuity for reasons other than the intrinsic merits of the programme. Finance Ministers in other countries have borne witness to the same difficulty. There does in fact seem to be only one reliable solution: to exchange one programme for another – a 'trade-in', as the jargon has it. The gradual extinction of an old programme over a suitable period may seem to a department a reasonable price to pay for securing approval of a more expensive programme. To the Treasury the ending of what it regards as no longer justifiable expenditure, an achievement which it is not otherwise able to secure, is a boon in comparison with which the agreement to allocate available funds to a proposal of considerable merit is of no great consequence. Both sides will be content and progress will have been made.

Although the vast majority of cases arise, as these last examples show, from the initiative of the department itself in seeking additional finance, there are some occasions when the review of a programme undertaken on the initiative of, and in conjunction with, the Treasury will result in a proposal by the latter of a modification calculated to save expense. This is quite separate from the scrutiny of their own programmes continuously carried out by the various departments and, where economies can be found, resulting automatically in reduced expenditure. That reduction will tend to be balanced by increases in expenditure in other programmes arising from over-cautious estimating. It is however unlikely that the department will readily agree to the suggested modification: had that been the case it would have made the modification on its own initiative earlier. But agreement may be reached on some basis similar to one or other of those applying to disputes arising out of the department's initiative, as earlier described. A reference to the relevant ministerial committee will have to be made if agreement cannot be reached otherwise – in this case the Treasury would have nothing to lose in making such a reference – and in the unlikely event of the issue still being unresolved it would remain open until the next annual review when the department would be required to justify the continuing full rate of expenditure in the competition for scarce resources.

All the interim issues so far discussed – by interim is meant issues arising in between annual reviews – are assumed to be of moderate or minor importance. The really big issues, in resource and political terms, such as the question whether or not to continue a vastly expensive technological project, will not be dealt with in this way. It is likely that a separate *ad hoc* committee, chaired by the departmental Minister and containing Ministers from all the departments closely concerned, including the Treasury, would be set up to monitor the progress of the project and to take from time to time any necessary decisions relating to its development. It would be likely to report regularly to Cabinet and if there developed serious disagreement in the *ad hoc* committee then a full discussion would take place in Cabinet where all the important policy issues could be thrashed out and decisions taken covering a stated further period or further allocation of funds. The decision would not be taken exclusively in the context of public expenditure but on a review of all the relevant factors including the high cost. The allocation of funds to enable any decision to be implemented would not be likely to cause any special difficulty inasmuch as, it being a continuing project, provision will have been made in the department's public expenditure budget at the time of the annual review. The provision may have related to a group of projects, and any exceptional increase in expenditure desired by the department would therefore have the effect of reducing the finance available for the other projects in the group.

Only one more reference need be made at this stage to the methods open to a Government of resolving issues arising out of a review of existing programmes. As a result of a special examination undertaken on the initiative of the Treasury, proposals may have been made for the serious curtailment of the work of one of the sections of a particular department. It is unlikely that much progress could be made on an issue of that kind where the necessary detailed knowledge of the work of the department would be known to very few Ministers and where the issues could not be put shortly to colleagues. The departmental Minister would naturally defend his department, saying with some justification that he was the responsible Minister, that he knew more about his own department than any other Minister, and that if the work of the particular section had not in his view been necessary, he himself would have ended it. The Treasury on the other hand would justify its intervention by referring to its responsibility for protecting the public purse and it would be clear to both sides that no progress was likely to be made through the normal machinery of government. It is on an issue of that kind, where a decision in two years' time will be preferable to permanent stalemate, that a Government can appoint a committee of enquiry of outside persons of knowledge and ability to examine the views of both sides, take what further evidence they require, and report their conclusions and recommendations to the Government. It is likely that the whole process will have taken a year or more and that as a result of the carefully sifted evidence and impartially argued conclusions, both sides will be prepared to accept some of the committee's main recommendations. They are unlikely to go as far as the Treasury would have wished; on the other hand the publicly expressed view of an authoritative non-governmental body would enable the departmental Minister to accept decisions which he could not have done on the basis only of his own departmental advice. So a decision will be reached and in due course implemented, Ministers will then begin gradually to accept the new state of affairs as normal, and it will be from that new position that the next argument, whenever it arises, will start.

The key action in that difficulty was the appointment of an 'outside' committee. More commonly this is the device adopted in order to promote a proposal for additional public expenditure in its very early stages. A typical example would be where a somewhat ill-defined proposal for satisfying an alleged need has been put forward from some particular source and is gathering a measure of public support. It may have originated inside a Ministry; it may have been made by some authoritative person or body outside Government. The important fact is that it has won the support of a departmental Minister who would like to see the suggestion tried out. As it – like most new proposals – will involve additional public expenditure, he will have to persuade his colleagues at the Treasury: but he knows he will fail to do that – and will fail if he appeals to Cabinet – while the proposal is rather uncertain. So in order to get clarity and greater authority and, more importantly, to put a little more steam into his proposal, he will suggest examination lose in making such a reference – and in the unlikely event of the issue by a committee of able men and women, the great majority of whom will be experienced in this particular area and able therefore to lend the weight of their experience to any recommendations they may make. The Treasury reaction will be the familiar one in this familiar situation. Their calculation will be that the majority of the committee, being experts in this field, will, after considering the evidence, be likely to conclude that theirs is the field in which more public money could usefully be spent. Nor will they, in the Treasury's estimation, be deterred from reaching that conclusion by the fact that the cost involved will fall on the public purse. So the Treasury will seek to oppose what it sees merely as the first of a series of connected steps leading to pressure for further public expenditure. The department will point out that it is sheer conjecture as to which way the committee will report; that if its report does favour further public expenditure that claim will have to compete with other claims in the annual review; and that it is surely being obscurantist to refuse to examine the facts. In these circumstances a Treasury Minister finds himself in a rather weak position: he knows from long experience that whatever the precise conclusions of such a committee, additional public expenditure will be involved and that the committee's report may not be capable of being delayed until the following annual review. But he recognises the difficulty of opposing an enquiry at that early – and apparently innocent – stage, and so the first step to a further commitment is taken. Not surprisingly this is an approach much favoured by Ministers in charge of spending departments.

All this is part of a continuing tug-of-war which Treasury Ministers find themselves engaged in – the spending departments wishing to improve their service to the public at the cost of more public expenditure, the Treasury wishing to protect the public purse by restraining the rate at which public expenditure increases every year. Treasury Ministers find themselves heavily outnumbered, and although they may persuade their colleagues to take a restrictive and – in the Treasury's eyes – responsible view at a particular meeting, that mood does not always last. Indeed, although it may be extremely inconvenient on practical and administrative grounds, constitutionally there is nothing to prevent Cabinet changing its mind at a subsequent meeting: that is, assuming that the first decision has not in the meantime been made public. But a publicly announced decision and, still more, a fully detailed printed programme of public expenditure will be very difficult to go back on. Publication is in fact the act which provides certainty and finality. It is indeed fortunate from this point of view that all Governments have since 1969 followed the practice of publishing an annual report on public expenditure followed by an important debate in Parliament. This report details public expenditure over a future period of five years. The various decision-making processes so far described refer to the focal year, and the reasons why that has to be Year 3, and why Years 1 and 2 are not really suitable for consideration at this point of time, have been explained. Little has, however, been said about Years 4 and 5, for the reason that they do not in fact come – at this stage – into the decision-making process. The figures shown for those two final years are not firm allocations decided on by the Government, for some of the necessary information is incomplete so far ahead. They are purely provisional figures indicating how public expenditure might continue to grow on the basis of existing policies remaining unchanged. The total growth will conform to the same pattern as was established for Year 3, and the main purpose of the figures is to enable Parliament and the public to have sufficient information to enable them to play their full part in shaping opinion. But all that is for a later chapter: in the present context of how decisions are made, the figures for Years 4 and 5 must be regarded as indicative rather than definitive. In the round, those figures provide a good indication of the likely level of expenditure and that can be very helpful to all concerned. But the figures for Years 4 and 5 do not represent a series of decisions on the detailed programmes: final plans cannot be based on those details, for the final decisions will be made either one or two years later.

It is only necessary to deal with one more aspect before attempting to draw together the somewhat tangled threads of this long description of the decision-making process. So far it has been assumed that the arguments which precede decisions have proceeded on the basis of agreed figures. Unfortunately that is not always so, and genuine doubts on the accuracy of the figures can arise. There are three main reasons for this: first, the fact that one is concerned with estimates of what will happen in the future; secondly, the fact that there are several ways of presenting the effect of the decision to be made; and the third, the fact that the decisive factor, the state of the economy, can never be assessed with precision and more than one course of conduct can be deduced from any given set of economic statistics.

It is surprising, having regard to the many future uncertainties involved, how accurate the estimates in total turn out to be. This is partly due to the great skill and experience of the many officials concerned; but partly it is due to the fact that with any large mass of statistics the under-estimates and the over-estimates will tend to balance one another so that the total remains largely unaffected. This turns out to be applicable to the public expenditure forecasts and therefore leaves a certain scope for argument about the figures of the individual programmes. As more techniques become available and as the passage of the years adds to experience, the figures become more reliable – but again in total – or in sub-totals – rather than in detail. Reference has earlier been made to relative price effect and shortfall, in both cases refinements of the total forecasts introduced to secure greater accuracy. But again, they are not of great help for the detailed forecasts. Moreover, in order to have 're-gard to prospective resources' estimates have to be made of the way in which the economy will develop – a notoriously fallible exercise. In short, the arguments which are based on the precise cost of individual programmes or, still more, on prospective economic resources, are not so securely based statistically as to be beyond challenge.

This is true also when it comes to choosing the most appropriate measuring rod for determining the effect of a series of public expenditure decisions: for there being more than one kind of effect, there is more than one kind of measure. The limitations of simple monetary measurement have been referred to earlier: there are measurements in terms of volume as well as in terms of cost: there is measurement by resource category and measurement of demand on output. The difficulties could not be expressed better than in two paragraphs in the 1971 White Paper on Public Expenditure (Cmd 4829). Paragraph 7 reads:

'The demand on output which results from public expenditure programmes is not accurately measured by the money expenditures; different forms of expenditure have different demand effects, and these may vary in different circumstances. As well as close analysis, a degree of judgement is therefore required to assess the implications of the programmes in terms of demand. Any measurement produced in this way is subject to reservations, but on this basis the estimated average annual rate of increase in net demand on output between 1971–72 and 1975–76 implied by the programmes of this White Paper is about 2.5 per cent in real terms. When allowance is made for public sector prices to move during the period relatively to those of the economy as a whole, as may be expected from the evidence of the past, this represents an average annual rate of increase in real cost to the economy of about 3.2 per cent.'

Paragraph 19 reads:

'In part 2 of table 3.2, on page 67, these comparisons are extended as the Select Committee on Expenditure have suggested (HC.549 page xix, paragraph 62) to the analysis of total public expenditure into the three resource categories used for that purpose in previous White Papers of this series – direct purchase of resources, transfers and purchase of existing assets. The main point which emerges is that the average annual rate of increase in direct purchase of resources between 1971–72 and 1974–75 is 3.9 per cent. As a method of expressing the implications of expenditure for demand on output, however, an analysis in this form is in principle less satisfactory than the direct assessment, in the manner described in paragraph 7, of the demand which changes in individual expenditures place on output.'

Anyone reading those paragraphs and the actual tables referred to, even if he did not pursue all the footnotes, could be forgiven for thinking that there were at least three different ways of expressing the statistical truth – each with its different measuring rod.

The third reason given as to why the figures could never be unchallengeable was the difficulty of assessing the economic situation precisely. It is not simply a question of finding out where one stands in relation to a number of fixed points; it is a question of finding out the general economic direction in which the country is moving, and at what speed – constant, accelerating or decelerating – and how far along that road we have already travelled. The answer can only be an intelligent guess because by the time all the necessary information has been obtained to pinpoint the position, we will not be there any more. Moreover, whatever estimate is made both of the situation and of the strength of the various economic forces propelling us, differing proposals can be put forward as to how to achieve the desired change of direction, one of which may involve increasing public expenditure, another reducing it. The economic picture painted by the Chancellor for the purpose of giving his colleagues the best and latest information available to him, and the measuring rod which he recommends them to use, are therefore inevitably open to challenge: it is only fair to add, however, that although this margin of error is known to them – especially to those who are professional economists – the figures are rarely challenged by a Minister for the purpose of enabling him to accommodate an additional item of departmental expenditure. He may say with justification that the actual figures may turn out to be different from the estimates; but he may not go on to say that they may turn out to be more favourable to his particular argument without the risk of the opposite eventuality being posed. All Ministers go to considerable lengths in trying to ensure that the factual background presented to their colleagues is accurate, and an unwillingness to accept that might be taken as a challenge to a colleague's bona fides. In fact if the separate calculations made by two departments result in differing figures being put before Cabinet, the normal practice would be to postpone consideration so that the figures could be agreed, or at all events reconciled; otherwise the time of Cabinet would be taken up in a wrangle as to the facts, instead of a discussion of the merits based on agreed or accepted facts.

These then are the various ways in which a Government, both during the PESC review and in the twelve months leading up to the next one, reaches its decisions as to the priorities involved in fixing the total of public expenditure and the detail of the constituent elements. If the picture that has been drawn is a somewhat confusing one, with no precise framework, with events overlapping, with decisions being arrived at in the best way possible rather than ideally, with cold logic being tempered by warm emotion, with strong forces pressing in different directions and with events refusing to stand still in the meantime, then it has been well drawn. Chaos and uniformity of approach are both absent; system has to yield to flexibility and tentative exploration. Colleagues find themselves changing allies with every new issue as identity of viewpoint and of departmental interest changes. Many decisions are as unpredictable as the mood of the House of Commons. But total agreement is finally reached because each Minister battling for his own point of view is determined that it shall be reached.

Chapter 5

Controlling Public Expenditure

It is not a simple matter to say with certainty where decision-making finishes and control starts, nor to define those processes which are part of the function of control as compared with those processes – very similar at first sight – which enable a decision to be varied in the light of changed circumstances. Where the amount decided to be spent is exceeded by the amount actually spent, the response of those who favour less public spending is to claim that public expenditure is 'out of control', and of those who favour more public spending to claim that public expenditure is being managed with wise flexibility. The conclusion must be that control refers to those processes which enable a decision to become effective. If that decision is regarded by some as being unnecessarily expensive, it is wrong to criticise the methods of control which result in the full amount decided upon being ultimately spent. Clearly the criticism should be directed against the decision and not its implementation.

But even such an obvious conclusion does not state the whole truth, for the decision, often enough, was not simply a resolve to spend £*x* million but rather a decision to provide a certain service which, it was estimated, would cost £*x* million. Now that is a somewhat different matter, for everyone recognises that estimates are fallible and that although they are absolutely essential, an error in estimating is to be distinguished from other causes of difference between the estimated figure and the amount actually spent (the 'out-turn'). Nor should it be assumed that the eventual difference will always be an excess of spending. If, for example, it was expected that the provision of the service would require the employment of 100 civil servants and in fact it was later discovered that by some reorganisation it could be provided by 95, nobody would regard the ensuing saving as other than welcome and sensible. The decision would be universally regarded as a decision to provide the service, irrespective of whether 100 or 95 persons were needed. Similarly one must accept – though this is admittedly more difficult – that the same remarks apply whether the number turns out to be 100 or 105. The essential point is that had all the figures been known at the time the decision was under consideration, it would still have been taken. The assumption is that this is so clearly the case that there is no need to consult the decision-makers afresh.

But what if the number turns out to be 200? Instinctively one recognises that this creates a different situation. Whether the difference arises out of an error in estimating or a change of plan or the discovery of a defect, the conclusion is the same: it cannot be assumed that the decision would have been the same if the new figure had been known at the time. In these circumstances one would rely on the system of control to prevent the expenditure being incurred for long at the new level without confirmation by the necessary authority. In the earlier case, the difference would be accepted and would be one of several differences – whether excesses or savings – which would be expected to arise out of the very difficult task of estimating future expenditure.

Control in this context, therefore, can perhaps be defined as the method by which a decision is brought up for reconsideration as soon as it is seen that its implementation is likely to incur expenditure greater than that originally estimated. But even this simple definition requires further clarification in two respects. First, the phrase 'in this context'. The important matter which arises after a decision has been taken is its implementation, for without this the decision is ineffectual. But the cost of so doing is mostly only one element to be considered by those who have the responsibility of giving effect to the decision. The task itself must surely rank first, the measure of the resources allotted to it second. It is of first importance that those 100 civil servants should understand fully what the decision-makers intended to achieve and should be put to work to achieve it. That is the administrator's responsibility. The way he is controlled and in turn the kind of control he exerts are of course important, but the control with which we are here concerned is not directly the administrative one. Our context is expenditure, and control is to be understood within that context.

Indirectly financial control can – and often does – affect the system of administration. If it is found that putting those 100 civil servants to work in a certain way is likely to incur expenditure well in excess of the estimate, thought will be given to carrying out the decision in a different way within the estimated cost. But that administrative change will have resulted from the exercise of financial control and it is that kind of control which is our primary concern.

The second point of clarification relates to the time factor: 'as soon as' it is seen that the cost is likely to be exceeded. The exact point in time when that happens is not susceptible of precise definition; indeed, it is very largely a matter of opinion. Public expenditure is decided upon for yearly periods; at the beginning of the period, a decision is made as to what is to be spent, all told, by the end of it. Now it may be possible, after three months have gone by, to foresee that by the end of the year the total provision will have been exceeded unless something is done to prevent it. That will, for example, be the case where expenditure occurs very evenly over the year and during that quarter more than a quarter of the total has been spent. But it cannot be foreseen with any certainty where that is not the case; in the light of all the circumstances, including of course previous experience, it may be judged likely or unlikely, with varying degrees of probability. But one cannot know for certain. In practice normal caution requires the holding back of expenditure in the earlier months so as to allow an appropriate margin to meet unexpectedly high demands in later months, and in this way it may well arise that less than the amount provided for is finally spent, because the demand in those later months turns out to be low and one cannot at that stage go back to the earlier period and increase the expenditure that was then incurred.

This is the familiar problem which faces everyone who has to accommodate his expenditure within a budget, whether in the field of public expenditure or not. He finds himself continually assessing and reassessing the future level of expenditure. If excessive caution is practised throughout, then every item in the budget will be underspent; and creditable though this may be from some points of view, and infinitely preferable though it may be to overspending on every item, nevertheless the simple fact remains that, assuming there was no large error in the original estimate, the decision which it was sought to implement will not have been implemented. The purpose of the exercise will not have been achieved. Excessive caution has therefore to give way to reasonable objectivity, and that being so it is inevitable that by the end of the year some items will have been underspent and some overspent. Happy is the treasurer or finance controller who finds that the two are broadly equal. But over the years the differences will in any event not be very great. In the field of public expenditure the figures are so large and the items so numerous that there is little likelihood of the net difference being substantial.

Financial control then, or, to be more precise, that part of it known as monitoring, will sound the necessary warning bells where there is the likelihood that expenditure for the year on a particular item will differ substantially from the estimate. Where the difference amounts to a substantial excess the probable course will be to invite reconsideration of the original decision. No bells will be sounded where no difference is foreseen. Should such differences nevertheless materialise, then the probability is that the amounts overspent will broadly equal the amounts underspent, at all events over a period of years.

What financial control cannot do, however, is to control uncontrollable expenditure, and examples of this are to be found however much a Government may seek to avoid entering into commitments – open-ended commitments as they are appropriately described – which do not permit of reconsideration with a view to reducing the resultant cost when this is found to be running at an excessive rate. Sickness benefit is a typical example. Having decided on the conditions and the rates for sickness benefit and having calculated, on the basis of previous experience, the likely expenditure for the ensuing year, it is not possible to go back on the decision when it is discovered that a totally unexpected epidemic of 'flu is pushing the expenditure far beyond the estimate.

To admit that there are areas of public expenditure which are strictly uncontrollable may seem to some a frightening admission, and it is certainly true that Governments try hard to avoid open-ended commitments because a series of substantial miscalculations on these might well adversely affect the management of the economy. But an examination of the circumstances of most open-ended commitments will show that they have been entered into because the loss of an opportunity to review the decision is not a very real loss. What, for example, could a Government do if it did review the sickness grant in the circumstances just described? It could not lay down that whereas everyone who got 'flu last year and the year before was entitled to sickness benefit, those who caught it this year were not; or that an attack of bronchitis this year attracted sickness benefit but that an attack of 'flu did not. The loss of the normal opportunity to review a public expenditure decision would be more apparent than real.

So too was this the case with investment grants, a matter which attracted considerable criticism at the time and does, therefore, merit some consideration. In order to give an immediate and tangible incentive to investment, the Government decided to pay a sum in cash to every manufacturer who bought new plant for his factory, the sum being a proportion of the amount spent. All the manufacturer had to do was to make his investment and then apply to the Government for his grant. The Government could estimate the likely cost, but it could not control it. An estimate was duly made for one particular year, based largely on the experience of the previous year. But in that earlier year manufacturers had been slow in filling in their application forms; in the year under review they speeded up enormously and as a result the grants came to far more than their estimate and the government department concerned came in for a great deal of criticism, for it had to keep applying to Parliament for more and more money to cope with the flood of applications. The basis of the criticism was that the department had failed to estimate, within many millions of pounds, what would be required and that the Government had got itself into a position where it could not control the situation – and that surely was the negation of good government.

It was perfectly true that the Government was caught up in the consequences of an open-ended commitment. The grant had been fixed for a given period and those entitled to it had only to make their claims. But how much did it matter? The investment grant was decided upon as a more direct means of encouraging investment than the previous system of investment allowances. Under the latter system an amount very similar to the grant was allowed by way of deduction from the tax that would otherwise have been payable. So in one case the Government was paying out more; in the other, receiving less. The net effect on the Exchequer was broadly the same, the only difference was that in one case it was much more visible. In short, here again the Government had entered into an open-ended commitment, appreciating that the consequential expenditure would not be controllable, because it knew that it was only denying itself a valueless right – the right to reconsider, when the level of expenditure would normally have warranted it, a decision which upon reconsideration would merely have been confirmed. It is not going too far to say that in the field of public expenditure, uncontrollable items are in the main of this character.

This generalisation needs, however, to be examined in the context of local authority expenditure, which is very substantial, accounting as it does for some 30 per cent of total public expenditure. Housing, law and order, local environmental services, non-trunk roads and, above all, education form the bulk of it. The first question that arises is the extent to which local authority expenditure can be described as uncontrollable, for which purpose it is necessary to divide it into its two categories of capital and current expenditure.

The former is, as stated earlier, subject to a measure of government control. For the major programmes of expenditure, such as housing, schools and principal roads, control is exercised by the setting of cost standards and the approval of starting dates for specific projects. For minor programmes such as recreation, school equipment and minor roads, which all told amount to about one-fifth of the major programmes, control is exercised through borrowing approval, thereby leaving the local authorities free to set their own priorities.

The current expenditure of local authorities falls into a different category. It is still substantial – two-thirds of local authority expenditure or 20 per cent of total public expenditure. It is, of course, all monitored by the individual local authorities, each with its own process of control and subject to public audit. Each therefore has its own set of warning bells and its opportunities to review its own spending decisions. What is at issue here is the extent to which the central Government can control the amount (the nature will be separately considered) of local authority expenditure having regard to the fact that the spending authority is not the Government but the local authority and that a condition of healthy local democracy is a measure of freedom in deciding what to spend. Theoretically the local authority can more or less spend what they like. In practice a procedure has been devised as a result of which local authority and central Government decide to like the same thing – even though a certain amount of self-discipline on the part of the local authorities and a measure of frustration on the part of the Government are involved.

The heart of the procedure is the rate support grant, a method whereby the Government provides about 60 per cent of the current expenditure on those local authority programmes of which it approves. It may be the case that the Government, while approving the programme, will find difficulty in accepting the level of expenditure incurred in carrying it out. It may feel that the maximum inducement to economy is absent when only 40 per cent has to be found locally. Indeed there are cases where the full effect of the various arrangements which exist to help special cases may result in only 10 per cent falling on local domestic rate-payers. Moreover a rise in local rates may not have the desired effect (desired by the Treasury at all events) of causing further economy in the implementing of local authority programmes. It may have the quite opposite effect of resulting in considerable pressure for an even greater contribution by the Government out of central funds to all local authorities. So the control over local authority current expenditure cannot be regarded as complete so far as the central Government is concerned – nor indeed would it be consistent with local democracy that it should be.

The balance of the finance is in the main derived from the rates; and in theory a local authority could double the size of one or more of its services if it was willing to finance the extra spending out of additional rates. Even if many local authorities were to decide to do so, that would not pose a special problem in terms of demand management. It would merely mean that in those particular areas the residents had to spend more of their income on publicly provided services and would accordingly spend less on items of their own choice. In practice, however, the deterrent of a publicly announced increase in local rate poundage is a sufficiently powerful one to prevent expenditure on a substantial scale being committed in this way. As a consequence the monitoring processes of the local authorities achieve the results desired by the Government of keeping that part of public expenditure which consists of local authorities' current expenditure broadly in line with its planned totals. Central Government, local authority associations and individual local authorities are in regular communication with one another and know one another's minds. If therefore local authorities decided to spend more than originally planned on one or more of their services, it would represent a deliberate decision taken in the knowledge of all the facts and, almost certainly, after many discussions with Whitehall. In those circumstances the fact that the Government has neither its own warning bells with regard to local authority expenditure nor the opportunity to reconsider an earlier decision – which was in any event a joint one – is not a real deprivation for clearly it would make no difference to the outcome. In short the Government has a sufficient overall financial control on local authority current expenditure, although in theory it is not susceptible to precise direct control by Whitehall. In fact, therefore, that expenditure does not represent an open-ended commitment by the Government, which could never be compelled to pay more than the agreed proportion of the relevant (i.e. approved) expenditure, the extra falling on the pocket of the local rate-payer. But if that occurred the extra would count as additional public expenditure and it is with the control of that expenditure that we are concerned, whether the spending authority is the central Government, a local authority or a public corporation.

As to the last mentioned, all that need be said at this point is that it is only the capital expenditure of public corporations – in the main, the nationalised industries – that enters into the calculation of public expenditure; and that this figure, which is very substantial, is subject to fairly close control by the Government – by the sponsoring department in the first place and finally by the Treasury.

There remains for consideration the financial control of one item, the spending of which is fundamentally different from all the others, namely the contingency reserve. For, with this exception, there is a standard pattern of decision-making followed, as the decision is implemented, by spending. This is not the pattern which applies to the contingency allowance, for by its nature it consists of a sum provided to meet the cost of decisions which have not and cannot yet be taken. True, a decision can be said to have been made in the sense that a definite sum has been provided; but the all-important decision of what it is to be spent on is not made at the same time as the provision of the funds.

What have to be considered, therefore, are the circumstances which give rise to this exceptional decision to provide money for spending on the unknown, exceptional both because for all other items of public expenditure it is the acceptance of the need to devote resources to a particular purpose which precedes the provision of the finance, and because, that need having been defined, the actual sum provided is a careful estimate of the likely cost of implementation; whereas in the case of the contingency allowance there is plainly no such basis for quantifying the cost. Essentially the reason is the fact that in estimating the cost of public expenditure over the years ahead, one is relying on the future course of events, and that only one thing can be said with certainty about the future and that is that one cannot be certain about it.

But that alone would not be sufficient justification for an additional provision, for the uncertainty might work either way – or, having regard to the magnitude of the figures, roughly balance out, that is to say, have no marked net effect on the total. But one knows from experience that in private life, in business, and even more so in Government, something unexpected and uncatered for is bound to happen which will inescapably give rise to additional expense in the months or years ahead, and the further ahead one looks the more certain is the additional expenditure. Experience also teaches that there is a measure of consistency about it all so that the task of estimating the likely cost – smaller in the immediate future, greater in the more distant – is not impossibly difficult. Against this background of experience it is no more than prudent to provide a suitable sum.

It is then the unforeseeable for which the contingency reserve seeks to provide. But there are degrees of unforeseeability; in addition to the completely unexpected event giving rise to expenditure there may be the expectation that, for example, a certain service may need to be expanded to meet a situation which has started to develop. A formal decision clearly cannot yet be made for the situation may still not arise. Alternatively the situation may have developed sufficiently for the need for expansion to be clear, but not sufficiently for the likely cost to be capable of estimation. But whatever the degree of uncertainty, the common factor is the impossibility in the circumstances of calculating the cost of each item. All that can be done, therefore, is to provide on the basis of previous experience a sum that, so far as concerns the overall management of the economy, can be spent; but which, so far as concerns the control of public expenditure, cannot yet be decided on in principle or in amount.

The provision of a sum described as contingency reserve in the annual statements of public expenditure is now well established. But this was not always the case. It was in fact not until 1968 that a decision was taken to provide a sum for unforeseeable expenditure at the same time as decisions were taken to provide specific amounts for each of the various programmes. Prior to that it is true that when indications were published of the likely shape of public expenditure five years on, some small allowance for contingencies had been provided (in 1966 the amount allowed was about $\frac{3}{4}$ per cent of the estimated total). But indications of the position in five years' time are very different from firm decisions taken for the immediate future. Five years is a very long time and all sorts of things may happen in the meantime; and it is only when firm decisions have to be taken as to the size of each programme and of the total of public expenditure that Governments are forced to choose between providing a contingency reserve or some service for the public.

It may be asked why, when experience in every walk of life and common prudence both point to the wisdom of providing for the unforeseeable, no such provision was made before 1968. The answer lies in the very great political difficulty of doing so. Against a background of resources never being sufficient to provide for the kind of public expenditure programmes that are desired by the Ministers most closely concerned with them, and against the same background of Ministers' proposals being cut down by a few million here and half a million there in order to reduce total expenditure to an acceptable limit, it is obviously going to be extremely difficult to persuade such Ministers that it is sensible that they should accept the cutting down of those services even further and, very possibly, the consequential criticism by both Parliament and public, in order to provide more than £100 million to meet proposals which no one round the Cabinet table is in fact making – as yet. The assumption in every such Minister's mind must be that but for the contingency reserve he would be able to secure the finance he so urgently needs. In any case, to deny an existing need in order to provide for a non-existent one is an extremely difficult course to propose. In fact it proved an impossible one until the course of events had demonstrated on more than one occasion that the political difficulties which arise from the lack of provision of a contingency reserve can be greater than those which arise from the cutting of proposed expenditure in order to make room for one.

Since 1968 there has been published each year a Government White Paper setting out a five-year programme for public expenditure, and it is of interest to observe that not only has a contingency reserve been provided in each set of figures but that the most relevant one has shown an increase each year. In 1968 the contingency reserve provided for the year 1969–70 was a figure equivalent to approximately ½ per cent of the total of public expenditure as then defined. In the December 1969 White Paper the comparable figure for the comparable year was roughly 1 per cent; in December 1972, about 2 per cent; namely £500 million.

Having secured a contingency reserve the next problem which arises is how it should be used, and to that question there is no perfect solution. First, there is the usual difficulty of timing, but to an even greater extent than normally. For with ordinary approved programmes of public expenditure it is not unreasonable to assume that if half the expenditure has been made by the middle of the year then the programme is probably on course. But how is one to cater for the unforeseen? Events might move rapidly; or they might move slowly. The majority of the expenditure might arise early or late. With the unforeseeable there is no telling.

With the partly foreseeable there arises the second difficulty, that of priorities. One of the situations that had been partly foreseen may have developed more rapidly than others where the need, once established, is likely to be regarded as more pressing. If all can be fully accommodated in terms of finance then the question of 'Which?' does not arise. But if – as is mostly the case – they cannot, or probably cannot, then it does. First come, first served may be a serviceable guide in many walks of life; with public expenditure first come, most deserved is not necessarily true. Many items will be of considerable merit and considerable size, and they will be agreed upon as between the department concerned and the Treasury in the usual way. Others will present more difficulty and will need to be decided on by the appropriate Cabinet committee and, if necessary, by Cabinet itself. In all these decisions the remaining size of the contingency reserve will be a very relevant consideration, but not a decisive one. On the one hand a new and most pressing need cannot be put entirely on one side just because the provision made at the start of the year on a not very precise basis is expected to be inadequate. Similarly it would be unwise to engage in a variety of new and not very pressing expenditures – probably involving long-term commitments – just because the provision happens to be available in a particular period as a result of an unusual absence of claims. In the event, therefore, the financial control of the contingency reserve will largely resolve itself into the decision-making processes associated with new items of public expenditure, but the funds remaining in the reserve will powerfully condition ministerial attitudes.

Having considered the area over which the financial control of public expenditure applies, and having decided what kind of expenditure can be accepted as being beyond that control, it is now possible to examine the broader aspects of control of public expenditure. How, for example, does the Government ensure that the public service which it decided to provide – and in respect of which the figure approved was merely the financial quantification – is in fact provided in the best possible way, and how does the public ensure that it receives good value for the money it provides for public expenditure?

The first condition of good administration is that the division of responsibility should be appropriate to the most efficient fulfilment of the task and that it should be clear. Within the central Government – local authorities and public corporations will be separately considered – the departmental structure is consistent with those criteria and has stood the test of time. Each department has its areas of government – it may be varied from time to time to suit changing circumstances but without affecting the general principle – and is responsible for both management and finance. The Minister is answerable to Parliament for the policy and running of his department; the Permanent Secretary – the top civil servant in the department – is the accounting officer responsible for all matters of finance and administration. That is all very clear, and the fact that responsibility for finance is put on the department in addition to the responsibility for administration is surely wise in that no element of doubt can remain as to where responsibility lies. Every encouragement is thus given to the exercise of that responsibility in the broadest way. The alternative system under which A incurs the expenditure and B, by way of a further check, meets it, leaves it open to B to say, in the event of anything having gone wrong, that such doubts as he might have had as to the wisdom of a certain act were removed by the knowledge that A had authorised the expenditure; and to A to say that his anxieties were similarly removed by the knowledge that B was prepared to sign the cheque. Where A incurs and meets the expenditure, and is answerable for both, there is no room for such mistaken assumptions.

The question then arises as to whether the advantages of such a system of overall responsibility are not outweighed by the disadvantages associated with the exercise of overall authority which is the necessary corollary. The answer is that they might be were the authority not matched by comparable accountability and were those exercising that authority not equipped in every possible way to do so wisely and efficiently.

That equipping is the responsibility of the Civil Service Department as to staffing and of the Treasury as to systems. (Until recently there was no Civil Service Department, the Treasury being responsible for the recruiting, staffing and conditions of service of the whole of the Civil Service.) There can be no room for anxiety on the score that an insufficient proportion of the able and very able men and women in the population is attracted into government employment: a comparison with the general level of ability in the academic world, in the professions and in business will serve to confirm this view. Indeed there is cause for anxiety the other way round: the fact that nearly two-thirds of those with 'further' education (i.e. formal education beyond school) find themselves employed in the public sector gives rise to concern as to whether the private sector is perhaps being under-nourished.

As to the best practice in administration and the latest developments in technique of control and evaluation, there already exists a large volume of literature to which it is not intended to add. Systems are continually developing, and there is continued argument as to which are worth installing having regard to the comparison between the cost involved and the benefits thought to accrue. What matters is that each department should be aware of the methods by which it might improve its own efficiency and that it should be able to rely on the Treasury as a store-house of knowledge and specialised instruction. Both are the case; and in order to be able to satisfy the demands made upon it the Treasury goes to considerable lengths to equip itself with the necessary information and to carry out the necessary research. But its role is not merely passive; it has the responsibility of ensuring that the departments are equipped in every way to carry out their functions as efficiently as modern science permits.

In short each government department exercises a degree of responsibility that is full and clear, and it is adequately equipped to carry out its functions efficiently. It is not the case that the Treasury is responsible for the efficiency of the administration of each individual department. It is certainly true that, as there is a widespread belief to this effect, the Treasury rarely escapes criticism if anything goes wrong with the running of any department. But that is a different matter and one which is not uncommon in the world at large. Moreover the misconception is not entirely without benefit, for the departments and the Treasury work the more closely and co-operatively in the knowledge that responsibility is thought to be shared in the world of politics and public accountability. What is wrongly thought to be the truth may be of very nearly as much importance as the truth itself.

Accepting, then, that the government machine is well able to give effect to government decisions in the field of public expenditure, what methods are adopted of ensuring that it in fact does so? There are basically two: the haphazard testing by the public and the methodical testing by Parliament. The citizen is in direct contact with the civil servant and can complain if he considers himself badly served. Often he will put his complaint to the department; sometimes to his Member of Parliament. In the latter event the MP may pass on the complaint to the relevant Minister and, when he receives an explanation, decide whether it is adequate or whether the complaint needs to be pursued further either by correspondence or by seeing the Minister or by raising it in the House of Commons. Alternatively the MP may decide that the complaint should be publicly aired in Parliament without any preliminary enquiry, if he feels that the circumstances warrant that approach. The great snag is that the parliamentary time available is far less than is needed; the MP will experience difficulty in getting a question answered in the daily question period of one hour, and even then the total exchange only lasts about a minute. He will experience greater difficulty in giving his complaint the half-hour airing that the daily adjournment debate provides. Nevertheless his question will not escape attention. Answers to every question have to be prepared and put before the Minister, together with a short summary of the facts. The Minister may feel that he ought to go into a particular matter in greater depth; so may a senior officer. The possibility of a public airing at some stage or other must always be borne in mind, and may in fact materialise. Whatever the action decided on by the Member of Parliament, it is clear that the right of every citizen without exception, in addition to his normal remedies, to place his complaint before his MP provides a valuable check on the functioning of the government machine, albeit a partial and haphazard one.

The checks carried out by Parliament through its committees and their officers are widespread, methodical and penetrating. They cover the activities of every department and are related both to what has happened and what is likely to happen. The system adopted provides for the appointment of two all-party committees of members of the Commons: the first, the Public Accounts Committee (the PAC) and the second, the Expenditure Committee (the successor to the Estimates Committee). Both are drawn from the political parties in proportion to their numbers in the House of Commons, but it would be quite wrong to assume that the preponderance of government supporters will result in the committee reports being always biased in favour of the Government or, indeed, that a highly partisan approach will be adopted by the members. The Chairman of the PAC is, by tradition, a member of the Opposition – frequently an ex-Treasury Minister – and so far as both committees are concerned, there tends to be a non-partisan approach. A number of reasons contribute to this. First, what divides parties is policy; but committees do not consider policy. Secondly, the common interest of all members is to foster good government and to criticise bad. Finally, the majority party is cured of any desire to exercise power unfairly by the realisation that sooner or later it will form the minority and will expect the new majority party to be guided by the pattern set when it was in power. In most cases, therefore, these select committees find themselves able to examine the issues before them with considerable objectivity. Were this not the case, the control by Parliament over public expenditure would be much weakened.

The PAC is served by a full-time officer of the highest calibre appointed in such a way as to secure and safeguard his independence. He – the Comptroller and Auditor-General – in turn employs a staff of over 400 who are engaged in perusing departmental files and investigating any activities that seem to require it. They have complete access to all sources of information and their enquiries enable the Controller and Auditor-General to draw to the attention of the committee matters of special interest. Some of these the committee may decide to investigate further by all the normal processes of calling for detailed reports and examining witnesses drawn both from the department concerned and – if appropriate – from the public. The PAC reports are in turn presented to Parliament and debated in the House of Commons and published to the world at large, together with the evidence in most cases. Matters of considerable public interest are picked up by the Press and receive very wide circulation. Every department and everyone in it is thus fully accountable for the action taken, the statement made and the letter written; full disclosure is the daily circumstance and full exposure the possible eventuality. Whether this system encourages too much caution and too little individual enterprise is an issue which is not of present concern. What it does achieve is the kind of financial and management control which makes it possible to claim that it is unlikely that substantial inefficiency can exist for long in any area of government spending without it being brought to light.

The traditional role of the Comptroller and Auditor-General was to act as the watchdog of Parliament, to ensure that the money voted by Parliament was spent on the purposes intended. Increasingly the emphasis has switched to management problems, to ensuring that the public gets value for money and that there is neither waste nor inefficiency. An examination of the cases reported to Parliament over recent years – themselves, of course, only a small proportion of the total number of cases investigated by the Comptroller and Auditor-General and his staff and therefore not a wholly reliable sample – would indicate that the second category, management, is some four to five times as numerous as the first. Of course some things are bound to go wrong with such a huge volume of expenditure – many thousands of millions of pounds – and with such a large number of individuals involved – some half-million non-industrial civil servants in the government service alone. But any error would almost certainly be an error of judgement and not an error in the field of financial propriety. It would be incredible if there were no reported cases where in the light of subsequent events a decision taken with careful foresight did not turn out to be the wrong one. But even at the risk of introducing a personal reminiscence into the record I feel bound to pay this tribute to the system and all those who operated it: I am aware of only one case of financial impropriety among those half-million civil servants that occurred during the whole of the six years when I was Chief Secretary to the Treasury; and no case has come to light of gross inefficiency or waste in the implementation of government policy. There can clearly be differences of view as to the wisdom of engaging in a particular field of research, or as to the wisdom of continuing with the development of a piece of technical equipment in an area beyond the established frontiers of science when the cost originally estimated has long since been exceeded. But these are policy decisions where the judgement of the Minister or the Government or Parliament has been brought to bear. The view may well be taken that in the light of subsequently ascertained facts, the original policy decision was an unwise one. That, if true, is however a comment on the decision and not on its implementation. The function of the system of control is to bring these facts and developments to the attention of those who made the original decision and who, in the light of these new facts, might wish to vary it. So long as that is happening the system itself is not failing in its purpose, and a decision to continue none the less with the original policy dispels any possible doubt.

But the work of the PAC alone, valuable as it is in bringing errors to light and thereby pointing the way to the avoidance of their repetition, is not enough. In the nature of things, the discovery may be too late – that is to say the stable door may be seen to be open only after all the horses have fled, whereas the escape of the first one should have set the alarm bells ringing. Moreover investigation into individual acts, valuable and essential though it is, tends to concentrate on the detailed aspects of implementation and not on policy implementation as a whole. These deficiencies of time and broad substance are made good by the Expenditure Committee, the successor to the Estimates Committee which existed up to 1971. As its name implied, its function was to examine the estimates of government expenditure presented to Parliament each year; that is to say, future expenditure as compared with the past payments examined by the PAC. The Estimates Committee tended to examine broad fields of expenditure, choosing a particular topic covering a number of estimates rather than a particular one or a particular group within a single department. In this way the Committee was able to form a judgement on the way a particular programme was being implemented – again, without querying the policy which lay behind the decision to provide that service or carry out that programme of expenditure. Nevertheless, the self-examination prompted by the Committee's questioning and the criticism expressed in its reports often succeeded in giving rise to such variations in the future implementation of the programme or to such modifications in policy as would achieve more efficiency and greater value for money. It was this combination of past and future, detailed and general, which gave the work of the Public Accounts and Estimates Committees their overall value.

The change in the name of the Estimates Committee to that of Expenditure Committee reflects an important development in the control of public expenditure. As will be more fully explained in a later chapter, the estimates which Parliament is invited to approve cover the expenditure of the central Government, including its contributions to the expenditure of local authorities. Public expenditure is a much bigger figure and a much more important concept, and it was largely the desire to wean Parliamentary interest away from over-concentration on the estimates (to the exclusion of everything else to do with spending) and to direct it to the really relevant issues of public expenditure that resulted in the decision to publish annually five-year public expenditure programmes. It followed that a committee charged with the limited responsibility of examining the estimates of central Government expenditure was no longer adequate, and accordingly its powers were enhanced by enabling it to look at the whole of public expenditure.

The change involved was slight in form but very substantial in content. It is therefore worth recording how the change came about, especially as it would appear to be typical of the way in which lasting changes occur on the British political scene. The necessary ingredients for a change would seem to be a very solid case in theory for the new proposal, evidence that the old practice is largely irrelevant, a suitably long time for the new ideas to be digested, an appearance of minimum change to disguise a radical departure, and a mainly irrelevant incident to act as catalyst.

The arguments in favour of the change were very strong, both economically and politically. As Governments came to intervene more and more in the circumstances in which business men carried on their activities and private individuals their lives, and as a very substantial and ever-increasing proportion of the wealth created by the community came to be used by Governments on behalf of and for the benefit of the population as a whole, it clearly became appropriate for Parliament to cease concentrating exclusively on the oversight of disbursements made by the central Government and to play its part in making the broad policy choices that the management of public expenditure involved. Three things were needed to make the change smoothly: the desire of MPs to interest themselves in public expenditure and their understanding of the much-reduced importance of the supply estimates; a favourable report by a Parliamentary committee setting out a practical scheme for implementing the change; and a favourable decision by Cabinet. An early opportunity was taken to put the new proposals forward in evidence to a suitable Parliamentary committee – but little response was evoked. The idea was too new and strange. A suitable opportunity was taken in the House of Commons to touch on the reducing role of the estimates. Here there was a reaction – a hostile one. The MP who was the Chairman of the Estimates Committee at the time made it clear that he was not going to have it said that the task laid upon his commitee was any less important or valuable than it had been half a century earlier; and the official Opposition spokesmen were not going to be taken in by a Treasury Minister who must have been attempting to take the spotlight off his incompetence by diverting attention to some less easily definable object like public expenditure. Accordingly, with two unfavourable answers, it would have been quite inappropriate to attempt the third – a favourable decision by one's colleagues in Government. Time was clearly needed for allaying suspicion and promoting support through understanding of the issues involved. In particular it was necessary to change the mood in relation to supplementary estimates – the method by which the Government of the day, having spent the money authorised by the original estimate, sought Parliamentary approval for additional expenditure.

History and the age-old power battle between Parliament and the executive had long invested the 'watch-dog' function of the House of Commons with great importance. By keeping control of the purse strings and in particular by keeping government spending down to the minimum, the MP could easily persuade himself that he was at one and the same time defending the liberty of the subject and preventing the abuse of power by the executive. The approval by the Commons of the original estimate had defined the figure which should be spent: to come to Parliament seeking approval for a supplementary estimate was clear evidence of incompetence or lavishness – or both; and the opportunity provided of criticising the Government and its spendthrift departments was too good to be missed. Now there is of course something still to be said for that approach; and no doubt there was a great deal to be said for it when the function of Government was much more limited and when financial probity could not be taken for granted. But put in the context of public expenditure and the management of the economy, what should be of value in the discipline of the estimates is the encouragement given to providing the desired service with the minimum use of resources, thereby leaving the maximum balance of resources for other much-needed purposes. Now the simple way to avoid the criticism attaching to a supplementary estimate is to take good care to see that the original estimate is sufficiently generous to cover any possible eventuality. On the other hand, the way to secure the minimum use of resources is to pare the original estimate down as far as reasonably possible – even though the occurrence of an uncatered-for event will result in the need to present a supplementary estimate to Parliament.

To begin with, therefore, the criticism of Parliament had to be accepted as the price to be paid for securing that very economy in the use of resources which Parliament itself desired. Gradually, however, patient explanation and repetition of the argument, coupled with consistency of conduct in other areas of financial control, combined to achieve a more objective viewpoint. The level of intelligent appreciation in Parliament is high, and the spoken word of partisan criticism is often accompanied by a silent but thoughtful appraisal of the subject of the criticism. However, what hastened the process of conversion was not the continuing criticism of Parliament but that of the outside world. World opinion had not been influenced by the process of patient explanation – it had indeed not been listening. To the outside world the steps in the argument were as simple as they were compelling. Sterling was under a cloud. Only if the British Government controlled its spending firmly might it weather the storm. Supplementary estimates meant that spending was out of control – and if one had any doubt about it, one had only to pop round to the street-corner paper shop in Zurich, Bonn, Paris or New York and read the headlines in all the 'solid' British newspapers. So one had better reduce one's holding of sterling and get back into dollars, Deutschemarks or Swiss francs.

The loss to domestic reserves consequent upon the submission to Parliament of supplementary estimates was so marked and so regular that something had to be done about it. One could not do away with estimates or avoid supplementaries; they were very much a part of the fabric of Parliament and still served an essential need – the control of cash. Moreover any attempt to do so in an international atmosphere of lack of confidence would undoubtedly have been read as justifying the worst suspicions and made matters infinitely worse. All one could do, therefore, was to overlay important-sounding but not very significant figures with figures of much greater importance; and hope that in the struggle for scarce headline space the lesser would yield to the greater. The more important figures would obviously be the public expenditure figures – published if possible round about the same time as, or even a little earlier than, the estimates and accompanied by the necessary explanations to demonstrate their altogether greater significance. If you really regarded yourself as a banker of international standing, the message must be that you had better study the figures that really told you what was happening about the expenditure of all public authorities in the UK, not merely of the central Government; and for five years ahead, not merely for the current year.

So the stage started to become set for the next act. Parliamentary opinion had by now become much better informed; the official Opposition had had confirmation from their contacts with the Whitehall grapevine that Treasury Ministers were not con-men but, as was to be expected, very tough operators; and a change which could well result in the powers of the Estimates Committee being increased rather than reduced was obviously something that every good committee man would wish to take seriously. The fact that increased pressure on sterling had been an incidental occurrence rather than an argument relative to the central issue meant that when, after devaluation, the pressure was extinguished, there was no halt in the progress of Parliamentary and other informed opinion.

Then, fortunately, a very competent Commons committee began sympathetically to reconsider the whole issue. Formal Treasury evidence supplemented by informal chats at not-so-casual encounters saw to it that great minds thought along similar lines and the committee's report included in its recommendations what had been excluded four years earlier. The climate of opinion in the House of Commons had made such progress that Government proposals supported by the all-party committee's report would clearly be accepted without difficulty. What remained therefore was to secure formal Cabinet approval of the change. But changes which involve, or are likely to involve, a transference of some power from the executive to Parliament find readier acceptance by the latter than by the former. Moreover proposals emanating from the Treasury, which therefore must presumably suit its plans, naturally require a hard look by the Ministers in charge of spending departments; and it was clearly seen that acceptance of the proposals would create difficulties for certain Ministers while at the same time being of real advantage to the Treasury. The difficulties centred on the reduction of future flexibility through having to make present decisions affecting five years' expenditure; and, more particularly, the premature disclosure of politically sensitive decisions (for example, the future level of pensions). The advantage to the Treasury was the reverse of the same coin – the inability to make changes. Treasury Ministers naturally seek to make expenditure decisions stick; that is to say, to prevent increases in expenditure, for the reverse does not arise. But this is a surprisingly difficult objective to achieve within Government. Changes in the domestic and more particularly in the international scene are mostly impossible to foresee and yet may result in very insistent demands for increased expenditure. The contingency reserve may be running out, and the alternative of finding room for the new expenditure by stopping an equivalent amount of already agreed expenditure presents obvious difficulties. It is always necessary to remember that the choice is not between good and bad proposals – that would make life very easy. It is between good and good. Each individual new proposal is not likely to be very large in relation to the total of public expenditure – especially in the very early years. With public expenditure running at £30,000 million a year, so the argument would go, how can it upset the country's economy to make it £30,002 million? Well of course, taken in isolation – as was inevitably the case, through time pressures – it could not. How many similar proposals for additional expenditure would come along in the future and be entitled to similar treatment could not be quantified and therefore could not be strongly pressed as counter-argument. How large a figure the £2 million this year would grow into in two or three years' time, it was probably too early to say. The result therefore was a strong tendency for the agreed figure of public expenditure to grow month by month. Certainly, the figure had been agreed, and agreed by Cabinet, the final authority in Government. But why should not a Cabinet change its mind? Is it not the duty of its members to take account of ever-changing circumstances and to review its decisions accordingly, as often as may be necessary? In fact it is obviously in the interests of good government that Cabinet should be able to change its mind whenever the occasion demanded it, and it would not be of much help to argue therefore that on this issue – the overall total of public expenditure – it was somehow or other wrong for Cabinet Ministers to exercise their judgement, which was the main justification for their holding Cabinet office, in the light of the new circumstances.

A Cabinet decision cannot lightly be reversed, and the onus of proof rests on those who would seek to make the change. But an extension in public expenditure is not seen as a breach of any fundamental principle. It is plain to see, therefore, that making Cabinet decisions stick is no easy matter. Aids to this end are not easy to find, but there is one which is extremely powerful – publication to the world at large. Once a Government has published its proposals in full detail and quantified the cost, it will go to considerable lengths to demonstrate that its strength of purpose and competence in management are such that forecasts are fulfilled. If there is any final barrier to the gradual increase of public expenditure in excess of planned commitments, full publication creates it. The readiness of Parliament, the Press and the public at large to criticise a Government for spending more than it planned to do, which was somewhat misplaced in the case of the supply estimates and was to a considerable extent the cause of the change under discussion, could now be used by the Treasury as an important aid in its task of controlling public expenditure.

From the Treasury standpoint, therefore, full publication was much to be desired, and having regard to Ministers' differing interests, a slight tussle in Cabinet was to be expected. But it was confidently felt that the major argument would prevail – that of extending democratic participation in deciding how nearly 30 per cent of the nation's annual wealth should be spent on community purposes. In the event, that is what happened. Ministers with little or nothing to lose gave their support to the proposed publication of public expenditure details over a five-year period. The greatest difficulty centred round the one Minister who combined a healthy and penetrating suspicion of every Treasury move with responsibility for the department which would be most affected by the change. Accordingly, the matter was not pressed to a conclusion at that meeting and steps were taken before the next Cabinet meeting to explain away the Minister's problems as far as that could be done. No undue difficulty was to be expected therefore in reaching a satisfactory conclusion at the next meeting. In the event the fact that full opportunity had been given for discussion and criticism at the earlier meeting, coupled with the equally important fact that by the time this final item on the agenda was reached it was already lunch-time (and most Ministers would be likely to have lunch engagements of one kind or another), meant that this important reform was finally approved by Cabinet without further discussion.

That it was important is perhaps best illustrated by quoting in full the views of the Select Committee on Expenditure, the committee set up as its name indicates to examine aspects of public expenditure and report to Parliament. In the introduction to their report on 'Command Papers on Public Expenditure' (the publication covering public expenditure for five years ahead fell into the category of Parliamentary papers known as a Command Paper), the all-party committee states:

'We feel that the importance of the Command Papers and Parliament's discussion of them cannot be overstated. The Command Papers contain the core of the Government's policy, and reflect its overall social and economic strategy. Similarly the debate on the Command Papers should provide the main opportunity for the influence of the legislature to be brought to bear on the programme of the executive. It should be among the most important events of the parliamentary year. As we emphasise in the following sections, a major development has taken and is taking place in the Government's control over public spending and in the information being provided to Parliament. It represents a very great achievement and we should like to pay a tribute to the Treasury for the work that has been and is being done.'

All party tributes to the Treasury for 'a very great achievement' are not paid daily in the House of Commons; indeed if any Chief Secretary hears the words 'Thank you' from the lips of a colleague he will immediately fear that he must have slipped up badly. But there can be no doubt that the Committee was correct in its assessment of the importance of the development that had taken place. It is put in world context by Sir Samuel Goldman, KCB – a most respected and very senior Treasury official – in *Public Expenditure Management and Control* (HMSO, 1973). He concludes: 'After many vicissitudes we have evolved a system for managing the public sector which despite many continuing deficiencies is probably superior to that found anywhere else in the world.'

It is interesting to observe in passing that the change came about when the necessary conditions earlier described were satisfied. The theoretical case in favour of the change was very strong; the old practice was seen to be becoming irrelevant in the context of economic management and the choice of priorities in public spending; four years had been allowed for digesting the new ideas – indeed the Plowden Committee as far back as 1961 had indicated that long-term surveys of public expenditure should be laid before Parliament and the public but had added 'It would be surprising if any Government were prepared to do this.' Then again, the change would not appear at first sight as being very fundamental – a few more statistics supplementing the estimates. Finally what triggered off the change had virtually nothing to do with public expenditure: it was the sensitivity of sterling.

An important element in the control of public expenditure is the sense of professionalism in the Civil Service. Indeed it is of such importance also in all the processes of deciding the amount and nature of public expenditure as well as, incidentally, the processes of Government generally – though this is not our present concern – that to omit an assessment of it would leave an account of the control of public expenditure incomplete.

It is first necessary to realise that the number of civil servants engaged on the decision-making processes of public expenditure and on its control is quite small. The exact number is of little significance: what matters is that those concerned are sufficiently few to be able to get to know one another well. Moreover they do, in fact, stay in one or other relevant post long enough to do so. They are highly skilled, loyal employees, but they move from one department to another and must needs take their loyalties with them. The changes will often mean that opponents become allies and vice versa. In such a continually changing pattern, what must – and does – emerge as the permanent qualification for the task of service to the public is individual integrity. This is seen as one of the main ingredients to promotion within the Service; it enables individuals to deal with one another on the basis of a loyalty to their profession to which temporary departmental loyalties must accommodate themselves. Conflicts of interest appropriate to representatives of different departments of Government must not be allowed to develop into hostilities. The enemy of yesterday would need to become the ally of tomorrow – a change too difficult to accomplish. Trustworthiness naturally becomes the basis of the relationship between these roaming individuals.

In this situation differences come to be settled on the strength of arguments based on fully disclosed facts. Facts withheld are an aid to the slick – an embarrassment to the straightforward. All this is particularly evident in the dealings of Treasury officials with those in other government departments – several of whom will have served in the Treasury and some of whom will have participated, while in the Treasury, in PESC negotiations. Departmental loyalties and responsibilities will result in the departmental case being fully made in any difference with the Treasury; overall loyalties and responsibilities will require all the facts to be carefully assessed and fully disclosed as an important aid to reaching the 'right' conclusion.

Reference has already been made to the difficulties that arise, in the context of PESC, in ascertaining the cost of 'present' policies and to the ability of departmental officials finally to reach agreement with their opposite numbers in the Treasury on what the figures should be. This process is repeated many times throughout the year in resolving the differences of opinion which inevitably arise over the cost of implementing the various programmes incorporated in the agreed PESC totals. For an important element in the control of public expenditure is that Treasury officials should keep regular contact with those in the departments who have the responsibility of carrying out the programmes and making the necessary day-to-day decisions. This does not mean interference in the department's sphere of responsibility; it does mean the kind of contact that will enable the Treasury official to be sufficiently familiar with what is happening for him to be able to assess fully and speedily any proposal put to him by the department to overcome difficulties met with in the course of implementing the various programmes. For difficulties do arise; difficulties, for example, of interpretation of the scope originally intended, which will arise in connection with borderline cases; difficulties in connection with the extra cost stemming from some new but unavoidable circumstance; difficulties in deciding whether the level or quality of service is that originally intended or whether some adjustment is required to prevent the original estimate being exceeded; difficulties in deciding whether, if additional finance is required, the demands by the public in other services provided by the same department have fallen off sufficiently to enable a comparable reduction in cost to be achieved. Difficulties of this kind are continually arising: it is inevitable that they should, given the numbers of human beings affected and the infinite variety in their circumstances and given the impossibility of foreseeing all the changes at home and abroad that occur during the course of two to three years.

Co-operation of a high order is required to enable all these difficulties to be overcome without damage to any of the services concerned or to the economy as a whole. Such co-operation can only exist between individuals who respect one another, understand their validly differing points of view and share a common desire to make the system work well. There is no place in such a system for the smart operator who obtains some temporary advantage over his opposite number through dubious methods. Professionalism, personal integrity and 'knowing your man' – and respecting him for what you know – are the essentials in making government work at the official level. In particular, they are the essentials in the control of public expenditure in its fullest sense. For there is no sense in which the kind of service provided can be regarded as an issue quite separate from the cost. The measure of national resources allocated to a particular public expenditure programme which the figure of cost attempts to describe, is an integral and necessary part of the process of allocating the right amount of resources overall which in turn is part of the process of managing the national economy. But that amount of resources can be used in so many slightly differing ways in carrying out the programme that to have regard exclusively to the figure would be to ignore the main purpose of the PESC decision, namely that of allocating the necessary resources so as to ensure the provision of the public service of the kind contemplated. It might for example be possible to carry out the service in several different ways at the same cost. Which would be the 'best' of these ways might well be a matter of individual judgement. Similarly an increase in cost might not necessarily imply an improvement in the service. Clearly, it is not possible to discuss cost in isolation from the question of quality. Accordingly it is not possible to control public expenditure of this kind with understanding and full appreciation of the factors involved unless there is added to the cool consideration of the figures of expenditure incurred a warm comprehension of the kinds of activity involved.

Most of what has so far been said on the subject of control of public expenditure has in fact contemplated that kind of expenditure which results from the provision of a public service: where, in the main, the greatest cost will be in the payment of salaries to individual civil servants (at national or local government level), who will be instructed in their task by their departmental superiors; where the head of the department will be accountable for the way the money is spent; where the detailed expenditure will be examined either by the staff of the Comptroller and Auditor-General's department or by the District Auditor; where certain aspects of the expenditure may be further examined by one of the select committees of the House of Commons or by the multi-departmental officials carrying out Programme Analysis and Review (PAR); and where the particular aspect of government policy may be questioned and debated in Parliament. There are, however, other kinds of public expenditure where the methods of control need separate consideration because, in the end, public money is not being spent on the instructions of a public servant but of a private individual who is not accountable to Parliament for his actions. In addition the benefit will not go directly to the whole, or to a whole section, of the public, but to a limited or very limited group. The most obvious examples lie in the field of aircraft manufacture and shipbuilding. The issues of public policy involved may be large but the number of direct recipients of benefit is small, and the decisions on how the available funds, whatever their source, are to be spent, lie in the hands of the management of the private firms concerned who may in the final resort be accountable to their private shareholders but are not accountable to the public.

In these very different circumstances the important question that arises in the field of control is how far down the line to follow the expenditure. The decision to provide financial assistance in the first place is a governmental decision arrived at in the way that public expenditure decisions are arrived at, as already described. Assuming – for the sake of clarity of the argument in the first place – that the expenditure takes the form of a straightforward subvention or grant to a particular firm, then the general purpose will have been clearly defined and Parliament will have been notified at an early stage. Problems of disclosure or intention do not arise: what presents the great difficulty is the question whether to attempt to control the subsequent expenditure by the firm, and if so, to what extent. One can eliminate questions of individual fraud or dishonesty: auditors and the law, not to mention several other deterrents, will see to that, whatever the circumstances. What is of concern is the achievement of the purpose for which the grant was provided.

It is clear that the decision to pay the grant should not be taken in the first place unless the circumstances favour the achievement of the purpose intended, including in those circumstances careful estimates of cost, commercial prospects, the competence of all concerned and the economic climate. What is not so clear is what more should be done by the Government to control the firm's subsequent expenditure. Some will argue that nothing more can be done nor indeed should be attempted. If the purpose is achieved, no questions will be asked; if it is not, then the answer to any criticism is that the cause of failure was unforeseeable and would have prevented a successful outcome whatever the extent of Government participation in the firm's management. Indeed, they will go on to argue, the situation would have been made worse by any such participation; for it would at best have diverted the attention of busy managers and directors from other necessary tasks and at worst have altered the decisions they would otherwise have taken, whereas it was on the basis of their capacity to take the right commercial decisions that the money was provided in the first place. Others will maintain that these arguments are all highly theoretical and that in fact it is just not possible, in political terms, to extract money from the public and yet not have some form of public accountability in the ultimate spending of it. Certainly it would hardly be possible to stand idly by and watch the money being lost. No matter how strongly it was argued that it was a matter of deliberate and carefully considered policy not to interfere with the freedom of knowledgeable men to manage their affairs in the light of their own experience, the argument would fail to carry conviction if things went wrong. In that event inactivity is called complacency, or even irresponsibility.

How then can one cope with a situation where it is impossible in political terms to do what is right in management terms? The immediate answer is for Governments not to get themselves involved in situations of this kind. Only when success can be guaranteed is it safe for a Government to assist – i.e. subsidise to some extent – a private firm. But this line of argument does not get one very far, for if success could be guaranteed, there would be no need for governmental assistance – the necessary financial help would be forthcoming from normal commercial sources. A possible solution is the creation of an agency through which governmental financial assistance can be directed to appropriate firms in such a way as not to attract the criticism which Governments, acting directly, cannot avoid. The disadvantage of such a course is that the powers and objectives of the agency, which will have necessarily been closely defined so as to serve the policy objectives of the Government, will not be capable of variation, as would have been the case if no such body had been interposed between the Government and the applicant firm. A Cabinet can judge each case afresh; a statutory agency can only act as is directed by the statute. Where the commercial considerations are uppermost, it is perhaps a good thing that political pressures are prevented from influencing commercial judgement unduly. But there may well be cases where political considerations are uppermost, such as for example the prevention of mass unemployment on the Clyde or the enhancement of national prestige through building a supersonic airliner. The profit and loss account of a private firm does not record the cost to the exchequer and the loss to the economy caused by unemployment relief and lack of work opportunities; its balance sheet provides no place among its assets for national prestige, from which other commercial firms may indirectly benefit.

The Government, therefore, may well have to retain that flexibility of manoeuvre which can only be achieved through direct action in cases where political considerations of one kind or another are the main factors in the decision to assist financially. It will once more then be faced with the dilemma already described. In fact it will additionally be faced with the problem of the firm's existing indebtedness to its creditors, if it decides to attempt to influence in any real sense the expenditure of the firm. For the law is held to provide – and although a Government can properly claim to be exempt from these provisions, it will not seek to do so for wise political considerations – that intervention in the management of a company which, speaking in round terms, is in financial difficulties may result in being saddled with the whole of the firm's liabilities. Now it may well be the case that the firm in question is appealing for Government assistance because it is in fact in considerable financial difficulty; in which case the attempt to control the expenditure of that aid by the firm, through intervening in the way its business is being carried on, may result in the cost to the Exchequer being very much greater than intended, a result which is the very denial of control. In these circumstances a Government may be compelled either to refrain from giving assistance, or to allow the firm to go bankrupt and to start again (if necessary the following day, in the same place and with the same staff) with a new company which has not inherited its predecessor's liabilities.

There is in short no simple answer to the question of how to control public expenditure where such expenditure takes the form of assistance to individual private firms, and particularly to those in financial difficulties. Nor does the answer lie in attempting to equip the Civil Service to carry out commercial tasks. It is of course sensible to bring into the Service, either on a temporary exchange basis or as a permanent addition, individuals with commercial experience. They will have more understanding of the way Governments work when they return to commerce; or if they remain in the Service they will bring useful background experience to certain of their duties. But *ex hypothesi* they will not have the keen commercial nose, the capacity to drive themselves and others and the sense of individual enterprise that characterise the successful man of business; they would not be remaining in the Civil Service if they had. Yet it is these qualities that are needed if a department is to intervene usefully in the important decisions of a firm receiving

Government assistance; and having regard to the difficult circumstances in which the firm is likely to be working, the decisions would probably be very difficult as well as important. No doubt men of great industrial experience and high calibre would be enlisted to serve on an advisory body, and clearly their advice would be most valuable in reaching the first decision – that is, whether to provide Government assistance or not – in cases where the commercial, as opposed to the political, considerations were uppermost. But they will inevitably be busy men – far too busy to take part in a regular monitoring service such as would be involved in an attempt to follow up and evaluate subsequent expenditure decisions by the firm itself, and without which it would not be possible to maintain that the Government had exercised full control of that item of public expenditure. The full-time civil servant would not be prevented in the same way from participating in all the necessary follow-up activities through lack of time – although it is to be remembered that those at the upper levels will often have to work very long hours indeed and be subject to great pressures. But his lack of experience in coping at first hand with the severe problems of an industrial enterprise in economic and financial difficulties and his lack of sympathy, or rather identification, with the commercial approach, will prevent him from intervening as usefully as possible at a critical point. The approach and standpoint of the civil servant and of the business man, reinforced by their training and experience, are markedly different in character and should be so, having regard to their differing tasks. It is a simple fact which cannot be overlooked in considering the control of this sort of public expenditure. The making of omelettes is a most difficult task for those who give high priority to the avoidance of breakages.

It is then extremely difficult to see a wholly satisfactory solution to the problem of a Government which, having regard to its general responsibility to control public expenditure, is faced with the need to follow up expenditure in cases where assistance has been given mainly on commercial grounds. It cannot, out of its own resources of skill and experience, effectively control the subsequent commercial decisions on expenditure of the particular firm; and it might be risking entering into an open-ended commitment – and every Government wisely seeks to avoid unlimited expenditure commitments – in relation to the firm's creditors. Nor can a Government, for the reasons given, secure, to the extent required for an effective monitoring service, the necessary skill and experience by the creation of an advisory body. It will be compelled, therefore, to rely on the well-tried device of an outside agency specially created for the purpose with clearly-defined statutory powers. Such a body would consist of men of the necessary calibre and experience to make the original decision as to the provision of financial assistance. They would not attempt to interfere with the subsequent management of the assisted firm for the reasons earlier described, and if the decision to assist failed to achieve its purpose, they would carry a share of the responsibility sufficient to enable the Government to sustain the remaining share of responsibility without unacceptable political harm. The conclusion stemming from the difficulties of effectively controlling public expenditure of this particular kind is that the cases where a Government provides financial assistance to particular firms on mainly commercial considerations should be kept down to a minimum. Economic considerations would seem to support this conclusion.

Where, however, political considerations are uppermost in the minds of a Government deciding to provide financial assistance, then it is the Government, and no other body, which will have the experience and the political judgement and which must therefore take full responsibility for its actions. It will, for the political considerations already mentioned, need to exercise a measure of control over the actual payments made subsequent to the original decision; and will accordingly need to retain to itself the flexibility which, in the earlier mentioned category of commercial assistance, will rest in the board of the assisted company. The Government will need to obtain the necessary economic and financial advice to enable it to make a balanced judgement; but it can obtain this from the kind of advisory body already described, supplemented if necessary by outside professional advice. It will be exceptionally fortunate if all this assistance can be afforded in time, for the sorry fact is that a Government very rarely has sufficient time to take all the advice it would wish to do, before being compelled by the pressure of events to reach its decision. It will mostly be able to avoid responsibility to the creditors of an existing organisation by starting a new one; and it will be able to limit its financial commitment to the new one by retaining the option to cease making further contributions. For whereas in the earlier 'commercial' cases the assistance would need to take the form of a single payment (or single commitment, which is for practical purposes the same thing), with 'political' cases (flexibility and initiative having been retained) the assistance will take the form of instalments paid from time to time as needed.

In both cases it has been assumed that the assistance contemplated is of a temporary nature, even though 'temporary' may well cover a period of three years or more. Where, however, it is contemplated that the assistance to the individual firm or firms will be more or less permanent, then clearly a different structure will be required to provide the appropriate degree of control over, and of public accountability for, the expenditure of public funds.. The pattern that suggests itself is that of the nationalised industry corporation or similar public corporation; nothing less would meet all the necessary criteria.

Closely connected with these issues, and sometimes indistinguishable from them, are certain problems in public purchasing which are concerned with accountability and control. The aircraft industry serves as a good example. Whether it is thinking of the defence of the country, of employment, of exports or of technical progress in engineering, a British

Government will always want to promote the interests of its domestic aircraft industry. This it can do in a variety of ways. At a minimum it can simply buy, as an ordinary customer, some of the planes on offer by a manufacturer; at a maximum it can provide the whole of the finance needed for the industry or for a constituent firm by the process of nationalisation. In between these extremes it can assist in a great variety of more or less limited ways, of which two are of particular interest in the field of public expenditure control. The first is the provision of a fixed sum towards the research and development (R. and D.) cost of a new type of aircraft, in which case the manufacturer knows that he has to face the total R. and D. cost, whatever it may amount to, less only the agreed fixed Government contribution. The second is the payment by the Government of the whole R. and D. cost, which it may decide to do where complete novelty of design might make it impossible for the individual firm concerned to contemplate the financial risks involved. The difference between the two methods so far as the contractor is concerned is obvious and not unimportant. In the first case, if the cost of R. and D. escalates to such an extent as to be beyond the resources of the firm, it may have to face bankruptcy. In the second, if the same escalation occurs, the Government will have to find the necessary additional finance and the firm's own financial position will remain broadly unaffected.

Only the second case presents any problem so far as control is concerned. For not only will the Government need to monitor the financial cost in the ordinary way, it will also need to assess the technical progress; and for that purpose to have the necessary expertise available to it. In this way it may be able to satisfy itself that the cost incurred at any particular stage, though considerably greater than that originally estimated, has been reasonably incurred; and when making the decision as to whether to carry on, notwithstanding the possibility of even further cost escalation, technical considerations will play a most important part. In addition it may well be the case that more than one country is involved in joint production and that political considerations – such as national prestige – assume unusual importance. The decision-making process will as a result be more complex and lengthy; indeed, the contractual arrangements between the countries jointly concerned may be such as to prevent a decision to change course being taken without the consent of every country. In that event, one country may have to consider what could amount to the unilateral breach of an international treaty – a course not to be lightly undertaken. But essentially public expenditure control would be playing its full part, that of giving the original decision-makers the opportunity, when the cost is beginning to exceed the amount contemplated, of varying their decision. It cannot do more than that. It cannot, for example, turn an original incautious decision into a sound one; it cannot prevent an unforeseen expense from materialising; it cannot eliminate the costs consequential on a decision to alter course or to halt production – and in certain cases these, having regard to the commitments originally undertaken, may be very substantial indeed.

The dividing line between governmental assistance and public purchasing, as these examples have demonstrated, is an extremely thin one, easily crossed and sometimes imperceptible. It is rarely the case in aircraft manufacture that a contribution towards R. and D. is totally divorced from the possibility of a future purchase, either by the Government directly in the case of military aircraft, or indirectly, by means of suitable inducement to a nationalised airline in the case of civil aircraft. What is of interest in the field of expenditure control is the method by which it is achieved. No separate agency need be involved; for the major considerations are not those of industrial management, in which it has been suggested a Government is ill-equipped; nor are they those of political judgement, in which a Government is supremely well equipped. Rather are they the scientific and technical ones, where uniquely the Government is well equipped, partly as a result of having the most important aircraft research establishment in the country and partly as a result of the enlistment into its ranks of technical experts in order to meet the continual need, in the day-to-day work of aircraft procurement, to call on expertise of this kind. The Government can therefore act directly and retain such flexibility as it desires in the incurring and monitoring of public expenditure in this field.

The central Government is a very substantial purchaser, buying about 5 per cent of the total output of all manufacturing and construction industries. In total the figure is in excess of £1,500 million a year; in detail, the percentage of each individual firm's turnover taken by Government purchases varies from the insignificant to the very substantial. The Government is, therefore, the most important purchaser in total and in many cases the dominant customer. In considering its policy as purchaser the Government must therefore take account of its overall responsibility to protect the public purse, to promote efficiency, to increase exports and reduce imports, to foster increases in regional prosperity and to promote good labour relations. So far as defence is concerned it must also ensure that security is maintained and that there is an adequate domestic manufacturing potential in the event of hostilities. Protecting the public purse mostly means nothing more complicated than buying in the cheapest reliable market, and the achievement of the other elements within the purchasing policy does not in most cases conflict with this major principle. But it has to be recognised that the considerations to which a Government must have regard are wider and more complex than those affecting the ordinary commercial buyer. He will best serve the interests of his firm by taking account of some elements other than the cheapest price, such as reliability in production and promptness in delivery. To do otherwise could result in the cheapest purchase being the most expensive in terms of his profit and loss account.

But that account takes no note, for example, of the cost of unemployment, as any Government must. In short, value for money has to be judged against a wider background in the case of the Government and public expenditure control must similarly take account of that fact.

A great deal has been done within Government to secure all the benefits of centralised purchasing and co-ordinated buying policies, bringing in, as far as practicable, local authorities and nationalised industries as well. Indeed, it is difficult to think of ways in which the Government could make the maximum use, in the national interest, of its strong position as a buyer, which are not already being attempted. The only possible exception is that of promoting anti-pollution policies, a matter dealt with more fully in the final chapter.

Two other departures from the basic principle of securing economy through competition between suitable suppliers merit separate consideration. Both have in common the control problems related to new and untried design. In the first place, the supplier is responsible for the design; in the second, the Government as customer.

It may well happen that there is more than one way of designing an article to fulfil a clearly-defined purpose. How to arrive at the cheapest method may be for the Government to do the design and then submit it to a number of suitable manufacturers for competitive estimates of price. An alternative method is to invite a very limited number of manufacturers – possibly one only – to consider the requirements and to prepare a suitable design, with or without the guidance of a proposed design from the Government. The advantage of this procedure is that the manufacturer may have had more experience in fulfilling that – or a very similar – purpose than the Government; or it may be aware of weaknesses in the proposed design; or it may be equipped to produce one answer more economically than another. The disadvantage is that it will not be possible to obtain competitive quotations in the ordinary way and that complaints on the score of favouritism may be made – and not easily defended publicly in Parliament – by those manufacturers whom this procedure will have excluded. It is clear, however, that in order to harness all the experience available this departure from orthodoxy may be justified, at all events for the first batch of articles where more than one batch is contemplated. It may even be possible to obtain most of the benefits of competitive quotation by persuading the manufacturer at this stage to accept the remedy applicable to the second set of cases referred to at the start of this paragraph and about to be described, namely the remedy of post-costing: but that is a separate and more important issue with something of a history.

Two-fifths of Government purchases – a figure in excess of £600 million a year – are made from suppliers who do not secure the order in the first place by the normal method of competitive tender. That is a large proportion and a large figure, yet much of what a Government needs is so specialised that, for a variety of good reasons, the order has to be placed with a particular supplier. How then is the safeguard against excessive prices, which is normally achieved through open competition, to be secured? The 'cost-plus' form of contract under which the manufacturer's price is simply the total cost incurred – whatever it may amount to – plus an agreed percentage addition for profit, is no longer regarded as satisfactory since it gives no incentive to efficiency and economy. The alternative preferred is to fix the price at, or as near as may be to, the start of the job on the basis of a detailed exchange of information on all the elements entering into the manufacture, including profit. The rate of profit used to be modest and a manufacturer who ran into unexpected production difficulties – for whatever cause – would soon be making a loss on the contract. So he would seek to level things out by making a large profit – sometimes as large as possible – in the successful jobs. This could be done by improving on the estimated cost of manufacture through greater efficiency, to the great benefit of all concerned. However there were two other methods, both costly to the taxpayer, of securing a hidden margin or series of margins at the time the price was negotiated; or permitting some impropriety in the books and records. As a result, wholly excessive profits could be made by a manufacturer and one or two scandalous cases did, in fact, come to light and were the subject of much Parliamentary investigation and public debate. A solution had to be found whereby real enterprise could be rewarded and extravagance, or worse, avoided, remembering the whole time that competitive tendering was in the nature of things impossible. First it was necessary to provide industry with a 'fair' margin of profit; that is to say, the same average rate of profit as was secured on non-governmental work. Secondly, the Government would, in appropriate cases, need to have access to the suppliers' books, where the true result would be recorded, to ascertain the profit – or loss – actually made. Finally, where an exceptionally high profit emerged it would be necessary to ascertain whether it was due to faulty estimating or increased efficiency. After very lengthy negotiation, agreement was reached on the basis of an independent review body, whose decision would be binding on both Government and contractor, being appointed to establish in any particular case whether any reimbursement was due to the Government. The review body got off to a very good start under its independent chairman and worked well; nor has any 'scandal' since come to light. It would appear that enterprise is being rewarded and the public purse protected.

Chapter 6

The Supply Estimates

Money means the command of resources; and the spending of a certain sum in a certain way is in fact the allocation of that amount of resources for those purposes. Governments and local authorities spend very large sums, and it is of the essence of democracy that the people should, through their elected representatives, play a full part in deciding what those sums should be spent on. Although most of the money to be spent is provided in the first place through national and local taxation, which also needs to be authorised by the same representatives, it is none the less the case that the spending of revenues is something quite separate from the raising of them. Clearly any one sum could be spent in so many different ways. Whether the Government spends on defence twice as much as it spends on education or half as much, is for the Government to propose but for the House of Commons to decide. It is noteworthy, but not surprising, that the oldest of all the Standing Orders of the Commons is the one which says that Government spending must be expressly authorised by that House; nor is it surprising that much of our constitutional theory and parliamentary practice has over the centuries developed around the use by Government of the power of the purse. The accretion of power to the executive which would result from Parliament ceasing to have the final control of expenditure would be so substantial that what remained of the system of self-government would no longer justify the description of a parliamentary democracy.

The control by Parliament of Whitehall's expenditure must, therefore, be fully maintained; and so too must the control of town hall spending by locally elected councillors. Both kinds of spending enter into public expenditure, and the question that arises is whether in the light of the control of public expenditure there is any need to continue the control of the actual payments made by the central Government and by local authorities; if so, to what extent?

That question is quickly answered in relation to local authority expenditure. Whitehall exercises considerable influence over it and is able, for the purposes of controlling the economy of the nation and of presenting to Parliament a clear picture of the total of planned public expenditure, to estimate with reasonable accuracy the probable amount that local authorities as a whole will spend. But that is a far cry from precise control over the spending by each local authority which must, therefore, in the interests of healthy local democracy, be carried out by the representatives of the local citizenry. Nor is this need lessened by the fact that Parliament has to vote the money provided out of national taxation towards local authority needs. For that is indeed only a contribution – albeit a very large one – towards local spending and not the total of it. Local authorities derive their income partly out of national taxation via the Government and partly out of local taxation, that is to say, in the main, locally levied rates on business and private premises. Local authorities need, therefore, to continue their procedures of submitting estimates of annual expenditure for approval by the general body of councillors, the actual payments made being subject to careful internal verification and to full external audit. Again, the question whether the control of central government spending should be continued must be answered in the affirmative; but the reasons are by no means as obvious as in the case of local government and need more detailed discussion. The best starting point for this discussion is perhaps a consideration of the reasons for that control hitherto. There are basically two: the first the political one, the second the technical. The political reason which has already been referred to is extremely important. The right to spend one's own money one's own way is a considerable freedom for it largely conditions the quality of one's pattern of living. Where part of an individual's money is taken by the community and used to provide some of the living conditions which he would otherwise have provided himself, then the right to share in deciding how that money should be spent is an important right. If what is provided by the community is the same as the individual would have provided, well and good. If as a result of the benefits of large-scale provision (e.g. a place in the school as compared with a tutor in the home) or if, as a result of the process of redistribution of incomes, the individual enjoys more of the things he wants, even better. If, on the other hand, for one reason or another, part of what is provided by the community is not what the individual wants and if the process of redistribution results in his no longer possessing the resources necessary to provide what is lacking, then his standard of living is altered; and that represents an unwelcome interference so far as he is concerned. It is tolerable only if, as a member of the community, he has had the opportunity of sharing in the process of reaching a decision as to how his – and other people's – money should jointly be spent; and if he is satisfied that there are effective systems of monitoring the spending so as to achieve full value.

Clearly the importance of the political reason has been much reduced by the emergence of methods of controlling public expenditure as such. Keeping to the earlier example of education, a parent who is concerned with the kind of service provided is not able to follow through the various payments made by his local authority together with those of his local education authority (which may well not be the same) added to those of the University Grants Commission, supplemented by those of the national Government. So his best opportunity for control in the sense of influencing the outcome is in relation to the figures of public expenditure. For it is there that he can find the overall proposals for achieving the educational service the Government has in mind irrespective of which part is provided by which spending authority. In short, he will best serve his purpose by concentrating on public expenditure and not on the individual expenditure estimates of the various authorities, including in particular the supply estimates of the central Government. Educational expenditure is but one example, albeit a large and important one, where the preservation of the rights of the individual at present under discussion no longer requires the same concentration on government spending: all told the political argument for continuing the control of government spending has been much reduced and overtaken by the need to control public expenditure.

This is not the case, however, as regards the technical argument which, although of less importance than the political one, is still of greater importance than its description would indicate. 'Value for money' is an oft-recurring theme in any consideration of public spending, and provided the concept of 'value' is not narrowly defined, is indeed a most important criterion. Moreover the generally accepted assumption that you are liable to be more lax in the spending of other people's money than of your own adds zest to the pursuit of those who have such enormous sums of other people's money to spend, i.e. the Government. Whether it be true, incidentally, that government departments behave in this way is an entirely different story. A great deal will depend on the standard set by the Treasury and in turn by the Chief Secretary to the Treasury. To recollect that the most frequent comments on the Treasury's attitude were 'candle-ends mentality', 'miserly old Treasury' and 'dead hand of the Treasury' is to be reminded that the Treasury is rarely accused of being over-generous! As to the attitude of Chief Secretaries they quite properly set a standard in dealing with the public purse of a strictness that they would probably be slightly ashamed to apply to their personal financial dealings. However that may be, the general assumption of the danger of laxity in public spending and the consequent belief that carelessness will be found if sought sufficiently long – or at all events that it is the knowledge that inquiries may well be made which prevents the kind of action which is worth inquiring about – serve to entice the hunter with the hope of a quarry.

Making sure, then, that a Government is obtaining value for money in all its public spending is making sure that that Government is acting efficiently, which is much to be desired in the interests of the whole community. The fact that some of the reasons for pursuing inquiries are less valid than others does not detract from the need to be vigilant. It follows that the process of authorising, incurring and verifying government expenditure need to be such as to facilitate these inquiries and to pinpoint the areas where prima facie inquiry should be undertaken. The processes in question are indeed designed with that end, among others, in view and the developments which have taken place over the years and which are still occurring greatly facilitate that kind of investigation. If the same high standard of efficiency is to be maintained, then the strict conditions attached to government spending can only be relaxed to the extent that they are replaced by safeguards of equal value in relation to public expenditure. That, at present, is simply not the case, and until the procedures for public expenditure have been developed in such a way as to secure equal safeguards, those in relation to government spending and particularly in relation to the supply estimates need to be continued.

But it is not only necessary to ensure that the Government spends the public's money in such a way as to secure a high level of efficiency, it is also necessary to avoid any kind of impropriety. The British Civil Service is justly famous for its integrity. It may be that the same high level would continue to obtain if the financial checks and safeguards were reduced. But no one can guarantee that, for no one knows the extent to which the desire to maintain integrity is sustained by the knowledge that any misdemeanours would be likely to be discovered. In the absence of such a guarantee it is surely wise to maintain all the procedures that have accompanied such a praiseworthy record and which are well designed for this purpose.

Then again, the time-scales for public expenditure are not the same as for central Government expenditures. The latter are most conveniently dealt with on an annual basis whereas public expenditure, as has already been explained, looks forward over five years and more. The need to look thus far into the distant countryside and take a general view of the topography is not easily compatible with a detailed examination of the immediate surroundings. They are not necessarily mutually exclusive; but it is far better – and easier – to carry out two separate surveys than to attempt all in one observation.

But the difference in time-scales involves a further problem – that of the shrinkage in the measuring rod as each year goes by. The reality of public expenditure is not a series of monetary statistics but a deployment of resources – men and women spending their working hours engaged on given tasks. Money is the most convenient measure and the statistics make it possible to understand what is happening. The expenditure of a given sum of money means the deployment of a certain amount of resources. But if, for example, salaries rise each year, then that same sum will pay for fewer men and women, that is to say, will command a lesser amount of resources, as the years go by. As the measuring rod is money and what is being measured are resources, an adjustment will be required in order to secure true comparisons between different periods. Now the two most obvious questions to be asked in assessing public expenditure are, first, how does one year compare with another; and second, how does the amount actually spent (the 'out-turn') compare with what was authorised (the estimated expenditure)? The prices at which producers sell their products and workers sell their labour rise – or very occasionally fall – at different times in differing degrees. The comparison of prices at two different dates can, therefore, only be determined subject to a margin of error. When the comparison involves, as it does, payments spread unequally over each of fifty-two weeks, then the margin becomes wider. Moreover the ingredients of public expenditure do not vary in price equally – some go up more than others, and as a result the margin of error becomes the more substantial.

Looking at the general shape of public expenditure, that degree of possible inaccuracy does not falsify the picture; it does not matter greatly that the further one peers into the distance the less precise is the outline. From the standpoint of firm financial control, however, this defect is well-nigh fatal. It is essential to have regard to a given precise sum and trace through its authorisation and its expenditure both in its amount and in its purpose.

This is precisely what the supply estimates and the relevant procedures provide: a request to Parliament for authorisation of a precise sum for a stated purpose and its subsequent allocation to that purpose so that the expenditure can be compared precisely with the authorised sum. If for any reason the estimate was inadequate in amount then a supplementary estimate must be presented to Parliament to cover the additional sum required. This precision certainly involves some limitation of flexibility, but from the point of view of financial control that is not only inevitable but desirable. Parliament, for the compelling democratic reasons already given, must continue to maintain its authority over the expenditure of public money; the executive must therefore be specific in its requests. Nor will the permanent head of a department who is accountable for the payments made by his department lose any sleep through abiding by the simple rule that you only spend what Parliament has authorised.

The purpose of the supply estimates procedures, then, is to enable Parliament to control the expenditure of the central Government; the purpose of the White Papers on public expenditure is to enable Parliament to bring its influence to bear on the Government in shaping public expenditure. These are different purposes and each is important in its own way. The figures are of course related to one another; it is therefore convenient and helpful to know how the total of public expenditure is divided between the three spending authorities (central Government, local authorities and public corporations). Similarly it is helpful to know which of the payments made by central Government enter into public expenditure and which (such as contributions to local authorities) do not.

Gradually the growing size of public expenditure and its increasing share of the national product have attracted the administration appropriate to its importance: a senior Minister, a high-level group of officials within the Treasury, a top-level inter-departmental team to carry out an annual survey, a Government White Paper each year disclosing the full figures for the five years ahead, a select committee of the House of Commons to examine the figures and report to Parliament, and an annual two-day debate in Parliament which will in due course, it is expected, 'be among the most important events of the parliamentary year'. Some of these developments and what they might foreshadow will be discussed in greater detail in a later chapter: for present purposes it suffices to say that it is not surprising that public expenditure has overshadowed the estimates as the subject that matters in political terms. Similarly the procedures in connection with the estimates appear to have been downgraded in terms of political importance: the days which, as an integral part of the parliamentary calendar, had to be allocated for discussion of different categories of the estimates, known as supply days, gradually came to be used as days on which the Opposition could debate a topic of their choosing or a series of topics involving government expenditure – as every act of a Government does, in greater or smaller measure – so that the House of Commons could examine and criticise government policy in an area where it appeared to be particularly susceptible to criticism. Indeed the name has now been changed from supply days to Opposition days so as to symbolise the removal of a direct link with the estimates. But all this represents in the main a change of form rather than of substance, for the major purpose behind Parliament's control of government expenditure is its control of the underlying policies. What therefore remains of permanent importance to a parliamentary democracy is the control by Parliament of government spending; and the precision in all respects of the supply estimates – a precision which is neither essential nor possible where five-year public expenditure programmes are concerned – renders them the only suitable instrument for the purpose of financial control.

Chapter 7

The Chief Secretary and the Treasury

The real function of the Chief Secretary to the Treasury is to assist the Chancellor of the Exchequer. He may or may not be a member of the Cabinet; if he is, then additionally he will have to carry out the duties which are common to all Cabinet members, still bearing in mind his responsibility to the Chancellor. It would be sensible, therefore, to look briefly at the role of the Chancellor before considering that of the Chief Secretary.

During the past half-century the position of Great Britain has altered radically. From being the head of a great empire, commanding greater resources and a higher standard of living than most of her near neighbours, she has become one of a large number of members of the Commonwealth, commanding no greater resources and a lower standard of living than most of her neighbours. As a result, the problems of foreign affairs and defence have diminished while those of providing a living for the community have increased; and this in turn has meant a comparative increase in the responsibilities of the Chancellor of the Exchequer. In the last decade he has had to carry heavier burdens than any of his colleagues other than the Prime Minister, and his status and importance have been fully recognised.

As head of the Treasury – the senior, though by no means the largest, department in the Civil Service – he is responsible for the management of the economy including all economic, financial and fiscal matters, for the Departments of the Inland Revenue and of Customs and Excise, for the Bank of England and for sterling as an international currency – to mention only the most obvious of his many responsibilities. In the course of managing the economy he will be concerned to ensure that there is a reasonable balance between available resources and the demands made upon them, including those arising from the totality of public expenditure. It is not surprising that he should require the assistance of three Treasury Ministers, chief among whom is the Chief Secretary to the Treasury, charged traditionally – among his other duties – with the task of assisting the Chancellor of the Exchequer, to the extent required by him, in all public expenditure matters.

The tradition is not an old one, indeed the office was first created in 1961 and reflected both the growing importance of public expenditure and the growing difficulty of controlling it. In order to give the holder of the office sufficient standing he was made a member of the Cabinet, and the office remains one of Cabinet rank whether or not the Prime Minister of the day chooses to invite his Chief Secretary to join his Cabinet. As a Cabinet Minister he would receive the same remuneration as every other Cabinet Minister (excluding the law officers) and when not in the Cabinet he would be paid more than any Minister other than one in charge of a department.

Whether or not the Chief Secretary to the Treasury is a Cabinet Minister is a matter for the Prime Minister, depending on the desired size of the Cabinet, the political balance within it and the standing and requirements of the man himself. Insufficient time has elapsed since the creation of the office to draw any reliable conclusion. It would, however, seem that the question is a marginal one but that there is unlikely to be room for the Chief Secretary to the Treasury in a smaller-than-average Cabinet. What duties are allotted to him in addition to public expenditure matters is again a matter for arrangement, this time with the Chancellor of the Exchequer. As has already been seen there are many aspects of the Chancellor's duties where ministerial assistance would be of help; and there may be some where the Chief Secretary's previous ministerial experience or professional training may have equipped him to be of particular help. Then there are certain tasks in which all Treasury Ministers must share, though by no means equally. These are the regular answering of questions at question time in the House of Commons, piloting a Finance Bill through Parliament each year (or more often), dealing with the constituency correspondence of MPs and attending the many Cabinet sub-committees where Treasury interests are involved – which means practically all. As number two at the Treasury the Chief Secretary will have to fill in for the Chancellor whenever he is unable to attend a meeting or keep an appointment – a not unusual occurrence having regard to the pressure of work resting upon him and the regularity with which unexpected issues of importance arise which demand his presence. In order to be capable of filling in at very short notice the Chief Secretary will need to keep himself generally informed on a wide range of the Chancellor's activities by reading the important papers and attending certain internal meetings. Additionally, of course, every Treasury Minister will, as an MP, have to visit his constituency regularly and deal as best he may with his substantial constituency correspondence, for which purposes he must not receive any kind of assistance from his department whether clerical, typing or by way of transport facilities. The same restrictions apply to any party committees he may have to attend or party papers he may have to write, or party meetings he may have to address. The civil servants and the various facilities in the Treasury are there to give him every assistance in his ministerial work but, quite properly, not in his work as a constituency MP or as a member of his Party. For the latter purposes he must privately provide such secretarial assistance and office facilities as he may need and also his own transport. Finally it must be remembered that although Parliament is not in continuous session throughout the year, HM Government has to function every day.

The conclusion to be drawn from this by no means exhaustive list of the various duties falling upon the Chancellor and the Chief Secretary is that however matters are arranged, both will have an extremely heavy burden of work. So the first point to be made about the role of the Chief Secretary to the Treasury is that he will have to be capable of working well for very long hours. Eighty hours per week would be quite normal, with stretches of 100 to 105 hours per week on peak occasions. One Chief Secretary achieved this remarkable output over a period of three months through adopting a pattern of six and a half working days per week – the other half day being allotted to physical exercise and relaxation – and working something in excess of sixteen hours each weekday. The remaining eight hours a day were spent on sleep ($5\frac{1}{2}$), personal ($\frac{1}{2}$) and two meals of one hour each, the third being a working lunch (or dinner). The pattern at the weekend had to be a little less arduous so as to accommodate constituency visits. No doubt marginal improvements could be made on this pattern, but a person working those hours is clearly pretty fully stretched and in danger of becoming over-tired. A lot will depend on individual sleep requirements – a topic of conversation that can be relied on to engage the interest of statesmen over the dining table in many an international gathering. These requirements vary, and although sleeping habits may be capable of some adjustment the really busy Minister finds that the volume of work he can undertake will in the final analysis depend on his need for sleep. One can, of course, help oneself by supplementing the sleep periods and by adjusting the severity of the particular task to the degree of tiredness. A fifteen-minute journey in the back of a reasonably comfortable car, driven by a chauffeur who has been fully advised as to 'when and where', gives an opportunity for a ten-minute cat-nap – and very refreshing it is. Then again there are certain tasks which are less demanding than others and these can be left to the end of the day – say between midnight and 2 a.m. – when the reading of papers for information purposes only puts much less of a strain on a mind beginning to tire than does a complex problem requiring a final decision.

Any really busy Minister will find himself waging a continuous battle for sleep as part of the exercise of organising his physical and emotional resources to the maximum. A Chief Secretary is, of course, greatly helped in this exercise by the challenge of the job and the variety of the work. The Treasury is in a real sense at the cross-roads in Government and every kind of problem will sooner or later find its way on to his table. The challenge provides its own stimulation and interesting variety its own response. The generally accepted explanation is that the adrenalin courses round one's body the faster, creating new sources of energy. Whatever the explanation it is certainly true that the interest and great variety enable one to apply oneself for longer periods than would otherwise be possible and that the challenge of the job itself creates a feeling of well-being and a sense of keener awareness and quicker understanding.

There is nevertheless the danger that an over-tired Minister may make a 'bad' decision (that is to say, a decision different from the one he would have made if he had not been so exhausted) and the question arises whether it is sensible to attempt to govern a country with over-burdened Ministers. Why not lean more heavily on officials and appoint an additional junior Minister if necessary? And does not all this simply demonstrate that a Chief Secretary who is unable to delegate is inefficient?

It is certainly the case that a Chief Secretary to the Treasury will have to work hours that by any ordinary standard can only be described as excessive. I well remember being somewhat surprised that at the end of my very first day at the Treasury I was handed the usual red leather box containing a fair number of papers that had to be read before the morning. I asked my private secretary how often my predecessor had found it necessary to take a box home with him. The answer was short and clear: 'Every night, Chief Secretary.' That was evidently the norm; and it is certainly the case that the preparation of work within the Treasury is so programmed that most of the papers needed for a particular day – though certainly not all – will appear for the first time in the overnight box of the immediately preceding evening. That is what is expected of a Minister, quite apart from the question of whether the volume of work resting on the shoulders of officials or the urgent nature of the particular matter makes earlier briefing impossible. Indeed various consequential arrangements stem from this practice. The Chief Secretary might, for example, find on reading the papers that he needs some additional information before attending the relevant meeting the following morning and that that meeting, an early one, is timed to begin prior to the officials' normal starting time. He need have no anxiety: the official chiefly concerned would, as a matter of standard practice, come in specially early so as to be available for consultation if required.

The overnight box, then, is a well-established part of the system; and it is the overnight box which necessitates much of the overtime. Nor would its average contents be reduced by earlier briefing: one evening's load would be a little lighter, but the preceding one a little heavier. Moreover there would be the positive disadvantage that the Minister would have a bigger burden on his memory – a very relevant point when each day brings its rush of events and its extra load of facts and figures to be absorbed and remembered. So the conclusion to be drawn from the practice of the overnight box is that no matter how hard officials try – as indeed they do – to reduce to a minimum the work falling on their Minister, the inescapable remaining load is extremely heavy.

A Minister is greatly assisted by his private office, which goes to lengths unparalleled in the business world to relieve him of as many tasks as possible. He does not have to think of what his engagements are for the morrow, what papers he will need or how he will get to wherever he has to go: his private office sees to all that and gives him each night a card showing all his appointments and movements for the following day. His papers will be collected and handed to him, his chauffeur ready in the car. He does not have to think about telling his officials what needs to be done as a result of a telephone conversation with a colleague – or indeed anyone else. His phone call – no matter how private – will have been listened-in to by his private office and they will automatically do whatever is required. The same applies on a foreign visit – or an all-night sitting in the Commons on a Bill in which the Minister is engaged. The right officials will be there at the right time, the necessary briefing will be in the Minister's hands; he will be spared all unnecessary tasks and every possible expenditure of time or energy. His private office will do all the arranging, all the following up, all the anticipating. The difference between the approach of the private secretary of the top level industrialist and of the Chief Secretary's private secretary is symbolic; the former arranges his boss's business life, the latter, his Minister's life.

Without doubt, then, the Minister's private office do everything possible to help. So, too, do the officials in his department. Briefs are kept reasonably short and drafted with great clarity. One important question is whether officials put papers before Ministers which need not go to him at all, for an obvious way of reducing his burden of work is to reduce the number of papers reaching him. It is simply not possible to draw a hard and fast rule as to which papers should or should not be put before a Minister, but the general experience is that existing arrangements work well. As one would expect, the tendency is for rather too much than too little paper to be submitted, for three main reasons. First, common sense tells one to err on the safe side – especially as a Minister does not have to read very far to find out that that particular paper might well have been omitted. So the disadvantage of sending up too much need not be very great. Secondly, Ministers are there to resolve political questions and officials to draw to their attention any matter which might have political content. This is an important part of an official's task of keeping his Minister out of avoidable trouble; and indeed a Minister could be greatly embarrassed if, unknown to him, a decision (probably a fairly straightforward one) had been reached which had unwelcome political repercussions although perfectly justifiable on other grounds. As so many issues arising in the course of government have political aspects, it is inevitable that possible political content will necessitate a large number of papers going to a Minister which he might otherwise not have needed to see. The third reason is the plain fact that civil servants like cover: a junior official will put a recommendation to his senior, rather than decide the matter on his own authority, where he is in any doubt as to whether the senior would wish to be consulted. Similarly a senior official will obtain the Minister's approval to a proposed course of conduct as to which he is in no doubt himself, where he thinks the Minister should take the final responsibility. This habit may be time-consuming but is an inevitable concomitant of democratic government. The elected representatives make the decisions and therefore take the responsibility. An official goes to great lengths to know his Minister's mind and the way in which the Government as a whole are thinking; but there is nothing like being quite sure and the way to achieve certainty is to get the Minister's initial on a piece of paper. If therefore the Minister believes that the elected representative should make the decisions and the permanent official should carry them out, he will accept the need for frequent consultation as to his views; and it is not in the greater sharing of work between the Chief Secretary to the Treasury and his advisers that any measurable reduction in his burden of work is to be found.

The appointment of an additional junior Minister, on the other hand, could in certain circumstances take part of the load off a senior Minister. But in addition to statutory limitations there may be substantial political difficulties in increasing the overall size of a Government, and the nature of the work may be such that a large effort on the part of the new Minister and of his additionally engaged staff may reduce the load on the others by comparatively little. The tendency therefore is to postpone the appointment of an additional Minister as long as is humanly possible.

The real issue is a deeper one: whether it is sensible to continue a system under which a Minister in the House of Commons has to carry out three separate functions – his departmental duties as part of the executive; his House of Commons duties as part of the legislature; and his constituency duties as representative of the citizens of all parties in a particular area. There are great advantages in this system: the Member of Parliament is brought into direct contact with the problems of ordinary people in his constituency; the Minister has continuously to account to Parliament for his actions and to justify his policies; and as both a Minister and an MP he is made aware of the feelings and views of constituents and parliamentarians. But mounting pressures on all three fronts will at some stage require a fundamental alteration in a system which grew out of quieter times. The degree of required intervention by a Government in the affairs of its people ever increases; the work of Parliament has increased so greatly that some of its tasks (such as those in connection with the supervision of delegated legislation) can no longer be fully carried out; and constituents come more and more to their MP for help and guidance. But any such change is a matter for the future; in the meantime the system remains unaltered and top civil servants occasionally give passing thought to these problems and conclude that so long as the system continues to produce a score or so of men and women who are capable of surviving under these enormous pressures and of working satisfactorily for these extremely long hours, then no fundamental rethinking is called for. Kitchens are expected to be hot, and if you can't stand the heat you'd better get out.

There is a strong temptation, therefore, whenever one is asked – as frequently happens – what are the main qualities required of a successful Minister to reply that there are three: the first, a strong constitution; the second a strong constitution; and the third, a strong constitution. Not a very complete answer, but it puts the matter in perspective. If a further three qualities are insisted on, then they would be strength of character, ability to get on with people and intelligence – in that order. But these comments – and indeed most of what has been said about the work load – refer to senior Ministers generally, including the Chief Secretary to the Treasury. Perhaps a few further comments which refer exclusively to the Chief Secretary are worth making. The first is that the general consensus among senior Ministers is that the job of the Chief Secretary is one of the most arduous. So long therefore as Ministers in general, under the existing system, are compelled to work long hours, the Chief Secretary will be expected to be up among the front-runners. The need to assist the Chancellor of the Exchequer in addition to carrying out his own duties in relation to the control of public expenditure makes this inevitable. The Chief Secretary to the Treasury is the No. 2 Treasury Minister and must therefore be ready to stand in for the No. 1, the Chancellor, as often as the latter's enormous responsibilities require it. I well remember dropping in on the then Chancellor to discuss a difficult issue and finding him with no less than three red boxes demanding his immediate attention. As it was after midnight, I insisted on relieving him of those papers that were complete in themselves and which did not require familiarity with earlier events. Even so, the remaining papers were not completed before 4.00 a.m.

There are many occasions when a Chief Secretary will have to relieve a Chancellor in some way or other. To be of real help he must complete the task handed to him satisfactorily without troubling the Chancellor further. He must foresee and avoid any action that will prove troublesome for the Chancellor – in short, he must have 'safe hands'. But hands are not rendered safe by five-finger exercises on the piano; they are made safe by taking the trouble to find out all about the task in hand before taking action – and that takes time.

Thoroughness is inevitably time-consuming, but a Chief Secretary has the one job where time cannot be saved at the expense of thoroughness. It is the detail which is at issue in the control of public expenditure as well as the principle. There is no need, of course, to get involved in the minutiae: a good working rule is that anything less than half a million pounds must be dealt with at official level without troubling the Chief Secretary. (That may seem a large sum, but in relation to an expenditure of £20,000 million it is really quite small: to be precise, 1/40,000 of the total.) But application to detail is an essential part of the Chief Secretary's approach, be it in relation to tax legislation, to individual items of public expenditure, or to the various elements in the processes of control that go to make up the annual cycle of authorisation, payment and verification. To be Chief Secretary to the Treasury for six years means that a total in excess of £100,000,000,000 of the public's money will have been spent on the public services during his period of responsibility for the safe arrival of the money at the intended destination. To be able to record that – as far as is known – not £1 was lost on the journey is a tremendous tribute to the integrity and skill of the British Civil Service in general and of the Treasury in particular. It is also consistent with the standard of thoroughness and watchfulness set at the top.

Six years, incidentally, is an unusually long time to serve in one job in any Government – too long, if one is to consider only the comfort of the Minister. But there are good reasons for departing from the normal practice of changing jobs more rapidly. A departmental Minister brings to his department his stock of experience and new ideas. After a few years some of his ideas will have been incorporated in legislation or in legislative proposals, others will have been shown to be unworkable or unacceptable to his colleagues. Not a great deal will remain – probably less than could be expected from a newcomer to the office; and similarly he himself would probably be able to make a bigger contribution in some other department. Certainly he will have become more familiar with the detailed aspects of his departmental responsibilities; but this is something which, though valuable, counts for less in the case of a Minister than of a permanent official and is not of sufficient weight to alter the balance of the argument. However, in his work in the control of public expenditure – proposals for altering the tax code are an entirely different matter but that work is quite separate – a Chief Secretary does not initiate; he responds. It is for the departments to originate new policies and to put their proposals to the Treasury if – as mostly happens – expenditure is involved. There was perhaps a touch of both exaggeration and sacrilege in the comment of one disappointed Minister to the effect that the departmental Minister proposes but the Chief Secretary disposes, but it was an accurate observation on who takes the initiative. Any ideas a Chief Secretary may have as to how a department's purposes may be achieved at lower cost will be a useful contribution to any discussion; any ideas he may have as to how mankind may be greatly benefited at the cost of a comparatively small increase in a department's expenditure must remain unspoken. He might even – one day – become a Minister in that department, though that is unlikely; he might – one day – enjoy the freedom of a member of the Opposition to put forward suggestions, and that is very likely. But be that as it may, what a Chief Secretary cannot do – if he wants to remain Chief Secretary – is to take the stance that he is a person who knows of good ways for a department to spend money which its ministerial head has not yet thought of. He cannot both promote expenditure and restrain it – and, whatever the dictionary may say, when it comes to public expenditure control means restraint.

So a Chief Secretary may come to the Treasury bubbling with ideas on improvement and reform – and all involving comparatively little extra expenditure – but so far as concerns the work of other departments, he cannot take any initiatives. In the early days of office this can seem very frustrating. Every politician knows for a fact that his own ideas are the best and it seems irresponsible to deny a waiting world the benefit of their expression. Indeed on one such early occasion I asked my private secretary how many times, judging from his experience, would a Chief Secretary be likely to initiate proposals in the field of public expenditure. His answer was as accurate as it was short. 'Never.'

The exhaustion of a stock of ideas is not such an important argument, therefore, when considering the optimum length of service in the post of Chief Secretary to the Treasury. On the other hand, increasing familiarity with the work is, for it is probably the case that more than in any other single department does this increasing familiarity save time. In short, as compared with other ministerial offices, the advantages of a long stay in office are greater and the disadvantages less. Moreover, the coincidence of previous professional experience in a similar field may be a fortunate one. It so happens that some of the skills acquired during the course of many years' experience as a practising accountant are the same as those required for the rapid and fully effective execution of some of the duties of a Chief Secretary to the Treasury. One of several examples is the responsibility of the Chief Secretary in connection with the annual supply estimates presented to Parliament. This is a task which could take days or could take weeks, for the estimates are very bulky and run to several volumes in their printed form. The trained eye – or the reputed sixth sense – enables one to read rapidly through the pages where everything is (one hopes) straightforward and to concentrate on those matters requiring further explanation or closer attention. This is not to suggest that the background knowledge acquired by a doctor is an essential pre-requisite for a Minister of Health or by a teacher for Minister of Education – although only a lawyer can carry out the duties of a law officer and it is interesting to note that both senior law officers (the Lord Chancellor and the Attorney-General) also retained their offices throughout the six years of the Labour Government, from 1964 to 1970. On the contrary, it is clear that a Minister is there to use his judgement, and all the facts and advice he needs are made available either out of the resources of the Civil Service or by consulting outside experts. It would be very dangerous for any Minister to rely on his own knowledge in reaching a judgement, for however wide his experience it must be extremely limited in relation to the great width of most of the issues coming before him.

Before leaving the topic of the burden of work resting on the shoulders of busy Ministers, a personal footnote may help to clarify the meaning of the word 'burden' in this context. It so happens that I found it necessary to work extremely long hours continuously for six years during a period of very great pressure at the Treasury. I was well above average age as a Cabinet Minister; yet the consequent strain on my health was such that in the whole of that period I was compelled to take off only two days (through a bout of 'flu). Fortunate is he who has plenty of work to do of the kind he likes doing!

Certainly the job of Chief Secretary to the Treasury is one of the most varied and interesting in the Government. There are few issues which do not find their place on his desk at some stage or other, be they domestic or foreign. He is in regular touch with all his colleagues and familiar with their problems and their aspirations. He has a great deal to do in the House of Commons and is continually meeting men and women with considerable responsibilities in industry, commerce and the professions, and statesmen of other countries. He knows of – and plays some part in – most things that go on in the Treasury, and the Treasury is the place where things happen. His responsibilities are man-sized, his influence not inconsiderable, and he exercises a measure of power. Although there is little outlet for original thinking in the control of public expenditure, his other work in the Treasury – particularly in the field of tax legislation – can give him all the opportunities to put forward his own ideas that his limited time will allow him to use. He is advised and assisted by officials of the highest calibre and looked after by a private office who will go to any lengths to ensure that nothing prevents him from keeping his nose to the grindstone for sixty minutes in every hour.

But he is the 'no-man' of the Government, and this produces certain stresses. One Chief Secretary was introduced to this aspect at the very start. On telling him of his appointment, the Prime Minister said, 'I want you to be Chief Secretary. You'll have to make yourself unpopular with all your colleagues. I think you'll do the job very well.' End of interview.

What distinguishes the task of a Chancellor of the Exchequer from that of any other departmental Minister is his relationship to spending. To put it simply, the departmental Minister wins political bouquets through spending more; the Chancellor through taxing less: and it is the taxes which produce the spending money. But it goes a good deal deeper than that. Being a senior Minister is the crowning experience in a politician's life. It may also be a very rare one. Age, election results, health, availability of the particular job – all these and many other factors have to be right before a man who is eminently fitted for the task may be entrusted with office. So when the opportunity does arise – and it may not last more than two or three years – there is a great desire, and a great sense of urgency, to make the most of it. Whether it is a desire to play one's part fully as a member of the team so as to demonstrate how right the electorate was to give it its confidence and how right it would be to do so again; or whether it is a desire to win the respect of one's colleagues and fellow-parliamentarians as a Minister of outstanding quality (and one capable, therefore, of even greater responsibility); or whether it is a desire to make a lasting contribution towards improving the lot of one's fellow-man, for which purpose one has spent a great deal of one's life equipping oneself, matters not. The result is the same: a great urge to self-fulfilment through the expenditure of thought, energy, long hours, one's stock of carefully prepared ideas – and money. Apart from the last mentioned, the departmental Minister can supply the lot – and is raring to go; and he will be fully supported by immensely able advisers who will add their knowledge and skill in improving his ideas in every possible way. Money? Well, he says to his chief official, that can't be a stumbling block: the cost will be so small in relation to the benefits to be derived, and the Treasury's got lots of it. At this point the official may suggest that the Minister have a word with the Chief Secretary, a suggestion which is readily adopted, for is not the Chief Secretary a colleague and friend, imbued with the same political ideals and equally anxious to see the new Government succeed?

And so the scene is set for the first heartbreak. For the Chief Secretary will receive him with the warmth of a friend and the sympathetic understanding of a colleague. But he may well see a different path to success – a path skilfully devised between inflationary pressures on one hand and under-employment on the other, a path leading to that greater economic growth which will provide the very resources under discussion – in perhaps two or three years' time. Meanwhile first priority must be given to strengthening the economy and that means that this particular proposal, excellent though it is, will have to be, not turned down quite, but postponed for a while in the same way as the many other proposals already reaching the Treasury. In fact the meeting provides a convenient opportunity for the Chief Secretary to tell the Minister that he was just on the point of having a word with him and asking him, in their common desire to make a success of the Government's economic policy, whether he would be good enough to have a look at some of his department's planned expenditure with a view to rephasing some of it so as to help in reducing the excessive pressure on available resources.

This is not a real conversation – though it might well have taken place; but it is a very real theme on which there are endless variations, and the first impression left on the Minister, understandably angry at being baulked in this way, is that the Chief Secretary is being unduly cautious and is merely reflecting the views of his officials. However, the Chancellor, with his greater political wisdom – so his thinking will run – will immediately understand that Governments succeed by being bold and doing things – of which the Minister's own proposal could well be the most meritorious. So off will go a letter to the Chancellor appealing against the Chief Secretary's decision: and the scene is set for heart-break number two.

Now clearly it would be impossible to run the Treasury on the basis that every time the Chief Secretary said 'No' to a Minister, all the latter needed to do was to appeal to the Chancellor. The authority of the Chief Secretary would soon be completely undermined and as a result he would fail in his task of relieving the Chancellor of some of his burden and some of the political odium; and any Chancellor stands in need of relief under both these heads if he is to succeed in his own much more important and immensely difficult task. Moreover, it would be a waste of both Ministers' time, for the general principles on which the Chief Secretary to the Treasury was working would be the same as those on which the Chancellor would reach his conclusion – co-ordination within the Treasury will have seen to that. For a Chief Secretary must at all times strive to ensure that the decisions he takes are those which the Chancellor would have taken. It is the Chancellor who is the Minister responsible for running the Treasury and the Chief Secretary who is there to assist him. If there is a possibility of two views emerging, then it is for the Chief Secretary to seek to persuade the Chancellor to his point of view or to accept that of the Chancellor, before committing the Treasury by his answer. He must at all costs avoid putting the Chancellor in the position of having to choose between two undesirable courses, that of letting down his Chief Secretary by reversing his decision, or supporting him at the cost of doing something which he, the Chancellor, regards as unwise.

So back will go a letter explaining much of this – in the nicest possible way – and reaffirming the Chief Secretary's decision. The Minister now finds his proposals blocked by the whole might of the Treasury, and reading between the lines he probably concludes that whatever the Chief Secretary had decided would have been supported by the Chancellor; so the Chief Secretary is the nigger in the woodpile still, and the question that remains is whether to take the matter to Cabinet. But it is not necessary to pursue the story further, for the decision to go to Cabinet will never be lightly undertaken and will depend on a number of factors which have been discussed in an earlier chapter. What is of relevance here is to underline the fact that the denial of money to a Minister may amount to as much as a denial of his opportunity of self-fulfilment, and that is a difficult thing for any man to have to take. No Chief Secretary, if he is wise, will do that to a colleague without a smile on his face and understanding in his heart.

The final test then of whether a Chief Secretary to the Treasury is succeeding in his task is not the degree to which public expenditure is overspent or underspent, important as that is; it is the degree of warmth left in his personal relationships with his colleagues. Ministers need to build a successful team if a Government is to succeed, and without overall success their individual achievements in their separate departments – albeit more immediate and more satisfying – will not be enough. Without co-operation by all concerned there can be no team, and the difficulties in the way of co-operation are so great that a strong desire to co-operate is needed for it to be effective. This applies, of course, to all Ministers, for each one finds his interests and those of one or other colleague in conflict from time to time. The will to work together is normally sufficient to overcome these clashes of interest. But with the Chief Secretary it is all clash – or so it seems to the others. They describe him as having three functions: to give them too little money for their annual budget; to say 'No' to any necessary new development during the ensuing twelve months; and from time to time to take back part of what had previously been given because of yet another financial crisis (due to mismanagement by the Treasury, of course). An over-simplification, perhaps, for every Minister knows that someone has to do that job and that it has to be done well if the Government is to succeed, painful though that may be so far as he personally is concerned. But it serves to underline the need for the Chief Secretary to do everything he can to maintain good personal relations. He must study his words of refusal most carefully, he must do whatever he can about timing, he must help his colleagues in every possible way (there are many courtesies which rightly count a great deal, as they relieve a busy Minister, even though they press hard on the available time of the Chief Secretary), and he must show that he has studied the Minister's proposals fully and understands them and, indeed, as far as is possible, that he identifies himself with the Minister in his point of view. This is not difficult, for it is nearly always the case that the proposals have great merit and have been worked over many times in the department so as to remove any difficulties of administration before they are put up to the Treasury. If the Chief Secretary cannot provide the cash he can at all events leave the Minister feeling that, had the money been there, his proposals would have been agreed and that the Chief Secretary has done his best to be helpful.

'I don't know anybody who says "No" as nicely as you do' was a frequently heard remark, and it was very necessary that it should be so. The point has been well put by Professors Heclo and Wildavsky, the experts on public expenditure in the USA, in their examination of the function of the Chief Secretary in the United Kingdom. 'He who indulges other men is not surprised to find warm regard; he who can win their affection while depriving them of worldly goods has reached an extraordinary height of diplomacy reserved for a few.' That is the target which the Government Scrooge aims at in his relations with his colleagues, the spending Ministers.

So far as the Chief Secretary's relationship with the Chancellor of the Exchequer is concerned, special considerations come into play; that is to say, in addition to those which normally apply to the relationship of a number 2 to a number 1 in any very large organisation. There is the usual dilemma that if the second-in-command, in order to ensure that everything he does is exactly what his Chief would have wished, consults the latter on nearly everything, he will not be relieving the burden on him to anything like the necessary extent. But if the number 2 puts the relief of that burden ahead of all other considerations, then there may be occasions when the decision taken is inconsistent with what number 1 would have decided. This is a familiar dilemma in many kinds of organisation but it presents special difficulties in this area of government. The normal remedy of a closely defined policy which will govern both number 1 and number 2 and so avoid the need for consultation between them save in the most exceptional case, cannot be relied on to the same extent as in most non-governmental organisations. This is partly due to the fact that at this level of government so many issues are exceptional: it is indeed the deliberate attempt of the permanent officials in any department so to organise their administration that only the abnormal or the exceptional or the politically sensitive issues reach the desk of the Minister. Partly it is due to the fact that finance enters into nearly every aspect of government and to lay down, within the Treasury, definitive policies governing every aspect of the whole field of Treasury work would be impossibly laborious and excessively restrictive; and it would, if attempted, be out of date by the time it was completed. For policies need to be flexible and to take very rapid account of new developments. Managing the economy of a country is not unlike walking a tight-rope, except perhaps that there is no safety net provided for the man who pursues a necessary adjustment too far.

Then again the need for care in ensuring consistency throughout a Government – and especially in the Treasury – is so much greater because, working always under the glare of the arc-lamps of publicity, there is little chance of any inconsistency escaping unnoticed; especially when it is remembered that there is a large body of capable and experienced men and women, known as the Opposition, always on the alert to search out every action of the Government with a view to proving it wrong. But the remedy of close and regular consultation between these two senior Treasury Ministers on matters under the control of the Chief Secretary is simply not available because of the pressure of events. They will in any event be seeing each other several times a week in the normal course of the Chancellor consulting his senior officials on major issues and new policies – the Chief Secretary will find himself sitting at the Chancellor's right hand at the large table at which his advisers and secretaries will be sitting. These and similar occasions are excellent opportunities for ascertaining the way the Chancellor's mind is moving but quite inappropriate for discussing a detailed matter falling within the Chief Secretary's responsibilities. Even the 'quick word' at the end of such a meeting before leaving the room is rarely available, because so often the meeting has had to finish promptly in order to avoid keeping the new arrivals in the outer office waiting for their appointment. And so it goes on. Meal times very rarely provide the opportunity for a chat, for the Chancellor (and the Chief Secretary to a lesser extent) has to attend many official lunches and dinners and to maintain regular contact with many others inside and outside Whitehall.

The answer lies in the Chief Secretary being as fully aware as is possible of the general approach of the Chancellor on all major political issues and of the way his mind is working over a wide area of policy. It is in fact these many contacts that make that possible, coupled with the fact that these two men, with a shared political philosophy, will have known each other and worked together in politics inside and outside Parliament for many years. The solution – other than in the quite exceptional case – is for the Chief Secretary to ask himself two questions before reaching any conclusion. What is his own answer? What is the answer the Chancellor would give if asked? In the vast majority of cases the two answers would be identical. In a few cases the Chancellor would, he knows, give a different answer; and it is that answer which will be the one given unless he feels the matter important enough to raise with the Chancellor, in whatever time is available. In the exceptional case, where it is impossible to conjecture what the Chancellor's view would be, even bearing in mind that the same senior official within the Treasury would be offering the same official advice to the Chancellor – were he handling the matter himself – as has been offered to the Chief Secretary; and where quick consultation between the two private offices – for private secretaries also are very familiar with their Minister's point of view – has not removed the doubt, then the Chancellor will have to be consulted in the most appropriate manner having regard to the time available. The issue, the official advice and the Chief Secretary's reasoned recommendation (all if possible on a half sheet of paper) will generally suffice but a short discussion may be needed in addition, especially if one of the reasons cannot conveniently go on the record.

The position at a Cabinet meeting is somewhat different, for every member of the Cabinet has an equal responsibility for ensuring that the best possible decision – to which everyone is then committed under the principle of joint Cabinet responsibility – is reached. In addition to his departmental loyalties and responsibilities, therefore, a Cabinet Minister who is in charge of a department has to bring his judgement to bear on issues not affecting his own department. Where his own department is affected, he knows that in order to enable Cabinet to reach a balanced judgement he must press his departmental view strongly for no one else will do it, or is capable of doing it, for him; and he will be assumed to be making the best possible case for his department whether in fact he does so or not. For him therefore to understate his own department's case, or to respond to an opposing view with the neutrality of an independent chairman, is to deny his own department the full and strong presentation of its case which it is entitled to expect from its spokesman. In practice, therefore, a Minister is not troubled by any conflict between his view as a member of Cabinet and his view as head of his department.

All this is well understood, but it does not quite cover the situation of 'double-banking', i.e. where two Ministers of a single department are members of the Cabinet. It is an unusual situation, but not an extremely rare one, and arises where the work of a department is very large and the number 2 Minister has rather special responsibilities. A senior Minister at the Foreign Office with the special responsibility of handling a large and separate matter – such as the negotiations for joining the European Economic Community – is a good example. Clearly no problem arises on departmental issues: the Chancellor is the head of the Treasury and would naturally expect the Chief Secretary to support him on any issues he raised at a Cabinet meeting, for there can be only one stance with regard to a Treasury proposal. Where the issue is one raised by the Chief Secretary, then similarly the Chancellor will, at the appropriate point in the discussion, speak in support of him. There will be occasions when it is clear that the discussion is not going very well for the Chief Secretary and the Chancellor may deem it wise at a certain point to offer a compromise rather than face the likelihood of complete defeat. But this is well within the overall concept of mutual support on a Treasury issue as between two Treasury members of the Cabinet. It is on the whole better for the standing of the Treasury, and certainly for that of the Chancellor, that it should be left to the Chancellor to offer the compromise. He will gain a little credit in the eyes of his colleagues for seeming to be less demanding than the full Treasury position, as explained by the Chief Secretary, would require; and he needs to build up as large a credit as possible against those occasions when he will have to ask for considerable sacrifices from his colleagues. Nor need the partial defeat of the Chief Secretary be very damaging, for everyone knows that both sides cannot come out of a Cabinet meeting covered in glory. Indeed, at a less important level, it must be remembered that in Cabinet the Treasury is always heavily outnumbered in terms of basic interests as between those who want to spend more (the departmental Ministers) and those who want to spend less (the Treasury). A Treasury matter is likely to make better progress, therefore, if the members of Cabinet are feeling well disposed towards Treasury Ministers: and one of the few things which may help to promote a temporary feeling of benevolence towards the Treasury on a particular issue is the partial defeat of the Chief Secretary on the previous one.

It is clear then that the Treasury gains strength by the addition of a second Treasury Minister in the Cabinet. The corollary is that some departmental Minister will find himself in a weaker position than would otherwise have been the case, and might feel momentarily there was an element of unfairness. Certainly the arrangement does place on the Chief Secretary an additional reason for being extremely diplomatic and for handling his Cabinet issues so that as far as possible he may win the argument (which indeed he must do in the interests of the economy as he judges the position) without defeating the man.

Little needs to be said with regard to those important issues which require every Cabinet Minister to state his view but which contain no real Treasury interest. In fact this will not often be the case, but when it is then the Chief Secretary must express his own judgement.

Whether the Chief Secretary is a member of the Cabinet or not – and even when he is not a member he will be invited to attend Cabinet meetings whenever an issue affecting him is under discussion so that he can put forward his own case – he will be involved in a great number of matters at ministerial level. It is not surprising, therefore, that many of his colleagues regard him as having considerable influence and the view has been expressed – but this is, perhaps, an overstatement – that he 'can influence a larger number of more important decisions than almost any other Minister'. Yet he rarely hits the headlines: Heclo and Wildavsky describe him well as the 'unsung maker of major decisions'. The reasons are not far to seek. Although it is probably the case that the decisions reached as between a departmental Minister and the Chief Secretary to the Treasury are of some importance and often of considerable public interest, it is for the departmental Minister to make any announcement that he thinks appropriate, either inside or outside Parliament, for he is the responsible Minister. So far as Treasury matters are concerned, the Chancellor is the responsible Minister and will be expected, in the normal course of events, to make any necessary statement on all major matters. Similarly it will be for the Chancellor to announce any new development so that in the many speeches the Chief Secretary to the Treasury is called upon to make he will be denied that newsworthy ingredient, something new. In practice, therefore, he will be limited to talking about known events and, unless he wants the Press to start writing about 'splits' in the Treasury, his analysis of and reactions to them must coincide with the Chancellor's. All this makes for sound government and absence of publicity for the Chief Secretary to the Treasury. He is a ministerial back-room boy and will be able to do his best work while that situation continues.

Chapter 8

The Way Ahead

As one walks along Downing Street towards No. 10 a name-plate on the door comes into view. It is hardly necessary to get close enough to read it, for everyone knows that the Prime Minister works there. But the more curious are rewarded, for they find that in fact the inscription is 'First Lord of the Treasury', and it is interesting to realise that this most powerful of offices grew out of the Treasury and its functions and not, as might have happened, out of the well-established departments headed by the great Secretaries of State. The amount and nature of government spending are the results of some of the most important decisions which a Government is called upon to make in the exercise of its powers, and its authorisation and control by an elected Parliament among the most important methods whereby a democracy prevents excessive power passing into the hands of the executive. For the individual, the nature and size of public expenditure determine to a considerable extent the quality of his living. Prime Minister, Government, Parliament and People: that is the measure of the importance of public expenditure.

A considerable assessment of its importance is contained in the reports of two all-party committees of the House of Commons. In 1969 the Procedure Committee stated that 'Government decisions, both about the level of public expenditure as a whole and about the way in which the total amount of public expenditure is allocated between its various components, are among the most important which Ministers take'; and added that the annual debate on the public expenditure White Paper 'could and should come to occupy as important a place in parliamentary and public discussion of economic affairs as that now occupied by the annual Budget debate'. In 1971 the Expenditure Committee took a similar view of the same publication (known as a Command Paper). They reported, as already mentioned: 'We feel that the importance of the Command Papers and Parliament's discussion of them cannot be overstated. The Command Papers contain the core of the Government's policy, and reflect its overall social and economic strategy. Similarly, the debate on the Command Papers . . . should be among the most important events of the parliamentary year.'

An internal survey of public expenditure had been conducted by the

Government in 1961, but the first public expenditure White Paper to be published was in December 1963. That was a good but modest start: the figures it contained were the estimates of total public expenditure for the year 1963–64, three-quarters of which had expired by the date of publication, together with those of the year 1967–68 on the assumption that the Government's policies and programmes remained unaltered throughout the period. In short they omitted the most important piece of information: what the Government were actually proposing to do in 1967–68 and in each of the intervening years. Nevertheless, it was a useful beginning.

Looked at in retrospect, progress was in fact rapid – although at the time it did not seem so. The five years which followed the publication of the first public expenditure White Paper saw the establishment of the public expenditure surveys as the framework within which the Government were taking all major decisions on expenditure. During the same period an all-party report was published accepting the Government's proposals on the presentation of the public expenditure figures to Parliament and recommending an annual two-day debate. The change of Government in 1970 did not prevent, or even delay much, the setting up of the Expenditure Committee in place of the previous Estimates Committee, a change which corresponded logically with the new developments.

These developments – and there were others, though of less importance – took place in a comparatively short period, and if the same rate of change were to be maintained, then other developments would follow which it would be necessary to describe. But change does not work in that continuous way – at least, not externally. Following an apparently quiescent period it erupts from time to time to the accompaniment of a number of rumbling noises – all rather like a volcano. It may well be that new ideas are gradually burrowing their way into men's subconsciousness while externally all remains unchanged. But whatever the processes by which men accustom themselves to new ideas, it is an observed fact that change comes in spurts, one development paving the way for another and those two creating the need for the third – and all within the accepted new philosophy. That is what happened with regard to public expenditure. The pressure for more government spending grew at the same time as the automatic restraint imposed by the Budget was much weakened as a result of the new concepts of demand management and unbalanced budgets. Moreover budgets were concerned with the economic situation in the short term, and government spending could only be considered for the years ahead: it followed that the long-term commitments involved in much of public expenditure could not sensibly be looked at only in the context of the annual budget. The new freedom resulted in public expenditure increasing year after year, and, worse still (according to the accepted tenets of the time), the rate of increase became greater than that of the national product. That critical situation demanded action: accordingly a Minister was appointed with the responsibility of controlling public expenditure and new administrative methods were devised to assist him in that task. Understanding of the social and economic importance of public expenditure grew and Parliament adjusted its procedures to the new requirements.

What remains to be done can best be discussed in relation to Government, Parliament and People in turn. But before turning to what is being done and should in the future be done in relation to Government, it might be well to clear up certain doubts about the practicability of what has been done. These relate to the forward look of five years and the extent to which that conflicts with the freedom of the people to elect their own Government at intervals of not more than five years. What, for instance, is to happen to a particular public expenditure programme which is planned and costed over the following five years when there could be a change of Government well before the expiration of that period? Might not that Government not only favour a change in the rate of public spending in general but also have a specific mandate arising out of its election manifesto to end the very service provided for in that particular programme?

The British genius in politics lies in its capacity to resolve theoretical conflicts by flexibility in practice. It is undoubtedly the constitutional position that no Government in Britain can bind its successor. But the need to reconcile that complete freedom with the limitations that the practical necessities of life put upon it did not arise for the first time in connection with long-term public expenditure commitments. International treaties, undertakings and even arrangements have to be honoured by the countries which are parties to the agreement irrespective of the political outlook of the domestic Government. If this were not so there could be no purpose in having an agreement. Mostly, of course, there is little change in foreign policy upon a change of Government in Britain and the desire to avoid a predecessor's commitments rarely arises. But where it does the sense of obligation is given the greater weight. So too in domestic affairs there is a wide measure of agreement between the main political parties about existing arrangements and about the general direction of future development – although there is often a difference of view about the desirable pace of that development. As a result, the area of possible conflict arising out of long-term programmes is not very great. But where it does exist it has to be recognised that it is in the nature of public expenditure programmes to give rise to long-term commitments and that the alternatives facing any Government are either to involve a possible successor or not to start a particular programme at all. The former course is taken, and Governments of all parties accept that their freedom to govern is affected in this way; that a longer period of time than is thought desirable may have to elapse before the old can be replaced by the new; and that government is a continuous process which probably benefits rather than suffers all told from the difficulties placed in the way of rapid changes affecting large numbers of people.

The conclusion which emerges from this short survey is that there is nothing in the practice of Governments in this country to prevent the reasonable planning of and provision for short-, medium- and longer-term public expenditure programmes. But the assumption throughout has been that the changes of Government in mind were changes from a Government commanding a majority in the House of Commons to a Government of another party similarly placed. It has further been assumed that such a change would not be accompanied by a major constitutional change. It is necessary therefore to consider whether, in the event of either of these assumptions proving to be erroneous, the conclusion reached might be invalidated.

It is, however, difficult to envisage circumstances which would lead to a different conclusion. If, for example, a general election resulted in no party having an overall majority, then the subsequent Government would either be a minority party government or a coalition. If the party in power were the same as before, then clearly it would not wish, out of a desire to satisfy a different philosophical approach, to go back on its public expenditure commitments. If the party in power was previously in opposition, then it would be less likely as a minority government to make as many changes as it might have done if it had been returned with an overall majority – and that eventuality has already been covered in reaching the conclusion already described. If, finally, the government rested on a coalition of parties, then there would be positive support in the new Cabinet for a continuation of those programmes which gave rise to the commitments. In short, the circumstances most likely to lead to the cancellation of a previous government's public expenditure commitments is the straightforward one of a change from a majority government of one party to a majority government of another, and that was one of the assumptions in mind when reaching the conclusion that there was nothing to prevent the starting of public expenditure programmes which involved expenditure over a number of years ahead.

The other assumption was an unchanged constitution. But what would happen if there were a major change – if, for example, there were a major devolution of government to a part of the UK – and Scotland comes first to mind. There is no need to consider complete separation because public expenditure in the UK would merely become public expenditure in the UK as reduced. The figures would be smaller; everything else would be unaltered. But even if the constitutional change took the form of a moderate devolution of governmental powers there would still be no need to alter the conclusion under consideration, for it would merely represent an extension of existing practice. It is already the case that the Secretary of State for Scotland has the responsibility for carrying out certain UK services in Scotland for which the relevant central government departments have the responsibility in England and Wales. The building of a hospital in Scotland is but one example. In short, the present control of public expenditure already allows for the principle of devolution by the central Government whether to a small or a large region and there would be no need therefore for any fundamental changes in the system if a constitutional change of the kind contemplated were to occur.

In this context it would be appropriate to remove a further area of doubt about the period of commitment and to consider what should be the future policy of Governments. Reference has already been made to the apparent change of policy which arose when the Conservative Government took over from its Labour predecessors in 1970, and which is evidenced by the significant alteration in format of the annual public expenditure White Paper. In essence this change amounted to the removal of the distinction between, on the one hand, the first three years and, on the other hand, the last two years of the five-year coverage. Prior to 1970 the figures for the former period represented estimates of what it would cost to carry out the Government's decisions; for the latter period they were provisional allocations of resources subject to final decision later by the Government. Publication of the figures of the first three years tied the Government to them; those of the last two years left the Government free to alter them as much as they desired within the limitations imposed by the practicalities of the situation. For once a programme is decided on, then depending on its nature a commitment is in effect being entered into for a longer or shorter period. But the size of that commitment is open to considerable variation in the future – particularly so in the distant future. The programme can expand or contract – the pace of development can vary. The possibility of suitable variation – rapid variation is always a theoretical possibility but the cost in sudden unemployment, damages for breach of contract and wasted expenditure may be very high – may be slight in the immediate future but may be quite considerable in later years.

Year 1 of the period covered by the White Papers is the current year; and as the date of publication is likely to be November or December and the year ends the following 31 March, there will be only about one-third of the year left and the figures will be made up more of actual money spent than of money estimated to be spent in the future. There will, in short, be no room for variation in those figures. Year 2 will be the year commencing in three or four months' time only, in respect of which firm decisions will have been taken by the Government after most careful consideration only a year previously, or possibly a little less. So here again there will be little or no flexibility in the planned expenditure. Year 3 is the year starting in fifteen months' time which became the focal year in the practice of the Labour Government. The publication of those figures is the first disclosure of the Government's final decisions. There will have been considerable argument within the Government before reaching those decisions. For continuing programmes the amounts argued about will have been limited by the inherent flexibility within the programmes for variation upwards or downwards without incurring unacceptable results and unacceptable costs. But there will have been some worthwhile area of flexibility – greater in the case of some programmes and less in the case of others – without which the argument would have been almost wholly academic. In fact the main reason for choosing that year as a focal year was that it was the first year with a worthwhile measure of flexibility. This then was the total period covered by government decisions; the period starting some three-quarters of a year before the date of publication and ending two and a quarter years after it.

Year 4 covers the period ending nearly four years after the date of publication, a considerable period ahead. Some programmes will still not be fully under way by then, such as the production of a batch of new military aircraft, but most programmes will be capable of some variation, possibly quite large in many cases. It is impossible to generalise, but in order to get some idea of the amounts involved it is worth pointing out that an overall flexibility of 10 per cent only – not a large figure considering the length of period ahead – could well amount to some £3,000 million. Now that is a substantial sum by any reckoning; and for Year 5 clearly the figure would be considerably more – perhaps of the order of £10,000 million. But the absolute amount is relatively unimportant: what is important is the fact that Years 4 and 5 present a large area for the exercise of choice.

Who will finally exercise that choice is not in dispute: it will be the Government of the day, carrying out a central function of government. 'Gouverner, c'est choisir' puts it well. What is of immense concern is whether Parliament and People will share appropriately in those decisions, whether they will be fully consulted; whether their interest will be fully engaged; and whether they will be given every assistance to enable them to cope with the issues involved so that an informed, widespread, public debate can ensue. How all this might be done will be described shortly; what needs to be pointed out at this juncture is the simple fact that if the Government publish only decisions and not the information upon which later decisions will be based, then there will be no opportunity for any others to participate in the process of decision-making.

Now that is precisely what the new Government did: that is the nub of the matter. In removing the distinction between the two periods (the first three years and the latter two) they did not of course alter the degree of flexibility inherent in the programmes. That is determined by the nature of the programmes. What they did was to deny the possibility of full participation by Parliament and People.

This is not a theoretical argument, for there is nothing theoretical about whether some twenty Cabinet Ministers have met together, possibly several times, in order to resolve some of the most difficult issues before a Government, the choice of priorities over the whole field of public expenditure. Command 4578 makes all this quite clear: in it the Government states that, subject to certain minor exceptions which are quite irrelevant to this particular issue, 'the totals given in this White Paper for the various programmes are those which the Government *have decided upon* for the purposes of managing public expenditure up to 1974–75' (that is to say, up to a final date some four and a quarter years ahead).

The view of the newly-created Expenditure Committee is well worth noting again. At the end of its first parliamentary session it reported, on 29 July 1971, that 'The debate [in the Commons] on the Command Papers should provide the main opportunity for the influence of the legislature to be brought to bear on the programme of the executive. It should be among the most important events of the parliamentary year.' It would be reasonable to assume that in making these assessments this all-party Committee was representing the general view of the House of Commons. But it is very unlikely that, in the changed circumstances, this influence could be brought to bear. As the Government made firm decisions for Years 1 to 5, Year 6 gave the first opportunity for directly influencing the Government before it took decisions. But six years is a long way ahead – much too far to attract busy men and women away from their tasks relating to the immediate future. Indeed it is so far ahead that it is a matter for conjecture whether suggestions and comments should be addressed to the Government or to the Opposition, for a general election is bound to intervene before the sixth year has started. If these two stumbling blocks are not in themselves sufficient to deter a would-be reformer, then there is the final deterrent of lack of information. Only a Government can, from its own resources, build up a picture of the likely course of public expenditure in several years' time. Without that picture there can be no basis for constructive criticism by Parliament. Yet the Government only covers five years in its publications and for all of those the public expenditure programmes will have been decided.

The first act of a Government desiring participation by Parliament and public in the great debate on choices in public expenditure is, therefore, to limit its decisions to the earlier part of the five years for which full figures must continue to be given and to leave the later part undecided. Where the earlier part should end is not of fundamental importance provided there remains a worthwhile later part. But for practical purposes the break, if it did not come at the end of Year 3, could only come at the end of Year 2 and for the reasons already given that is nothing like as suitable as Year 3. In short, the first requirement is a return to the practice that held good prior to 1971.

Still considering only the role of the Government in relation to public expenditure, it is next necessary to see whether better systems can be adopted or more significant information can be provided so as to enable the decision-making process to be improved, for the description given earlier makes it clear that the term 'scientific' could hardly be used to describe the whole of this process. There are in fact two recent developments which merit examination in this context – Programmes Analysis and Review (PAR) and Central Policy Review Staff (CPRS). Their advocates herald the former as a distinct improvement in method and the second as an improvement in administration. Others see them as unnecessary, as doing no more than is already being done, as being a waste of effort or even a cause of confusion. CPRS is often likened to the fifth wheel on the coach. It would probably be helpful, therefore, to consider the general problem of aids to decision-making so that these two innovations can then be considered against that general background.

To err is human, and no doubt the usual explanation will be offered that with better information the error would not have been made. Rarely is it admitted that the fault lay with the judgement of the decision-maker. Now it is of course undeniable that the better the information, the more likely is it that the decision will be the right one. But there must come a point – even where time and circumstance have allowed the collection of all the information required – where adding up stops and judgement starts. Mostly some of the information needed will not, for one reason or another, be available and it is still the case, as ex-Premier Clem Attlee so perceptively commented, that the test of a good Minister is his capacity to reach the right answer on the basis of inadequate information. It is still the case that however great the help given by new methods and formalised disciplines, there is no substitute for men of ability applying their minds to the task. They will exercise their judgement wisely and in all probability they will, unaided, ask themselves the very questions that the formalised methods require answering. Those with inadequate powers of judgement will 'get it wrong' from wherever it is that the computer stops.

PESC – which might itself conceivably be described as one such formalised method – certainly produced one result in decision-making which, it could be alleged, might not otherwise have been achieved. The very fact of having to estimate the cost over a period of five years, if only in order to fill in the blanks in the columns provided, meant that no new programme could be started on the basis that it only cost very little in Years 1 and 2 without those concerned being made aware of the (possibly substantial) cost in Years 4 and 5. It is true that a wise provider of finance would automatically seek that information without the promptings of the public expenditure surveys; but they made certain that the question would not be overlooked.

It was felt by some that this discipline produced two complementary results. It made it more difficult than would otherwise have been the case to start new programmes; conversely it gave greater security to existing programmes. It became necessary, therefore – so the argument continued – to devise some method of testing the justification of continuing programmes. To subject a carefully selected number of them to full and objective analysis and review would, it was felt, achieve this purpose. Now it must be true that if it were agreed all round that of a department's total tally of, say, twenty-five programmes, one particular programme was clearly at the bottom of a list of priorities; and that there was a fixed ceiling for that department's expenditure which could in no circumstances be altered; and that a new much-to-be-desired programme would undoubtedly rank much higher in priority were it to be included in the list: if all that were agreed to be so, then the exclusion of that new programme through the application of the PESC five-year look at its cost could conceivably result in the existing low-priority programme being continued.

The whole of these conditions are, in practice, never satisfied. To take the most obvious one, the departmental ceiling is not a fixed steel and concrete structure; it is on the contrary movable and tends to rise when the pressure in the room below ceases to be containable, in spite of the whole weight of the Treasury seated above it. It is merely a limit which exists so long as everyone concerned accepts it. Then again, no department is willingly going to make itself vulnerable by agreeing that a particular programme is well at the bottom of its list of priorities. In the absence of agreement the only objective approach would be to subject all the department's programmes to a PAR exercise in the hope of reaching a consensus on a list of priorities. But that would be a mammoth task incapable of achievement. In fact it is, as has been earlier mentioned, extremely difficult to put an end to continuing programmes, quite irrespective of the effects of PESC: the best hope lies in agreement with the department on the basis of new lamps for old, i.e. £x million for a new programme if an old programme costing £$\frac{3}{4}x$ million is discontinued.

But all this is a matter of opinion: what is a matter of fact is that – so far, at all events – no PAR study has resulted in a change of policy. However, that position may alter in time, and in any event the conclusion to be drawn from it is not that no benefit is to be obtained from PAR – on the contrary there are worthwhile benefits which will be described shortly – but that PAR is not the only or the best method of dealing with the problem of old programmes which may have partly outlived their earlier usefulness.

Nor does PAR seem to satisfy another criterion in the way originally claimed. The importance to the community of a particular programme cannot be assessed entirely on the amount of public expenditure incurred. There are indeed many important programmes pursued at comparatively small cost; but in the argument about public expenditure it is natural that those programmes involving large sums should receive most attention. It was, therefore, felt that some machinery ought to be devised for scrutinising the smaller programmes which might otherwise escape proper examination, and that PAR was suitable for this purpose. That argument may be theoretically correct – although here again the assumption that a department will not review, of its own initiative, at suitable periods, its small-cost programmes unless there is a formalised system of so doing, remains to be proved. On the other hand, it would be very surprising if it were regarded as appropriate – at all events for a considerable time – to devote the time and talents of a weighty body to the examination of any programme where substantial sums of public money were not involved. Again the simple fact is that each of the fifteen or so topics subjected to PAR studies in 1971–72 involved significant amounts of public expenditure.

One further practical aspect needs to be mentioned before attempting to make a general assessment of the value of systematised re-examination known as PAR. The proof of a report lies, as with the pudding, in the digesting of it. It helps mankind little that a fine report should be produced and then laid to rest in a cubby-hole. It must be read and, if appropriate, acted upon before its purpose can be claimed to have been fulfilled. Now the PAR reports are thorough and weighty; each one is, in fact, a book. They are addressed to senior Ministers – each one of whom has no time to read a book. This rather noteworthy drawback is attempted to be overcome by the department concerned – which will have participated fully in the drawing up of the report – preparing a summary; and it is that summary which will be read by those who will have to decide what action is needed.

Programme Analysis and Review is a process involving studies of the kind which have customarily been carried out by the responsible department, mainly on their own initiative, but occasionally prompted by the Treasury or by special financial pressures. The very fact that Ministers and departmental heads always need more money than they are able to get in order to carry out all their policies as fully as they would like, means that they are under continual stimulus to see where money can be saved. PAR studies are different in that the programmes are selected and examined jointly by the department, the Treasury and the Central Policy Review Staff, a small body of considerable ability recruited for the purpose and described in more detail below. The studies themselves are not new, nor was it unusual to create an inter-departmental working party from within the Government to look at a particular issue, to include representatives of the department mainly concerned and of the Treasury, and to service it from the Cabinet office secretariat (a small group of skilled civil servants drawn from the departments, but in no sense any longer attached to them or representing them, in order to serve the Prime Minister and the Cabinet as a whole). PAR thus represents nothing new in principle; but it does represent a considerable extension of existing practice, with more people engaged and consequently more reports. These reports are not disclosed to Parliament; and conceivably they would not be as valuable or as objective if they were written with that disclosure in view.

An assessment of the Central Policy Review Staff (CPRS), the other important innovation referred to earlier, will inevitably raise the question of the extent to which a Prime Minister is entitled to influence the thinking and the policies of a departmental Minister. In theory policy is for the Cabinet where the Prime Minister has the responsibility and authority of being the Chairman but is otherwise only *primus inter pares.* In fact every Minister knows who appointed him and who can remove him. However, what is not in dispute is that the Prime Minister is responsible for the co-ordination of policies as between departments and for seeing that each new policy is, until a Cabinet decision to the contrary is taken, consistent with the overall stance of the Government as revealed in the party manifesto at election time. To do that he must be aware not only of what every department is doing – every Cabinet Minister sees to that and consults the Prime Minister at an early stage of a new policy proposal – but of the impact and side effects which any new departmental proposal may have on other departments and on government policy as a whole. The Treasury only performs a part of this function: they are the one department which has to know what every other department is doing, but their test is whether any new development fits in with the overall economic and financial strategy of the Government. That is an important part, but not the totality, of government strategy. So the Prime Minister traditionally carries out this function with the assistance of the Cabinet office.

However the new Conservative Government of 1970 concluded that the Cabinet office was not equipped to carry out this task in sufficient detail. It also decided that there was a need to provide Cabinet Ministers who had no departmental interest in an issue that was coming before Cabinet with an objective non-partisan assessment of the particular proposals in addition to the information and argument set out in the paper circulated by the department responsible for the new proposals. Such an assessment would also take into account any contrary arguments circulated by any other department which was closely affected by and opposed to the new ideas. One way of providing the necessary manpower would be to increase the Cabinet secretariat. But to secure an 'outside' view might be better in the sense that a fresher and more objective approach would be taken and this would mean recruiting some staff from outside Whitehall. In this way the CPRS unit came into existence, a body which was to take nothing for granted, would have access to Cabinet committees (but not to Cabinet), and would be responsible to the Prime Minister. It would also brief him on PAR studies, in which it would participate; and being, like the Prime Minister, free of departmental responsibilities, it would be able to concentrate on the long-term view as opposed to the short-term, and on the strategy rather than tactics.

Clearly these arguments add up to a pretty solid case, and if CPRS were to achieve most of these objectives it would be assured of an existence longer than the life of one particular Government. Cabinet Ministers might find it helpful; the Prime Minister certainly would. On the other hand the departments generally would feel that one further obstacle – though certainly not an insuperable one – was being erected in their path. The Treasury, which traditionally dealt with the uncommon issue which did not relate to a particular department, might find the lines of demarcation difficult to draw; and it would tend to look askance at another body which claimed some authority on economic policy and resource allocation. Finally the Cabinet office, which was responsible for providing analytical assistance to the Prime Minister, would find its role diminished. All this gave rise to hesitation, however, rather than opposition; and the general view is that CPRS has proved to be moderately effective. It is not specially concerned with issues of public expenditure, but the scope of its work includes issues which have their public expenditure aspect – as so many issues do. The fact that it has the responsibility of looking at problems in the round and with regard to their long-term effect should prove beneficial, for there is never a lack of those who will press the short-term view in politics and one more voice calling attention to the long-term issues will go some way towards providing a balanced view.

These then are the major developments in recent times affecting the process of decision-making in the field of public expenditure. What remain for consideration are those changes which are still under discussion. There is apparently only one substantial change which could reasonably be regarded as a possible runner: to model the British administration of public expenditure somewhat on the pattern of the American by moving it closer to the Prime Minister. One version of this idea would be to combine the Cabinet office, the Civil Service Department and the supply divisions of the Treasury (those which deal with public expenditure) and to make the Chief Secretary to the Treasury the Prime Minister's chief adviser in this area. CPRS would be closely linked with the new grouping. It is of course possible to separate the functions of the Minister in charge of public expenditure from those of the Chancellor of the Exchequer. The Secretary of the Bureau of the Budget, as he is known in the USA, is but one example.

Frequently countries find it convenient to have two separate finance ministers, each with his own department. Between them they are responsible for economic policy, foreign financial policy, domestic financial policy, taxation and public expenditure. Where the dividing line is drawn varies between one country and another and from time to time in the same country. In the United Kingdom, for example, the Labour Government of 1964–70 experimented with an Economic Ministry (headed by the deputy Prime Minister) as well as the Treasury (without its Economic Minister) but in due course returned to the traditional pattern of a single finance ministry, the Treasury, headed by the Chancellor of the Exchequer and assisted by the Chief Secretary to the Treasury, the Financial Secretary to the Treasury and an Economic Minister. But the public expenditure function has never been removed from the Treasury, and although it could easily be done, it is not easy to foresee whether it would be an improvement on the present situation. The attempt to separate economic policy from financial – on the basis of defining the former as having to do with the long term and the latter with the short term – failed partly because the dividing line was not always very plain but mainly because it proved in most cases impossible to consider either in isolation from the other. There had, therefore, to be a great deal of duplication of effort – a circumstance inevitably giving rise to the possibility of friction. When it began to look as though the work of the two departments might need to be merged again, there was never any doubt as to which would remain and which would cease to exist. The Treasury held the purse strings, was old established, and could carry out the whole of its traditional functions without leaning at all heavily on the Economic Department. The reverse was not true.

None of this provides a precise guide as to the likely success of a division of Treasury functions of the kind under discussion. The dividing line would presumably be between revenue and expenditure and only the latter would, of all the Treasury functions, be withdrawn from it. This dividing line is a clear one and on the whole easy to maintain; moreover once the overall totals had been decided upon as part of the function of managing the economy, the details of revenue could be considered in isolation from the details of expenditure – at all events in most cases. But not in all. For instance, a switch – in whole or in part – from investment grants to investment allowances (the former being a subsidy to the manufacturer, the latter a relief to the taxpayer) would result in a reduction in public expenditure matched by a fall in tax revenue. Although, therefore, the net financial position of the State would remain unaltered, both revenue and expenditure would be affected and the decision to make the change would have to be a policy decision agreed to by both the Treasury and the new Public Expenditure Department. Similarly there would have to be co-ordination of policy between the two departments on such issues as whether to reduce the scale of a particular public service, thereby reducing public expenditure, or to leave it unaltered but to achieve the same financial effect by making a charge to the user in certain cases. The former method reduces expenditure, the latter increases revenue; the net result may be the same. But all these are merely examples of the need for co-ordination and consultation. That is a very normal part of good government and by no means creates insuperable difficulties. The division of the work of the department therefore is not the problem. The real issue is whether the Treasury would suffer and whether the Government – including the new department – would benefit.

One result of the new proposal would be to put the new Expenditure Department on the same basis as all the other departments in having a precise agreed budget within which the departmental Minister would have to work. The practical effect of this would be to make the task of containing public expenditure within agreed limits, including the contingency allowance, a fraction easier by creating this further barrier to pressures for increased expenditure. In that respect the new arrangement would be advantageous: not because it is always better to spend less rather than more in public expenditure, but because it is always better to decide policy with more regard to merit than to pressure, and whatever the method of administration in an active democracy, the pressures for more expenditure are always considerably greater than the reverse. A small step towards achieving the distant goal of balanced pressures is therefore to be welcomed.

To a much lesser extent there would similarly be a slight gain to the Chief Secretary to the Treasury. As number 2 in the Treasury he is felt to be very near to the public purse; he may not have his finger on the purse-strings but he is in daily contact with the man who has. As a non-Treasury Minister – the Minister of a separate department – he would find the argument of the fixed ceiling of public expenditure easier to maintain, for he would be incapable of giving more than he had to give, and the remedy of an addition to the overall total of public expenditure would be, and be seen to be, an argument of principle involving the Chancellor of the Exchequer and the Cabinet in a consideration of the state of the economy. In a sense too the Chancellor would find life a little easier. He has a most difficult task, technically and politically. For although he may be respected both for his office and his great qualities, it is not given to any man to tax and be loved. Three annual budgets is the maximum political life of a Chancellor and any method whereby the erosion of his store of goodwill can be avoided is much to be recommended in the interests of enabling him to carry through his unwelcome duties. The proposed re-organisation of administration of public expenditure would concentrate the requests for more money for individual programmes rather more than at present on the Chief Secretary to the Treasury to the exclusion of the

Chancellor. And this is right, for although it does not make the Chief Secretary to the Treasury's prime task of maintaining good relations with his colleagues any the easier, it helps the Chancellor more than it hurts the Chief Secretary. For, as already explained, he is the 'abominable no-man'; he is expected to say no as part of his abominable function; and it is realised that every Government has to have someone responsible for this function, at home and abroad. There are moments therefore when he may even be upgraded in his colleagues' estimation from an abomination to a necessary evil.

So far, therefore, it seems that the new proposal has several points in its favour, though whether they add up to a sufficient case for effecting so substantial a change is more doubtful. There is little doubt, however, that the removal, in the late 'sixties, of responsibility for the management of the Civil Service from the Treasury to the Civil Service Department created certain difficulties in the management of public expenditure and that the reunion of public expenditure and Civil Service management functions would be beneficial. On the other hand the proposal to hive off the public expenditure functions has two major disadvantages: the Prime Minister and the Chief Secretary to the Treasury would each become too powerful.

The Prime Minister is the First Lord of the Treasury; but that is a matter of history and courtesy, not of practical politics. He neither has any responsibility for, nor feels any special loyalty towards, the Treasury. On the other hand he always has had responsibility for the management of Government and the government machine – indeed only he, as the chairman of the Cabinet and as a Minister who is not otherwise involved in the work of a department, could conceivably discharge that function. His title of Minister for the Civil Service recognises that responsibility, and the fact that the day-to-day work of that department is done by another Cabinet Minister does not detract from it.

If the supply divisions of the Treasury were transferred to the Civil Service Department the Prime Minister would be responsible for public expenditure and the day-to-day work would be done by the Chief Secretary (under some appropriate new title). But the present limitation on the free exercise of his discretion, which derives from the right of a dissatisfied Minister to appeal to Cabinet, would effectively disappear. For it would not be conducive to good government – nor to a long life as a Minister – that there should be a direct policy confrontation between Minister and Prime Minister in Cabinet. The Prime Minister is a non-combatant chairman who guides the discussion and sums it up. He is a very powerful figure: to add to his powers that of final arbiter on all public expenditure disputes would represent an unwise and intolerable increase.

On the other hand it may be suggested that no Prime Minister would be so foolish as to allow a situation like that to develop. Certainly, he would not: on the contrary he would endeavour, even though the transfer had taken place, to maintain his normal posture of detached but understanding concern by playing no greater part in public expenditure matters than he had previously done. He would remain in the wings and leave the centre of the stage to the Chief Secretary. This would lessen the difficulty but not avoid it, for in any dispute the Minister of the spending department would know that in effect he was still dealing with the Prime Minister at one remove. He would feel free to argue with the Chief Secretary but not to the point of pursuing his disagreement to the Cabinet room; he would at the end of the day be compelled to accept whatever he had succeeded in persuading the Chief Secretary to offer. The latter, on the other hand, would have no reason to temper his enthusiasm by having to consider the likely effect of an appeal to Cabinet. In short, the arrangement would be so weighted in favour of the Chief Secretary as to be unacceptable as well as unwise.

It is difficult to see any way in which the proposal to transfer to the Civil Service Department the supply divisions of the Treasury could avoid these major drawbacks and be made to work satisfactorily. Yet it remains true – and indeed fairly obvious – that the reuniting of responsibility for the use of major national resources (which is involved in public expenditure), with responsibility for organising the use of manpower resources within the government machine (which is the task of the Civil Service Department) would be advantageous. The solution lies, therefore, not in considering whether or not to transfer further functions from the Treasury but in restoring to it the Civil Service management functions in question. Such a restoration has, in the view of some of those best fitted to make a judgement, much to recommend it in addition to the advantages which relate to public expenditure. But it is unnecessary for present purposes to do more than refer to two further reasons for the move which arise directly out of the management of public expenditure.

In order to carry out their programmes, spending departments need money and manpower. They come to the Treasury for the first, to the Civil Service Department for the second. Clearly they ought to go to one authority for both. The Treasury criterion is the use of a given amount of resources measured in financial and economic terms. The Civil Service Department will mostly be working to a fixed target of aggregate numbers. The two criteria should coincide; but they may not, with resulting tension all round.

The second reason relates to the supply estimates. As already explained, the consideration by Parliament of these estimates is one of the major constraints over the executive by the legislature. They occupy a most important place in our Constitution. They are presented to Parliament by the Chief Secretary to the Treasury and it is on him that Members of Parliament rely for the accuracy of the figures, the fairness of the presentation and, above all, the judgement that the expenditure involved represents the minimum needed. It is in full awareness of these responsibilities that the Chief Secretary every year examines with care each estimate submitted to him by his officials. Whether he spends a long time or a short time on each, whether he seeks further information or clarification, whether he approves, criticises or withholds approval, all this will depend on the circumstances affecting each estimate. He will gladly devote the necessary time to the task because he recognises that it plays a central part in the internal control of public expenditure in addition to its parliamentary aspect. He must, for example, find exact confirmation in the figures of all the agreemonts reached with the various departments on a great number of different issues throughout the year. Finally he will take the one action needed to set in motion the whole process of the provision of funds by Parliament: he will attach his signature to each estimate – and for 1973–74 they totalled some £18,000 million.

But he will not feel wholly satisfied: he will derive what satisfaction he can from the realisation that in one area – fortunately the only one – he has done the best he can in the circumstances. But that is not the best he could have done in different circumstances. That area is Civil Service manpower, an item which appears in practically every estimate. He will see the detailed make-up of the item in the figures supplied by the Civil Service Department; he will examine, compare and test-check. But in this one area alone he will not apply his judgement – he will instead be compelled to rely on the judgement of his colleague in charge of that department. It matters not whether that judgement is wiser or less wise: the point is that of all the expenditure for which he is answerable to Parliament this is the one area where he accepts responsibility partly on good faith instead of wholly on his own judgement. The restoration to the Treasury of responsibility for staff numbers and management services would remove that incongruity and should serve to promote the efficiency and economy with which public expenditure programmes are carried out.

It does not appear, therefore, that there are major alterations which the Government should make in the near future in order to improve its management and control of public expenditure. It will probably be the case that when Parliament and people have developed a stronger interest in this topic and have exhibited a greater desire to participate more closely in the important choices which have to be made, some reforms will be required to accommodate the new desires. Over the next few years, however, such developments seem very unlikely, and until they have taken place it is not possible to prescribe the appropriate alterations in the method of administration. In the meantime the existing arrangements will serve both to ensure what is required at present and to stimulate the improvement in detail which is already taking place. Considerable progress has, for example, already been made in securing accurate comparison of different years' results on a constant price basis, but greater accuracy is no doubt capable of achievement and the studies which are already taking place into methods of improvement should continue. Similarly there is need to continue the progress already being made in the conversion of financial statistics into figures defining economic effects. When one is concerned with the allocation of resources, which is what decisions on public expenditure are, then it is necessary to realise that £1 million of expenditure does not have the same economic effect – that is to say, does not consume the same amount of resources – whatever the field of expenditure. The present methods of dividing public expenditure into broad categories corresponding to the economic effect of those payments, so far as the published figures go, supplemented by closer analysis internally and the use of conversion factors to produce greater accuracy, do go a long way towards enabling the relevant decisions to be taken; but no doubt continued study will produce greater refinement.

Then again there is the problem of verification, an essential part both of the process of securing the implementation of past decisions and of achieving a better understanding of the real effect of decisions as they are made in the future. There is the difficulty of price changes already mentioned; the problem set by the fact that the Government which is expected to produce the figures of actual expenditure and compare them with estimated expenditure only has direct control over part of the field of public expenditure; and a variety of difficulties associated with the fact that the science and control of public expenditure are comparatively new and developing all the time and that the world of public expenditure cannot stand still while examination and decision take place. Verification must be permeated with great understanding if it is to succeed, for what is really to be verified is whether, in the course of using economic resources of the amount decided upon, amenities and perhaps even human happiness have been increased – or alternatively inconvenience and perhaps suffering reduced – in the way and to the extent decided upon. These are not readily susceptible to the measuring rod, and the objective has been expressed in this way to make that clear. For it is not simply a question of making sure that the pounds spent and the pounds authorised coincide. It would certainly be possible to ensure that result with considerable precision by putting cost first and last and making everything else accommodate to it – much as Procrustes succeeded in accommodating every weary and hapless traveller to his bed. But it is for consideration whether the results would be any more beneficial.

The process of verification, that is, the measuring of achievement, is then a complex one, and indeed those who favour PAR will, with some justification, assert that nothing short of a full-scale review of the results achieved will serve that purpose. Certainly it is much more than comparing the number of pounds spent with the number authorised. That process is better defined as authorisation and is carried out to the extent possible: that is to say, the money spent by the central Government is provided in such a way as to ensure that it is authorised by Parliament. That is the function of the supply estimates and the associated procedure. It is for these reasons that that procedure needs to be continued, as argued earlier. But the full verification process is capable of some improvement as new and more accurate methods of measuring achievement are devised.

Finally there is the troublesome problem of the use of the contingency reserve, where again somewhat better methods of reaching a decision need to be devised. The difficulties have already been referred to in the context of the control of public expenditure, especially in relation to timing. For it is essential, if actual expenditure is to be contained within the decided limits, to retain the flexibility given by a reserve as long as possible. Yet there are new demands for more money arising almost weekly and some of these may well be connected with a sudden crisis which requires immediate attention. Then again it is well established that the only way of reaching sound judgements on public expenditure issues is to have competing demands: which implies delaying consideration of an individual requirement until several more have accumulated (as they undoubtedly will). There is no perfect resolution of this dilemma, but a reasonable solution probably lies in having a fairly full-scale review of public expenditure, including in particular the state of the contingency reserve, twice or three times during the course of the year when Cabinet can decide a number of disputed claims for more expenditure; and in relying more heavily than usual on the discretion given to the Treasury to make decisions on the more urgent demands in the meantime. Unless these processes are formalised there is the danger that decision-making will become ragged and that as a result the public purse will suffer.

There are, then, some areas where improvement should be sought in the management of public expenditure – it would indeed be a sorry state of affairs if the quest for better methods were ever halted – but no dramatic reforms can be anticipated in the near future. Nor is that a surprising conclusion to reach having regard to the major improvements achieved in the past decade and to the fact that this country is, as a result, in the lead among the Governments of the world – 'well in the lead' in the words of one Treasury spokesman, and 'I do not know of any country further ahead than us' in the words of another – in the control over public spending and in the information being provided to Parliament; and it is Parliament that should next be considered in order to ascertain whether there is scope for improvement there in the next few years.

In the middle of the nineteenth century Sir Francis Barine, who had been responsible for the setting up of the Public Accounts Committee (PAC), complained that 'the House showed so little anxiety with regard to this subject'. There were several reasons for this, the main one being that it was new. In due course the PAC came to be recognised as a most important committee and an essential part of the machinery whereby Parliament shares in the control of public spending. It does not lack recruits of the necessary calibre even though its work is mainly carried on behind closed doors in an upstairs committee room so that the outside world knows little of the Members of Parliament involved and of their work. By contrast speeches made and questions asked in the chamber of the House of Commons attract far more publicity and allow an MP's constituents to know of his activities. Gradually the custom grew up of having an ex-Treasury Minister from the Opposition as its Chairman. The committee is an all-party one, but as the members are chosen in such a way as to reflect the strength of the various parties in the House of Commons, it was felt that an Opposition member should be the chairman. The committee therefore is well equipped to function strongly and does so in practice. It is served by the Comptroller and Auditor-General and his large staff who have access to all government files; and when a matter of great and immediate public interest is examined and reported on, there is no lack of interest in the ensuing debate in the Commons. In other circumstances the committee works most effectively but quietly and few MPs take part in the debates on its reports in Parliament. The work is important and interesting and, inasmuch as the committee has a great – perhaps a too great – effect on the approach of the civil servant to his work, constitutes a considerable exercise of power. It is therefore satisfying work in many respects although a great deal of it attracts little or no publicity.

Three conclusions emerge from this short review. The first, which has a great bearing on the present position, is that lack of parliamentary interest in the early stages of a new procedure is no guide to the future. The second is that the apparent lack of interest associated with lack of publicity is not to be confused with real lack of interest in the important work involved; and the third is that as the PAC system works so well it is not surprising that there are no obvious ways in which it could be improved. It will always be the case that the brightest ideas come from men of talent; but this merely means that any system of the kind under discussion will work better if those engaged have more ability. That is a permanent situation affecting all such systems and all committees. But there never are sufficient brains to go round and it is impossible to get the most talented people for every job; and as already indicated, there is no shortage of able MPs willing to serve on the PAC.

The importance of the supply procedures has already been stressed and the need to continue with the present system of putting detailed estimates and supplementary estimates before the Commons for its approval. These two – PAC and Estimates – and everything they involve, together with verbal and written parliamentary questions, constitute a most effective part of the system of control over public expenditure. It is in two other directions in particular that improvement should be sought: in the closer involvement of Parliament in the choice of priorities represented by public expenditure plans, and in a more enlightened application of the important test of 'value for money'.

'Value for money' is a phrase which some, at the first hearing, tend slightly to despise as indicating an excessively materialistic approach and as offending their finer feelings. On second thoughts those conscious of Parliament's duty to search out waste or extravagance in the spending of the hard-earned money which the taxpayer has perforce contributed, recognise that the real issue is whether the resources so acquired ought to be used for one purpose rather than another; that resources wasted or used extravagantly mean the denial of resources that could have been used, possibly with great benefit to very many citizens, for another purpose; and that 'value for money' is the best test that can be applied. But of course the argument does not end there; nor is there a direct antithesis between the two points of view. For one is left with the question of how to define and measure 'value' and whether the definition should be wide enough to take into account those things which appeal to one's 'finer feelings'. Some account is clearly taken of this point of view already. The level of noise connected with air travel is a simple example. The Government, the airlines and every air traveller is prepared to pay something extra for the convenience of having noise kept down to its present level. Similarly the Government has spent public money on making the lives of those living near London Airport a little more pleasant by soundproofing their houses. In all these and many other ways Government, Parliament and People have decided that absence of noise is valuable and accept that it has to be paid for. It would be impossible to imagine a parliamentary committee taking the opposite view and issuing a report based on the principle that they are required to have regard to value for money and that only tangible things are of value.

It is in an acceptable extension, along these lines, of the test of 'value for money' that progress needs to be sought; and the fact that the value to be attached to these intangible benefits cannot be measured precisely is no argument for excluding it completely or for not attempting an approximate measure. The cost of accidents in the factory, or of the common cold in lost production, is counted as an important factor in several policy decisions notwithstanding that only the more obvious elements in the cost can be measured and that the cost in terms of human suffering cannot. Quiet, or the absence of excessive noise, is accepted as being worth paying for, so is fresh air to breathe, so are flowers planted in a public square or trees at the roadside. These intangibles which appeal to the senses are examples of the way in which society has already attached value to conditions where precision of measurement is impossible and must remain so, for different people would attach different values. The process needs to be carried a great deal further and Parliament has an important part to play both in putting before the Government of the day their assessment of the values attached to these amenities by men and women everywhere and in extending their view as to the elements that should form part of the cost in assessing 'value for money'. The immediate and obvious effects of noise, smells and ugliness are such as to cause the normal narrow calculation of costs and benefits to be revised. The future and less obvious effects may be of greater importance and have a dramatic effect on the assessment of value for money. Where mining takes place the cost per ton of whatever is produced will at first sight seem less in the case of the mine which leaves an ugly hole in the ground or an even uglier mountain of spoil, than in the case of the mine which spends a considerable sum in restoring the amenity of the lovely countryside. But the cost of restoration has not, in the former case, been avoided; it has, almost certainly, merely been postponed. It should therefore be taken into account in any assessment of value for money. Similarly the cheaper petrol which pollutes the atmosphere by producing more carbon deposit than the more expensive petrol may not be cheaper at all; and the cheaper cost of transport by road, achieved at the expense of air pollution, noise and the destruction of acres of arable land, may not be cheaper than the existing rail transport. Equally the reduced cost of producing food through the use of fertilisers that double the yield per acre, takes no account of the destruction of life caused through the drainage of the extra nitrogen into our river systems or of the even more fundamental ecological effects.

It is too easy to say that all this is far removed from the down-to-earth problems of public expenditure and that Parliament cannot exercise any useful influence where the considerations are so vague and that if it departed from its traditional attitudes in carrying out its function of protecting the public purse the resulting indiscipline would entail extravagance. For the influence of Parliament is very great. Both Houses play a most important part in moulding public opinion, and the House of Commons, beyond whose established majority view no Government can make progress for the time being, has an influence on the executive which is probably greater than is generally appreciated. For what is not always sufficiently realised is that the employer/employee relationship between Parliament and the civil servant is a real one, not merely a theoretical one. The Minister is the head of the department while he is there; the Permanent Secretary has a title which renders comment unnecessary. The membership of Parliament may change but the average MP remains a member for about five times as long as a Minister holds his appointment. Parliament is permanent; so is the Civil Service. It is only the Minister – and his junior Ministers – who are birds of passage. Moreover the Minister is in turn responsible to Parliament. The Minister is, of course, responsible to Parliament for the policy of his department and may instruct his officials not to answer questions on policy put to them by a properly constituted committee of the House of Commons, for it is the Minister who has to justify his policy, not the civil servant who merely carries out the Minister's instructions; and the body to whom the Minister must make his case is Parliament and not a committee. But in all other respects civil servants must (and always do) give such a committee all the information and every assistance they can. The cases of conflict between a senior civil servant's duty to Parliament and his duty to his Minister are rare in the extreme – and embarrassing to all in the extreme. Ministers and officials take great care to avoid getting into that kind of situation. But enough has been said to explain why the civil servant always has one ear cocked at Parliament and part of his mind on what he is going to say to the relevant enquiry committee about what he is doing at that very moment – should he ever be asked.

If, therefore, the question arose as to whether the Government should make a particular purchase from firm A who were able to quote a lower price than firm B through taking no account of the ultimate cost of restoring the amenity which the manufacturing process in question was in part destroying; and it had been established that firm B did include the cost of restoration and would otherwise have been cheaper; then it would be important to know whether Parliament took a strong view one way or the other on that issue. It may be suggested that that dilemma should be prevented by all firms being required by law to restore the amenity so that they would be competing on equal terms in that respect; and indeed this is already the position in many areas. No car manufacturer, for example, offers a vehicle which is cheaper by virtue of the fact that it is not fitted with a regulation silencer. But there are very many areas where there is room for question and as our knowledge of how to avoid the harmful long-term effects of certain manufacturing processes increases there will always be cases where the Government's purchasing policy, in harmony with the view of Parliament, could play an important part in encouraging a more forward-looking policy on the part of the manufacturer well before legislation became appropriate or possible.

Very many issues are raised when close consideration is given to the problems associated with the prevention of pollution and with the improvement of the environment. Some are not related to public expenditure but many are, and clearly the Government is in a better position to do something about it than any individual. Not only is it necessary, therefore, that Government and Parliament should, in a general way and over a wide field, turn their attention to the social and financial implications, but they should also combine to widen the interpretation of value for money. Parliament must also play a more active part in deciding the priorities of public expenditure for that is another way of describing an important element in the quality of life; and few things could be more important than that.

The first condition of the exercise by Parliament of a more active role in deciding priorities in public expenditure is that it should have the opportunity to do so. This means that the details of the various programmes should not be decided on by the Government so far ahead that no one else can play an effective part. That issue has already been fully described. Once that opportunity has been fully restored, then there is no reason why the machinery for participation which already exists should not be fully used. There is a duly constituted committee with all necessary powers to enquire into the various aspects of public expenditure, and there is provision for a full two-day debate in the chamber of the House of Commons where all members, Government or Opposition, committee members or not, can make their voices heard. The work of the committee should not be circumscribed nor their duties too closely defined. Clearly their enquiries will be varied, but two elements will be included. The first is the provision of material to assist Parliament by bringing out certain points and clarifying others; the second is the detailed enquiry into aspects of public expenditure directed to satisfying itself that Government policies are being administered in such a way as to achieve their purpose. There is no reason to doubt that members of wide experience and ability will continue to be attracted to the Expenditure Committee, and given the right men, the right machinery and the right powers, it is clear that the committee will function well and that its reports will play a full part in improving the control of public expenditure and in assisting Parliament to play its part in shaping public expenditure.

It is not yet equally clear that Parliament will rise to its full responsibilities in relation to public expenditure and use to the full the opportunities created for it. The debates on the annual White Paper have not yet attracted sufficient interest, and it would be unsafe to rely on the precedent of the PAC and to assert that this is merely history repeating itself. No doubt interest will grow as appreciation of the importance of the subject grows. But it would be wise to consider how that growth could be assisted.

The House of Commons is at its best in debating clear-cut, current issues rather than discussing general topics. The physical confrontation of the two major parties which derives from the seating arrangements and the fact that each is contending for the public esteem that will enable it to win the next election, greatly contribute to this as well as accurately reflecting the will of the members. Each of them in turn has to bear in mind the need to make a good impression in his own constituency and one of the most effective ways of doing this is to have his activities reported in the Press, whether national or local. He is certain to have many interests competing for his time, especially if he is also engaged part-time in professional or business work outside Parliament; and he will no doubt take some account of the likely publicity in deciding which parliamentary interest to pursue, although it would be wrong to lay too much stress on this point. A further aspect of this need to choose between competing claims on his time, especially if he wishes to see his family occasionally, is that an item of business in the House which, it is known, is not going to be followed by a division, provides one of those rare opportunities of being absent with impunity. Where, therefore, a combination of these factors occurs and there is neither a contentious issue before the House nor the likelihood of any publicity for any speech he may contribute nor the possibility of a division, then the attendance in the Chamber is likely to be pretty sparse, although the library and the lobbies will have their usual complement of members dealing with their constituency correspondence, doing research, preparing for a forthcoming debate, seeing constituents and so on. This is what is liable to happen to a two-day discussion of the general principles behind the Government's long-term decisions on public expenditure, and the fact that they are not immediate issues tends to lower the temperature even further.

It should not be difficult, however, to make such adjustments as would result in a reasonable measure of parliamentary interest being engaged, especially having regard to the fact that a modest attendance in the chamber – such as is seen during most of the long debates on the Budget each year – is not inconsistent with Parliament's playing its full part in the moulding of public expenditure policies. Where, for example, the Government of the day is proposing a considerable alteration in the policy behind certain programmes – and this is a fairly regular occurrence, especially upon a change of Government – then a debate could take place on the basis of a motion worded in such a way as to point the issue or issues involved and to result in a division being called. Again the debate could be divided into a number of separate topics, each intended to last no more than three hours or so, in order to concentrate the discussion somewhat and prevent the issues being lost sight of through the debate covering too wide an area. There are well-established precedents for this practice. There would be no great difficulty in producing background briefing material for those MPs who wished to take part in the debate but felt themselves to be inadequately informed about certain aspects: that is a normal service provided by the library. It would obviously be convenient and helpful to all if, in addition, the work of the public expenditure committee were so arranged that it reported, at some suitable time ahead of the debate, on those issues of special political interest.

The combination of these arrangements, all capable of being achieved without difficulty, would increase to a considerable extent the interest taken by Parliament in public expenditure and in the annual debates and would overcome, with one exception, all the restraints referred to earlier. But before dealing with that major exception – constituency interest – it would be as well to consider the position in the House of Lords where no constituency problems arise. What has been considered hitherto is the annual debate in the Commons and the ways of enabling members of that House to participate more fully in moulding public expenditure policies. The House of Lords is not faced with the same problems. The constituency angle is, quite obviously, completely absent: no peer has to consider his own re-election nor publicity in the local newspaper. The party battle is far less evident, for a number of reasons in addition to those just mentioned. There are, first of all, so many peers who owe allegiance to no party; that is to say the bishops, the law lords and the other independent members who sit on the cross-benches. These benches do physically contribute to a lessening of the sense of party confrontation which is seen in the Commons where virtually two parties physically oppose one another. Moreover there are not two parties, there are three; Conservative, Labour and Liberal – the last being sufficiently numerous to count in a way in which they normally do not in the Commons, taking a thoroughly practical standpoint. It is not surprising, therefore, that the House of Lords is at its best in wide discussion rather than narrow debates. Add to this the fact that so many peers are created because of their great experience and outstanding achievements in their respective walks of life and it becomes clear why so many of the discussions are of a very high level indeed.

Clearly there is a case, then, for discussions on certain aspects of public expenditure to be held in the Lords. The reason why this is rarely done – at all events in the explicit context of public expenditure – is reticence regarding money: for it is 'the other place' which deals with money. But the issue of principle which calls for full discussion does not in fact offend against this practice in any way. The real issue is how a given sum of public expenditure should be apportioned among the main programmes. The questions of whether additional taxation – and taxation is certainly not a matter for the House of Lords – should be levied in order to provide the finance for more public expenditure, or whether the total claims of public expenditure are necessitating excessive taxation, do not need to arise. The welfare services, education, law and order, defence – whichever aspect of public expenditure one looks at one finds peers with great experience capable of making most valuable contribution to a debate of this kind. Curiously enough the House of Lords also contains three ex-Chief Secretaries (and only four have, to date, held the office since it was first created) as well as three ex-Chancellors of the Exchequer and several ex-heads of spending departments on both the ministerial and the official side. It is worth noting also that debates on some aspect or other of the social services are frequent and always well attended.

It is clear then that the House of Lords could play a useful part in increasing the interest taken by Parliament as a whole in the way in which the State spends a large proportion of the nation's resources; and doubtless their discussions would in turn interest a wider public so that the impact of Parliament as a whole would be greatly increased. People would appreciate more and more the importance of public expenditure decisions in their effect on their own lives and that things could have been different – and perhaps more to their liking – if their views and wishes had been clearly formulated at the right time and expressed in the right place. It is at this stage that constituency pressures would begin to play their part, encouraging MPs to participate more in public expenditure matters in order to represent their constituents' interests and justify their giving priority to these debates because of increasing public interest and the resulting public discussion on radio, on television and in the Press. It is, of course, already the case that certain items of public expenditure such as, for example, the building of a new hospital in the locality or of a new road to bypass the town, are matters of considerable local interest and accordingly produce their quota of representations to the local MP, questions to Ministers and reports in the local Press. But what is needed in addition is the much wider discussion of public expenditure proposals in their context; of the larger decisions which are based on the choice of priorities rather than of the simple pressure for more expenditure on this, that and the other item. What will, it is hoped, come to be understood is that if the requests for the hospital or for the road are refused on the grounds of lack of finance, the time to press again is when the decision to spend less than is thought sufficient on hospitals or on roads, in order to provide more for other programmes, is being taken: that is to say, when the government proposals for future public expenditure are being discussed in the round by Parliament.

That greater understanding of the relevance of public expenditure, which is clearly a necessary pre-requisite of greater participation, will not be achieved – except over a very long period – unless deliberate steps are taken to put the basic information before the public in an easily digested form. The present display in post offices of posters showing the destination of income tax and the experiment of displaying PAYE posters in factories showing the effective rate of tax on typical earnings, point the way, as does the well-established practice of setting out, in the rates demand, where the money goes. These are partial and do not tell the whole story. What needs to be told, in simple graphical form – and there are so many examples available of how information of this kind can be shown in attractive ways in colour – is the build-up of the fund from taxes, rates and other sources and its disbursement in the various public expenditure programmes. The fact that the more the State spends on the community the more income it requires from the community is easily portrayed and easily understood. Those who press for an increase in old-age pensions know that that involves an increase in pension contributions; and in the same way the need for extra taxation to finance extra expenditure would become associated thoughts. The wider the understanding sought, the simpler the proposition must be. It is doubtful whether ideas of reducing certain programmes in order, within a given total, to increase others, can be readily formulated or convincingly expressed, but few propositions could be simpler than the one which states that in order to spend more you need more money. Tax demands and receipts could tell the story in simplified form; post offices and factories could carry more detailed displays. The Press, radio and television would all play their part in explaining the government proposals, the possible alternatives, and their effects on the lives of the reader, listener or viewer.

Essentially what is being suggested is that people should be given a greater say in the ordering of their lives – a thoroughly democratic principle with which few would disagree. Some of the things they want they choose themselves and pay for with their own money – their food, clothes, holidays, travel and so on; others are chosen indirectly by their representatives in local or national government and paid for indirectly by their rates and taxes – such as their security as a nation, their safety as citizens, their children's education, clean water to drink, sanitation and drains, health care and hospitals, books to read and art treasures to enjoy. The list is long and extremely varied, for the simple fact is that most of what the individual wants is best supplied by the community. The real dividing line between public and private provision may be drawn differently by different people and some may prefer to exercise individual choice instead of or in addition to the public one, such as in schools and hospitals. But for most people, most of what they want is community-provided, and the indications are that the share of public provision is likely to increase rather than the reverse. How then to combine the economy and efficiency of public provision with the satisfaction of individual choice is the question which the suggestions here made seek to answer. For fundamentally public expenditure raises questions about standards of living and, in a very real sense, the quality of life: questions as to how much of our efforts shall be devoted to improving those standards and how much to securing the greater happiness of future generations, just as we have inherited the legacies – some more acceptable than others – of the past. The price of greater freedom of choice is greater involvement by Parliament and People and is surely well worth paying.

Appendix

Table 1: *Public Expenditure: 1972-73 and 1976-77*

£ million at 1972–73 out-turn prices (including the relative price effect)

	1972–73	1976–77	*Average annual growth rate per cent*
Defence and external relations:			
1 Defence budget	3,003	3,304	2·4
2 Other military defence	61	93	12·6
3 Overseas aid	275	324	4·2[a]
4 EEC and other overseas services	205	362	1·2[b]
Commerce and industry:			
5 Agriculture, fisheries and forestry	582	479	−4·7
6 Research councils, etc.	141	137	−0·7
7 Trade, industry and employment	1,670	1,070	−5·5[c]
Nationalised industries:			
8 Nationalised industries capital expenditure	1,811	2,184	4·8
Environmental services:			
9 Roads	1,013	1,256	5·5
10 Surface transport	287	238	−4·6
11 Housing	1,415	1,241	−3·2
12 Miscellaneous local services	1,257	1,456	3·7
13 Law and order	847	1,079	6·2
14 Arts	41	50	5·1
Social services:			
15 Education and libraries	3,569	4,331	5·0
16 Health and personal social services	2,917	3,525	4·8
17 Social security	5,050	5,325	1·3[d]
Other services:			
18 Financial administration	446	354	−5·6
19 Common services	326	403	5·4
20 Miscellaneous services	101	114	3·1
21 Northern Ireland	711	715	0·1
Total programmes	25,728	28,045	2·5[c]
22 Debt interest	2,350	2,225	−1·4
23 Contingency reserve	—	700	
24 Shortfall	−200	−200	
25 Price adjustments	6	−331	
Total	27,884	30,439	2·5[c]

[a] Consistent with an increase of over 7 per cent in the true aid programme.

[b] The percentage figure excludes contributions to the European Communities as these were payable from January 1973 onwards.

[c] The percentage figure excludes investment grants.

[d] Based on benefits for 1976-77 at their present levels.

Source: Cmnd 5178 (HMSO, 1972).

Table 2: *Public Expenditure by Programme, in Cost Terms: 1968–69 to 1976–77*

	1968–69 *out-turn*	1969–70 *out-turn*	1970–71 *out-turn*
At 1972–73 out-turn prices including the relative price effect			
Defence and external relations:			
1 Defence budget	3,008	2,830	2,949
2 Other military defence	219	104	48
3 Overseas aid	228	233	221
4 EEC and other overseas services	164	157	157
Commerce and industry:			
5 Agriculture, fisheries and forestry	478	469	456
6 Research councils, etc.	111	120	128
7 Trade, industry and employment			
Investment grants	584	692	636
Other	803	743	751
Nationalised industries:			
8 Nationalised industries capital expenditure	1,960	1,738	1,907
Environmental services:			
9 Roads	780	844	952
10 Surface transport	299	263	217
11 Housing	1,408	1,364	1,364
12 Miscellaneous local services	931	953	1,050
13 Law and order	625	660	736
14 Arts	27	27	32
Social services:			
15 Education and libraries	2,951	3,027	3,199
16 Health and personal social services	2,403	2,467	2,669
17 Social security	3,346	3,572	3,818
Other services:			
18 Financial administration	301	307	292
19 Common services	187	226	250
20 Miscellaneous services	89	86	94
21 Northern Ireland	501	532	561
Total programmes	21,403	21,414	22,487
22 Debt interest	2,620	2,630	2,530
23 Contingency reserve	—	—	—
24 Shortfall	—	—	—
25 Price adjustments	990	866	602
Total	25,013	24,910	25,619

Source: Cmnd 5178 (HMSO, 1972).

£ million

1971–72 *provisional out-turn*	1972–73 *estimate*	1973–74 *estimate*	1974–75 *estimate*	1975–76 *estimate*	1976–77 *estimate*
3,020	3,003	3,213	3,123	3,283	3,304
58	61	67	71	86	98
244	275	270	281	294	324
156	205	246	294	324	362
505	582	561	534	505	479
136	141	134	132	132	137
493	350	193	97	37	18
813	1,320	1,657	1,570	1,367	1,052
1,722	1,811	1,991	2,167	2,160	2,184
897	1,013	1,086	1,153	1,199	1,256
224	287	262	256	252	238
1,263	1,415	1,413	1,304	1,261	1,241
1,117	1,257	1,372	1,369	1,390	1,456
791	847	897	958	1,021	1,079
35	41	51	47	47	50
3,384	3,569	3,756	3,909	4,122	4,331
2,772	2,917	3,074	3,216	3,367	3,525
4,427	5,050	5,217	5,259	5,311	5,325
321	446	345	345	350	354
280	326	340	356	377	403
109	101	105	106	114	114
615	711	716	716	705	715
23,382	25,728	26,966	27,263	27,704	28,045
2,450	2,350	2,300	2,275	2,250	2,225
—	—	350	500	600	700
—	−200	−200	−200	−200	−200
263	6	−234	−262	−301	−331
26,095	27,884	29,182	29,576	30,053	30,439

Table 3: *Public Expenditure by Programme, in Volume Terms: 1968–69 to 1976–77*

	1968–69 *out-turn*	1969–70 *out-turn*	1970–71 *out-turn*
At 1972 Survey prices			
Defence and external relations:			
1 Defence budget	3,093	2,901	2,863
2 Other military defence	206	123	76
3 Overseas aid	228	233	221
4 EEC and other overseas services	157	151	150
Commerce and industry:			
5 Agriculture, fisheries and forestry	458	445	437
6 Research councils, etc.	108	115	122
7 Trade, industry and employment			
Investment grants	549	646	587
Other	788	723	726
Nationalised industries:			
8 Nationalised industries capital expenditure	1,856	1,680	1,833
Environmental services:			
9 Roads	736	772	887
10 Surface transport	298	249	205
11 Housing	1,330	1,299	1,370
12 Miscellaneous local services	877	889	972
13 Law and order	649	680	705
14 Arts	27	26	31
Social services:			
15 Education and libraries	2,849	2,900	3,001
16 Health and personal social services	2,426	2,472	2,573
17 Social security	3,346	3,572	3,818
Other services:			
18 Financial administration	306	309	290
19 Common services	169	199	216
20 Miscellaneous services	83	81	87
21 Northern Ireland	480	512	544
Total programmes	21,019	20,977	21,714
22 Debt interest	2,620	2,630	2,530
23 Contingency reserve	—	—	—
24 Shortfall	—	—	—
25 Adjustments to 1972–73 out-turn prices and relative price effect	1,374[a]	1,303[a]	1,375[a]
At 1972–73 out-turn prices			
Total	25,013	24,910	25,619

[a] These figures include the following amounts for the revaluation to 1972 survey prices of the cash out-turns of social security benefits (see Chapter IV, paragraph 76 of 'Public Expenditure White Paper: Handbook on Methodology').

£ million

1971–72 *provisional out-turn*	1972–73 *estimate*	1973–74 *estimate*	1974–75 *estimate*	1975–76 *estimate*	1976–77 *estimate*
2,891	2,842	3,009	2,892	3,015	3,000
76	75	82	84	101	116
244	275	270	281	294	324
151	198	238	286	316	355
497	572	550	522	493	465
134	137	129	125	122	126
461	325	186	97	38	19
799	1,290	1,631	1,557	1,361	1,039
1,661	1,741	1,928	2,118	2,128	2,162
865	971	1,038	1,099	1,136	1,187
217	283	257	250	247	231
1,268	1,417	1,424	1,325	1,285	1,267
1,025	1,159	1,245	1,238	1,249	1,298
765	818	853	896	941	978
35	41	50	45	45	47
3,201	3,375	3,498	3,585	3,724	3,857
2,664	2,814	2,927	3,021	3,121	3,220
4,427	5,050	5,217	5,259	5,311	5,325
308	431	323	317	316	312
255	298	309	321	335	356
104	97	100	99	106	103
604	694	697	697	680	687
22,652	24,903	25,961	26,114	26,364	26,474
2,450	2,350	2,300	2,275	2,250	2,225
—	—	350	500	600	700
—	−200	−200	−200	−200	−200
993[a]	831	771	887	1,039	1,240
26,095	27,884	29,182	29,576	30,053	30,439

	1968–69	1969–70	1970–71	1971–72	
	969	816	569	249	

Source: Cmnd 5178 (HMSO, 1972).

Table 4: *Public Expenditure by Economic Category: 1968–69 to 1976–77* — *£ million*

	1968–69 *out-turn*	1969–70 *out-turn*	1970–71 *out-turn*	1971–72 *pro-visional out-turn*	1972–73 *estimate*	1973–74 *estimate*	1974–75 *estimate*	1975–76 *estimate*	1976–77 *estimate*
At 1972 Survey prices									
Current expenditure:									
Wages and salaries	5,999	6,072	6,257	6,537	6,696	6,932	7,077	7,258	7,456
Selective employment tax	167	161	164	163	162	164	167	170	174
Other current expenditure on goods and services	3,814	3,697	3,625	3,809	3,931	4,207	4,202	4,375	4,445
Subsidies	1,083	1,031	985	1,092	1,203	994	892	754	579
Debt interest	2,620	2,630	2,530	2,450	2,350	2,300	2,275	2,250	2,225
Current grants to persons	3,606	3,819	4,072	4,709	5,612	5,712	5,757	5,848	5,875
Current grants to private bodies	334	347	375	401	429	454	472	494	519
Current grants abroad	225	203	197	226	280	294	338	380	440
Total	17,848	17,960	18,205	19,387	20,663	21,057	21,180	21,529	21,713
Capital expenditure:									
Gross domestic fixed capital formation	4,658	4,475	4,743	4,594	4,978	5,336	5,467	5,491	5,575
Increase in value of stocks	31	23	91	6	134	125	146	134	119
Capital grants to private sector	846	937	899	827	780	857	714	667	669
Net lending to private sector	126	65	164	112	213	327	318	273	164
Net lending to overseas governments	66	91	87	81	80	95	104	104	111
Drawings from United Kingdom subscriptions to international lending bodies	24	18	12	14	31	42	40	41	46
Other net lending and investment abroad	9	21	32	54	355	419	408	368	298
Cash expenditure on company securities (net)	31	17	11	27	19	3	12	7	4
Total	5,791	5,647	6,039	5,715	6,590	7,204	7,209	7,085	6,986
Contingency reserve	—	—	—	—	—	350	500	600	700
Shortfall	—	—	—	—	−200	−200	−200	−200	−200
Adjustments to 1972–73 out-turn prices and relative price effect	1,374[a]	1,303[a]	1,375[a]	993[a]	831	771	837	1,039	1,240
At 1972–73 out-turn prices									
Total	25,013	24,910	25,619	26,095	27,884	29,182	29,576	30,053	30,439

[a] See note to Table 3.

Source: Cmnd 5178 (HMSO, 1972)

Table 5: *Public Expenditure by Spending Authority, Distinguishing Current and Capital Expenditure: 1968–69 to 1976–77*

£ million

	1968–69 *out-turn*	1969–70 *out-turn*	1970–71 *out-turn*	1971–72 *pro-visional out-turn*	1972–73 *estimate*	1973–74 *estimate*	1974–75 *estimate*	1975–76 *estimate*	1976–77 *estimate*
At 1972 Survey prices									
Central Government:									
Current	11,415	11,379	11,598	12,591	13,696	13,895	13,875	14,034	14,039
Capital	1,532	1,661	1,715	1,594	2,039	2,338	2,253	2,145	2,012
Local authorities:									
Current	3,813	3,951	4,078	4,347	4,617	4,862	5,030	5,245	5,449
Capital	2,164	2,060	2,251	2,227	2,508	2,590	2,481	2,442	2,449
Public corporations:									
Capital	2,095	1,926	2,072	1,893	2,043	2,276	2,475	2,498	2,525
Debt interest	2,620	2,630	2,530	2,450	2,350	2,300	2,275	2,250	2,225
Contingency reserve	—	—	—	—	—	350	500	600	700
Shortfall	—	—	—	—	−200	−200	−200	−200	−200
Adjustments to 1972–73 out-turn prices and relative price effect	1,374[a]	1,303[a]	1,375[a]	993[a]	831	771	887	1,039	1,240
At 1972–73 out-turn prices									
Total	25,013	24,910	25,619	26,095	27,884	29,182	29,576	30,053	30,439

[a] See note to Table 3.

Source: Cmnd 5178 (HMSO, 1972).

Table 6: *Gross Public Expenditure, Charges and Other Directly Related Receipts by Programme: 1972–73 (estimate)*

£ million

	Gross expenditure	*Receipts* *Charges*	*Other*	*Total expenditure net of charges*
At 1972–73 out-turn prices, including the relative price effect				
Defence and external relations:				
1 Defence budget	3,291	288	—	3,003
2 Other military defence	58	−3	7	61
3 Overseas aid	275	—	26	275
4 EEC and other overseas services	208	3	−11	205
Commerce and industry:				
5 Agriculture, fisheries and forestry	585	3	3	582
6 Research councils, etc.	143	2	—	141
7 Trade, industry and employment	1,699	29	142	1,670
Nationalised industries:				
8 Nationalised industries capital expenditure	1,811	—	[a]	1,811
Environmental services:				
9 Roads	1,036	23	2	1,013
10 Surface transport	297	10	1	287
11 Housing	1,415	—	121	1,415
12 Miscellaneous local services	1,315	58	9	1,257
13 Law and order	872	25	—	847
14. Arts	41	—	—	41
Social services:				
15 Education and libraries	3,769	200	2	3,569
16 Health and personal social services	3,111	194	227	2,917
17 Social security	5,050	—	3,105	5,050
Other services:				
18 Financial administration	448	2	−27	446
19 Common services	327	1	79	326
20 Miscellaneous services	131	30	10	101
21 Northern Ireland	719	8	86	711
22 Debt interest	2,350	—	956	2,350
23 Contingency reserve				—
24 Shortfall				−200
25 Price adjustments				6
Total				27,884

[a] The trading surpluses of nationalised industries are not included.

Source: Cmnd 5178 (HMSO, 1972).

Table 7 : *Net Total Benefits Received* (+) less *Total Taxes Paid* (−), *1972*

£ per year

	Range of original income: £ per year								*Average over all income ranges*
	Under 381	381–	557–	816–	1,194–	1,749–	2,561–	3,750 *and above*	
All households in the sample	+586	+491	+319	+170	−109	−340	−668	−1,374	−234
Retired households									
1 adult	+435	+229	+149	−10	−220				+355
2 adults	+646	+491	+342	+293	+28	−338			+461
Non-retired households									
1 adult	+409	+153	−20	−200	−440	−668	−1,109	−1,480	−286
2 adults	+660	+431	+286	+58	−270	−590	−991	−1,707	−568
2 adults, 1 child	+1,044		+245	+161	−220	−458	−757	−1,376	−447
2 adults, 2 children			+676	+265	−122	−302	−582	−1,181	−354
2 adults, 3 children				+356	+216	−21	−315	−1,305	−74
2 adults, 4 children				+618	+513	+141	−109	−1,351	+233

Source: Economic Trends, No. 241.

Table 8: *Income After All Taxes and Benefits as a Percentage of Original Income, 1972*

Percentages

	Range of original income: £ per year								*Average over all income ranges*
	Under 381	381–	557–	816–	1,194–	1,749–	2,561–	3,750 *and above*	
All households in the sample	695	205	146	117	93	84	78	73	88
Retired households									
1 adult	691	150	122	99	85				243
2 adults	668	205	150	130	102	84			192
Non-retired households									
1 adult	385	133	97	80	69	67	62	65	78
2 adults	532	193	142	106	82	72	67	67	75
2 adults, 1 child	1,163		135	116	85	78	75	72	80
2 adults, 2 children			199	126	92	86	81	76	85
2 adults, 3 children				134	114	99	90	78	97
2 adults, 4 children				158	134	107	96	79	111

Source: Economic Trends, No. 241.

Table 9: *Total Taxes as a Percentage of Original Income* plus *Cash Benefits, 1972*

Percentages

	Range of original income: £ per year								*Average over all income ranges*
	Under 381	381–	557–	816–	1,194–	1,749–	2,561–	3,750 *and above*	
All households in the sample	23	25	28	30	33	34	34	35	33
Retired households									
1 adult	20	22	27	33	32				24
2 adults	24	26	31	29	33	37			29
Non-retired households									
1 adult	23	27	29	34	37	36	40	37	35
2 adults	27	28	27	29	35	35	37	35	35
2 adults, 1 child	31		30	28	33	34	34	32	33
2 adults, 2 children			25	29	33	33	33	32	32
2 adults, 3 children				32	32	31	30	32	31
2 adults, 4 children				25	27	34	34	33	32

Source: Economic Trends, No. 241.

Table 10: *Average Taxes and Benefits per Household, UK and US, 1968*

(*per cent of original income*)

	US	UK
Original income (money factor income plus imputed rent)	100·0	100·0
Cash transfers	+ 9·2	+ 10·3
Benefits in kind:		
education	+ 7·7	+ 6·5
health	+ 2·0	+ 5·1
Housing subsidies		+ 0·6
Income tax	− 14·6	− 11·3
Social security contributions	− 8·1	− 7·2
Indirect taxation (including property tax)	− 12·5	− 19·8
Final income	83·7	84·2

Source: The Redistribution of Income by Nicholson and Britton (Bowes & Bowes, 1965).

Table 11: *List of Chief Secretaries to the Treasury*

The Rt Hon. Henry Brooke, MP (now Lord Brooke of Cumnor)	1961–62
The Rt Hon. John Boyd-Carpenter, MP (now Lord Boyd-Carpenter)	1962–64
The Rt Hon. John Diamond, MP (now Lord Diamond)	1964–70
The Rt Hon. Maurice Macmillan, MP	1970–72
The Rt Hon. Patrick Jenkin, MP	1972–74

Index